45 RPM

The History, Heroes

& Villains of a

Pop Music Revolution

by Jim Dawson & Steve Propes

Backbeat Books
San Francisco

Published by Backbeat Books
600 Harrison Street, San Francisco, CA 94107
www.backbeatbooks.com
email: books@musicplayer.com

An imprint of the Music Player Network
Publishers of *Guitar Player*, *Bass Player*, *Keyboard*, and other magazines
United Entertainment Media, Inc.
A CMP Information company

CMP
United Business Media

Distributed to the book trade in the US and Canada by
Publishers Group West, 1700 Fourth Street, Berkeley, CA 94710

Distributed to the music trade in the US and Canada by
Hal Leonard Publishing, P.O. Box 13819, Milwaukee, WI 53213

Cover and interior design by Richard Leeds – bigwigdesign.com

Library of Congress Cataloging-in-Publication Data

Dawson, Jim, 1944–
  45 RPM : the history, heroes & villains of a pop music revolution /
by Jim Dawson and Steve Propes.
    p. cm.
  Includes discographies, bibliographical references, and index.
  ISBN 0-87930-757-9 (alk. paper)
  1. Popular music—History and criticism. 2. Rock music—History and criticism. 3. Sound recordings—History. I. Title: History, heroes & villains of a pop
music revolution. II. Title: History, heroes and villains of a pop music revolution.
III. Propes, Steve. IV. Title.

ML3470.D38 2003
781.64'149—dc21

                                          2003052207

Printed in the United States of America

03 04 05 06 07   5 4 3 2 1

Contents

Introduction

The little record with the big hole in the middle was an elegant yet simple artifact from postwar America: seven inches of shiny plastic and bright, embedded paper. It was called "the 45" because of the revolutions-per-minute velocity required to bring it to life. Born not of necessity but rather from one man's pique, the efficient little 45 dominated commercial music for twenty-five years. Jazz, classical, theater, and other "adult" music were initially pressed onto the 45, but the format's time constraints and association with disposable pop music gradually sent these weightier genres to the LP. That's why in the 1950s and early sixties the 45 pretty much had rock 'n' roll and Top 40 radio all to itself.

This book is dedicated to disc jockey Alan Freed, who put the big-beat soul in rock 'n' roll and spread the jive on 45. [Photo courtesy of the Estate of Alan Freed; www. alanfreed.com.]

It was an effective troika. Commercial radio was a get-in-and-get-out medium that demanded lean and lithe popular music, with nothing wasted, and the go-go 45 was perfect for the quick payoff. Though often called "the three-minute record," in fact the 45 usually delivered its payload in far less time. (One 1960 No. 1 hit, Maurice Williams and the Zodiacs' "Stay," was barely more than a minute and a half long.) It's no coincidence that the ponderous intros, droning solos, and endless codas that later came to characterize popular music, especially rock, arrived just as the LP was replacing the 45 single in the hearts of many young Americans.

Mid-century kids had a special relationship with their 45 records that carried on into adulthood. Like Daniel Stern's obsessive character, Shrevie, in the 1982 film *Diner* ("Every one of my records means something!"), they could recite the labels, years, and flipsides of their favorite singles. They luxuriated in the vivid and mysterious logo designs, the tactile connection between vinyl and flesh, and of course the music, crackles and pops indelibly included, that jumped and purred out of their record players. Many will tell you even today that a recording sounds *better* at 45 rpm than it does

5

at 33 ⅓, not only because higher speed gives the listener more information from the grooves, but also because engineers usually spent more time on mastering singles than they did on the corresponding album cuts.

The only reliable connections that kids had to their favorite music were the ever-present radio and that diminutive disc (occasionally with a photo sleeve), doling out magic performances in small doses. They might spend hours waiting for the local jock to play a certain song, or dial the phone over and over trying to get through to the request line, which was usually busy. If they were lucky enough to actually have the latest record in their hands, they had to content themselves with only one song on each side. Someone today who listens in a single sitting to a twenty-song Greatest Hits CD by Buddy Holly, Fats Domino, Jo Stafford, or the Beatles can't appreciate what it was like to savor the A-side and B-side of the latest hit over and over again, until that artist's next 45 arrived at the local record shop six weeks later. To borrow from Dr. Samuel Johnson's quip about imminent execution, it wonderfully concentrated the mind.

Compiling this book, we generally confined ourselves to the United States because other countries adopted and later phased out the 45 at their own pace and marketed it differently. In most countries, including the United Kingdom, the 45 was introduced without RCA's early spindle system, so instead of the big hole in the middle their 45s had a built-in center—with a smaller spindle hole—that could be popped out if needed. Also, the seven-inch EP, abandoned in the U.S. in the mid sixties, carried on in other countries well into the 1980s and warrants another book entirely.

We've included in our description of each 45 not only the title of the song(s) and the name of the artist(s), but also the label and the number, because recordings were often reissued under different numbers or by different companies. Each 45, though mass-produced, was part of a unique pressing identity, with its own name, rank, and serial number, a fact taken into consideration on these pages.

Most of all, we wrote this book as an overview, not a collector's guide. Considering the millions of different 45s released over the past fifty-plus years, we avoided getting too involved with musical specifics. Besides, various 45-rpm price guides have that field wrapped up.

Today, as far as the music industry is concerned, the 45 is as dead as the rotary dial phone, but there are still a few indie companies pressing them up in limited numbers, as well as many thousands of 45 collectors who find it hard to listen to anything else. One thing's for certain. The 45 single has its own important niche in our cultural history. It's about time that somebody wrote a book about it—so why not us?

Jim Dawson and Steve Propes

CHAPTER 1

Record Revolutions

....

"Will [recording] not be like holding communion with immortality?"
—Emile Berliner, 1888

T hough Thomas Edison is often credited with being the father of the phonograph, his 1877 invention was a failed format—a wax cylinder shaped like a tube inside a modern roll of toilet paper—that went extinct in the early 1900s. The flat recording disc that became the industry standard for most of the twentieth century was the brainchild of a self-educated German-Jewish immigrant American named Emile Berliner, who in 1888 developed a method of using acid to etch sound grooves into a zinc-coated circular plate, then making rubber-coated copies and playing them back on a manually operated turntable with a floating needlelike stylus attached to an amplifier horn. When Berliner demonstrated his new "gram-o-phone" at the Franklin Institute in Philadelphia, it seemed whimsical to the Victorian mind, and the only client he attracted was a German toy manufacturer who hired him to create a talking doll and a small children's record player. In order to fit the hard rubber plates inside the company's dolls, Berliner miniaturized them to three inches in diameter, with less than a minute of sound capacity. His discs for the kiddie players were a little larger, five inches. The recordings were nursery rhymes, little songs and recitations. The playing speed was roughly thirty revolutions per minute, but since these toys had to be steadily hand-cranked, no correct speed really existed.

After Berliner formed his own United States Gram-O-Phone Company in Washington, D.C., he standardized his "plate"—that's what he called it—at seven inches in diameter and increased the speed into the neighborhood of seventy revolutions per minute, which gave him better sound quality because the extra velocity allowed the needle to extract more music per moment. In 1896 he hired a young entrepreneur named Eldridge R. Johnson to develop a spring motor that could be wound up, so that a talking machine could play recordings at a steady, pre-set speed. Four years later, Johnson replaced Berliner's primitive acid-etched zinc masters with his own much superior wax process and introduced the first mass-produced "record"—a cardboard platter covered with an Indian tree gum called *shellac* and pressed like a waffle by a metal stamper cast from a mold of the original recording.

Calling his new enterprise the Victor Talking Machine Company, Eldridge Johnson retained Emile Berliner's seven-inch disc size but decided in 1901 to introduce an alternate format: the 10-inch record, with a new standard speed of about 78 rpm, give or take a revolution. For several years Victor maintained both sizes, but even though the 10-inch record retailed for almost twice as much, the public came to prefer its fuller sound and four-minutes' worth of play, especially after the company began pressing music on both sides of each record in 1904. Victor finally discontinued the seven-inch plate in 1907, and for the next forty-two years the shellac "78" record carried the world's music, round and round. Victor (which became RCA Victor in 1946) would alone sell a billion 78s by mid-century. But then one day the company's top executive set out to kill the 78 and go back to their original seven-inch record.

So begins the story of the 45.

CHAPTER 2

Columbia Unveils the LP

T he 45 was the product of a snit: An egocentric genius believed that he was being humiliated by a rival.

In April 1948, William S. Paley, the 47-year-old patriarch of the Columbia Broadcasting System, invited RCA Victor's cocky little, bull-chested president, General David Sarnoff*, and his staff to the Columbia Records boardroom at 799 Seventh Avenue in Manhattan to see and hear firsthand the future of the record business: Columbia's glossy 10-inch and 12-inch microgroove Vinylite discs, the result of a quarter of a million dollars' worth of tinkering. As Paley's research supervisor, Peter Goldmark, demonstrated the new format's remarkable sound quality by playing a piece of classical music, Sarnoff remained silent but was visibly agitated. "With the first few bars, Sarnoff was out of his chair," Goldmark recalled years later. "I played [the microgroove disc] for ten seconds and then switched back to the 78. The effect was electrifying, as I knew it would be." Another Columbia executive, Howard "Scotty" Scott, recalls Sarnoff being more than electrified: "He was furious and chewed out his entire staff in front of Paley."

The 57-year-old Sarnoff realized that Columbia's new product was going to change the record industry. He had been a pioneer in commercial radio since the early 1920s, and in the 1930s he'd guided RCA's development and commercial application of television. He was less familiar with sound recording, but clearly this new long-play plastic record, which Peter Goldmark called an "LP" for short, had greater sound fidelity than RCA's traditional 78. Sarnoff could hear for the first time the quiet music passages without any of the extraneous hiss and crackle inherent in 78s. On a more practical level, he noted that the LP weighed half as much, was far less breakable and played at a much slower speed—33⅓ rpm—that allowed about fifteen minutes of music per side

*Sarnoff was commonly called "General" because President Roosevelt made him a brigadier general during World War II in honor of his communications work for the U.S. Army.

(or twenty-two minutes on the format's alternate 12-inch size). That was four or five times the capacity of a 78.

Sarnoff was especially galled because his own company, Victor, had unsuccessfully introduced the 33⅓ plastic record via its special Program Transcription series in the early 1930s. In fact, the man who had aborted the project was now standing right there in the room with them on Paley's side of the table: Ed Wallerstein, who had left Victor ten years earlier to become general manager of Columbia Records. It looked on the surface as if Wallerstein had purloined Victor's technology as he walked out the door. But as Wallerstein later explained, he pulled Victor's narrow-grooved, 33⅓ discs off the market in 1933 because "there were technical problems. Most of the records had been made from a vinyl compound, and the pickups [the tone arms holding the playing needles] available at the time were so heavy they just cut through the material after several plays."

The basic technology behind the long-play record had been around since 1927, when Western Electric's Vitaphone Company, searching for a way to make motion pictures talk, developed a 20-inch disc with enough capacity to hold eleven minutes of recording time—the same length as a reel of 35mm film. At 78 rpm, eleven minutes of full, state-of-the-art sound would have required an unwieldy 25-inch disc, so an architect at Bell Laboratories in New York named Dr. J. P. Maxfield, whose specialty was acoustics, calculated that 33⅓ revolutions per minute would be the optimum speed, but only if the playing surface were made of smooth, less-resistant plastic instead of shellac, to offset the loss of sound quality that accompanied any lowering of record speed. By the 1930s, radio networks were using a similar 33⅓ format to transcribe East Coast programs for replay on the West Coast three hours later. But these plastic "transcription discs" were too big and bulky for consumer use, and besides, they lasted only a few plays before the intense stylus pressure wore them out. Not until Columbia Records came up with a lightweight tone arm that applied only eight grams of pressure could these more delicate plastic records, made smaller in circumference for convenient handling and storage, be considered a marketable product. In other words, Columbia's major technological breakthrough was not the microgroove LP but rather the playback system.

After the demonstration, William Paley got around to his main reason for inviting his RCA counterpart up to his lair. He wanted to discuss a licensing deal under which Columbia Records would press RCA Victor's music on LPs—for a reasonable fee per record, until some point in the future when RCA installed its own long-play record presses. What this proposal boiled down to was Columbia temporarily controlling a portion of RCA Victor's manufacturing. Sarnoff told him he'd think about it, and left. As soon as he got back to his own office on the fifty-third floor of the RCA Building in Rockefeller Center, he gathered his engineering team behind closed doors and demanded to know why they'd allowed Paley to make a fool of him. He told them he had no intention of committing RCA's music to a Columbia Records configuration. One staff member suggested that since Columbia did not own a patent on the system, why couldn't RCA simply bring its own 1933 long-play prototype up to date and press its own LPs? The only thing they couldn't use was the term "LP," which Columbia had trademarked.

It was a reasonable alternative that would have saved RCA Victor and the entire recording industry a lot of money and grief. From a business viewpoint, RCA would have profited from cooperating with Columbia and adopting the new LP, as most other major record companies would do before 1948 was out, instead of turning to another format altogether and further confusing the American consumer. But Sarnoff wasn't interested. As he

David Sarnoff on the cover of Time, *1931.*

would directly, and sarcastically, tell Paley a few days later, "It's quite something for the great Victor company to take a thing like this from the little Columbia company." He wanted no part of anything Columbia could claim as its own. There also may have been, according to the trade papers at the time, a prior gentlemen's agreement between Sarnoff and Paley not to upset their mutually profitable apple carts by introducing any new record system. If this were so, Sarnoff would have felt personally betrayed.

William Paley seemed surprised, almost hurt, when Sarnoff rebuffed him. He later blamed it on Sarnoff's anger toward the fledgling CBS television network's habit of using big bucks to woo stars away from the NBC network, which Sarnoff also headed, as well as his grudge against Columbia for breaking Victor's traditional grip on the classical music market by undercutting its prices several years earlier. Certainly, the wars between the two record corporations and their new, corresponding TV networks had been bitter. But Sarnoff may have held an even deeper, more personal resentment against his rival.

Born in 1891 in a remote Russian *shtetl* and raised for several years by a rabbi uncle who forced him to memorize the Talmud, David Sarnoff emigrated to America at age nine, speaking only Yiddish, and grew up in the crammed, broken-down tenements of New York's Lower East Side, hustling from one menial job to another to help support his family after his father died. After teaching himself telegraphy, he went to work for the American Marconi Company and studied electrical engineering at night school. Gradually Sarnoff saw his future in the new "wireless telegraph," which by 1912 became known as "radio" because wireless transmitters radiated electrical signals in all directions.

On duty one night at his telegraph key at the Marconi station atop Wanamaker's Department Store in Manhattan, the 21-year-old operator was the first to receive a message from the ocean liner *S.S. Titanic*: "Ran into iceberg. Sinking fast." Over the next seventy sleepless hours, thanks to President Taft's order clearing all other stations off the airwaves, Sarnoff captured and relayed every transmission from the rescue ships that rushed to the disaster. His vigil transformed him into the first media celebrity. More importantly, those long lonely nights sitting at the telegraph gave him plenty of time to envision the possibilities of wireless communication.

Knowing that it could broadcast voices as well as signals, Sarnoff wrote a monograph in 1915 predicting that a "Radio Music Box" could "make radio a household utility in the same sense as the piano or phonograph." At that time, few in the wireless industry thought it had any commercial value because, since anyone could listen in on the messages, there was no privacy or exclusivity. But four years later, when General Electric and several other companies formed a subsidiary called Radio Corporation of America (RCA) out of the remnants of the bankrupt American Marconi Company and put Sarnoff in charge, he found himself on the ground floor of a fledgling industry he'd prophesied. A few years later, when RCA radios became a national sensation, Sarnoff proposed that the corporation set up a network of entertainment shows to sell more radios; this led to the formation of the National Broadcasting Company (NBC). He also proposed that radios and phonographs be put into the same cabinets, using the same speakers. And soon after that, in 1929, he used $150 million of RCA's high-flying stock to take over the Victor Talking Machine Company, complete with its Victor Records division.

William Paley was ten years younger than Sarnoff, born in America in 1901. Though Jewish, he was the grandson of upper-middle-class immigrants and aloof from the privations that most fellow Russian Jews, like Sarnoff, endured after arriving in America. In 1928, as an Ivy League–educated, socially assimilated, 27-year-old millionaire in his father's cigar business, Paley bought his way on a lark into a failing radio operation called the United Independent Broadcasters network, known unofficially as the Columbia Broadcasting Company because of its affiliation with the Columbia Phonograph Company. Within a few years he turned both enterprises into the main competitors of RCA's NBC radio network and Victor Records.

In his memoirs William Paley wrote, "From the earliest days of radio, when [Sarnoff] was the 'grand old man' and I was 'that bright young kid,' we were friends, confidants, and fierce competitors all at the same time . . . . [But] I always thought his strengths lay in the more technical and physical aspects of radio and television, while mine lay in understanding talent, programming, and what went on the air." Paley's successes, often at Sarnoff's expense, bear out his assessment, but it's doubtful that Sarnoff considered Paley a close friend. More likely he resented Paley and considered him an upstart, a Jazz Age golden boy, and somewhat of a dilettante.

Now that the damage was done, Sarnoff asked his staff for ideas. One executive reminded him that, in addition to the stillborn long-play system, Victor's Camden, New Jersey, record laboratory across the Hudson River had worked on several other unfinished projects over the years. One of them had been on the drawing board in 1938 but abandoned a year later when Sarnoff himself decided that with Americans still emerging from the Depression, they wouldn't be ready to invest in an entirely new record system. But maybe now, a decade later, with the postwar economy beginning to hum along nicely, it might be a good time to revive it.

Victor's engineers had originally planned this system in conjunction with a company-manufactured record player that solved the problem of listeners having to walk over to the machine at the end of each record, pick it up off the turntable and replace it with another. (Some 78 players did have automatic record changers built into their spindles, with a swinging arm that pushed down on the waiting platters to keep them hovering in place above the turntables, but they were slow and clunky.) This new player had been designed with a spindle that could stack several discs and drop them one by one onto the turntable whenever the tone arm automatically swung out of the way. Since the heavy, brittle 78 sometimes cracked or chipped when dropped even a couple of inches, the engineers had decided upon a smaller, lighter disc made of durable plastic. With records rotating together on a turntable, one on top of another, the label area in the middle of the disc, as well as a thin band around the outer circle, would have to be slightly thicker to prevent the delicate recording surfaces from grinding against each other. The designers had also reckoned that if this disc were going to be frequently dropped down a spindle, it needed a larger hole in its center to distribute friction and other stresses over a greater surface area and thus avoid the gouging that the small holes in 78s suffered after steady use. Thus the spindle would be larger and made of plastic instead of metal.

As for the new record's size, the research department had settled on Victor's original diameter from back in 1901: seven inches—or to be more exact, six-and-seven-eighths inches. The actual recording area could take up only the outer half, to prevent the distortion that naturally occurs when the grooves become more tightly concentric toward the middle. That meant that the recording surface had to be about an inch wide and roughly two-and-a-half inches from the center. The remaining innermost part would accommodate the "dead wax," the label, and the center hole (itself slightly more than an inch and a half in diameter). Putting the width of the recording groove (roughly three-thousandths of an inch), the acceptable level of distortion and other audio considerations into Dr. Maxfield's original 1927 formula, the 1938 RCA team had come up with 45 revolutions per minute as the optimum speed for their seven-inch record. (The more common explanation that RCA simply subtracted $33\frac{1}{3}$ from 78 to arrive at 45 is untrue.)

Now, ten years later, all they had to do was pull the old technology out of mothballs and fine tune it.

What David Sarnoff primarily liked about this abandoned project was that RCA Victor would have an altogether different format of its own instead of an imitation of Columbia's LP. He conceded, privately, that the long-play record would more likely capture the bulk of the theatrical and classical music fields. In particular, the 12-inch LP's full play time of forty-five minutes could handle many of the world's symphonies, ballet suites, and other great musical pieces, not to mention the lucrative Broadway and Hollywood musicals, all on one platter. The standard 78 was already heading for obsolescence as far as those markets were concerned. But what about popular music—Tin Pan Alley tunes, big band swing, hillbilly, blues, and jazz—that relied on three-minute performances best offered on smaller records? Fresh pop and novelty music were the meat and potatoes that kept the record business going because the public demanded new songs every week, and Columbia's LP was much too big, too outsized, to handle that realm. The LP was also too large to fit into the many thousands of jukeboxes across the nation, which were greatly responsible for creating and perpetuating hit records in those days before radio fully took over the business of record promotion. (In the early fifties, *Billboard* estimated that Americans punched 26 million songs a day on the nation's jukeboxes.) But a new, diminutive microgroove record with the same fidelity and durability as an LP could perfectly feed the ravenous pop music maw.

RCA Victor would also have a sales advantage because, unlike Columbia, it manufactured not only phonograph records but also the machines on which to play them. Back in 1889, Edward Easton had formed Columbia to manufacture the graphophone, a machine that played cylinders, but he'd abandoned the playback business a few years later after he began selling many more cylinders than machines. Even now, in 1948, Columbia had no direct involvement in manufacturing the equipment needed to play its LPs. Instead, as Sarnoff soon discovered, Columbia was giving away its technology to Philco Radio & Television Corporation, Hoffman Radio Corporation, Admiral Radio & Phonograph Corporation, and other manufacturers, depriving itself not only of an entire stream of revenue, but of the ability to maximize the interplay between two separate markets: records and machines. Today we'd call it the synergy between software and hardware. Sarnoff knew that RCA Victor had the advantage of being able to promote its 45 by practically giving away phonographs at cost.

Within days the seven-inch record was back on the drawing board, bundled under such secrecy that RCA Victor gave the project a code name, Madame X, and even came up with a subterfuge to hide the 45's existence. Since quarter-inch recording tape was becoming popular with several of the larger companies as a medium for studio recording, RCA let the word out that it was working on a consumer tape system that would make the record disc, including the LP, obsolete. Given the immature state of recording tape technology in 1948, the idea was preposterous enough that if William Paley and his Columbia engineers believed the rumor, they'd be gloating over Sarnoff's folly instead of wondering what his lab rats were really up to.

CHAPTER 3

Getting Up to Speed

O n June 19, 1948, Columbia chairman Ed Wallerstein formally introduced the LP to the press and the music industry in a banquet room at Manhattan's posh Waldorf-Astoria Hotel. He stood at the podium flanked by an eight-foot tower of 78s on one side and a fifteen-inch pile of 33⅓s on the other. "These," he said, nodding at the stack of 78s kept in place by a vertical shelf, "hold the same music as *these.*" He gestured down at the much smaller heap of LPs. It was a perfect visual image of compression, compactness, and efficiency. When he finished his speech, Wallerstein added a similarly impressive auditory display by playing a piece of classical music on one of his company's Masterworks 78s. After four minutes, the platter abruptly ran out of music in mid-passage. "Then, I took the corresponding LP and played it on the little Philco attachment right past that break [in the music]," he later recalled. "The reception was terrific. The critics were struck not only by the length of the record, but also by the quietness of its surface and its greatly increased fidelity. They were convinced that a new era had come to the music business."

And about time, too. The old 78 was mostly shellac, a word taken from the Sanskrit *lahk*, meaning "one-hundred thousand," because shellac was a product of the amber-colored, resinous secretions of countless tiny beetles (*Laccifer lacca*) feeding on the sap of rubber trees found only in parts of India and Southeast Asia. In the record-making process, shellac was used as a binder for various neutral filler materials, including carbon black (which gave records their dark color) and other powders, molded together by extreme heat. Among the ingredients always present were thousands of ground-up bodies of those insects that had produced the shellac in the first place. Their tiny carcasses seemed a primitive material for such an up-to-date industry as the record business.

By contrast, the main ingredient of the LP was a synthetic resin plastic. What we know as the commercial plastic industry didn't begin until 1907, when a Belgium-born American inventor named Leo Baekeland discovered a carbolic-acid- and formaldehyde-based substitute for shellac in his riverside barn near Yonkers, New York. He found that when he baked his liquid goo at a high temperature, it became a hard, translucent substance, molded into any shape he wanted. Baekeland called it Bakelite. His General Bakelite Corporation subsequently became part of the Union Carbide and Carbon Company (now Union Carbide Corporation), which improved upon Baekeland's original plastic and, in 1930, came up with a flexible compound of polyvinyl chloride and vinyl acetate called Vinylite, whose first major application was as a protective coating on the insides of beer cans to keep the beverage's natural salts from reacting with the metal. The second major application—and Vinylite's introduction to the record business—had been Victor's aborted microgroove project. Then, a decade later, Victor got another chance to exploit the plastic material when it signed a contract with the U.S. government to press V-Discs at its Camden plant for the Armed Forces Radio Service (AFRS) during World War II.

RCA marketed its new 45 system as a futuristic wonder.

The V-Disc project began after the American Federation of Musicians union went on strike in mid 1942 to get higher royalties from record companies to offset their perceived losses from radio and jukebox play. The companies refused to go along with these demands, so for the next two years musicians were not allowed to set foot inside a recording studio. However, the Armed Forces Radio Service convinced the union to sign a waiver to allow musicians to record exclusively for Allied troops around the world as part of their patriotic duty.

Once the ink was on the contract, the next problem was to find a replacement for shellac. The AFRS had already been having problems with most of its brittle transcription discs arriving in jigsaw pieces at military bases around the world. Worse, the Japanese were occupying French Indochina, America's main source of imported shellac, and what little was available had to be earmarked for electrical insulation as part of the war effort. To maintain a fresh inventory of music, record companies were forced to buy up old 78s and crush them into dust to add to the mix of new records. Since the Army was already using Union Carbide's Vinylite for electrical equipment and life rafts, the AFRS began to press their V-Disc 78s using a watered-down form of Vinylite called Formvar.

As the only outlet for America's top recording artists during the studio ban, the new V-Discs were an immediate hit with the troops. During the first week alone, 1,780 boxes, each containing thirty V-Discs and a complement of playing needles, were shipped to Europe and into the Pacific theater. By 1945, Victor's Camden plant had shipped more than four million records (along with 125,000 spring-wound V-Disc phonographs and millions of steel needles to grind into them). When troops remained overseas after the war as part of the Marshall Plan, the V-Disc project continued to provide them with music for another couple of years. Yet David Sarnoff and RCA Victor never took advantage of their position as V-Disc's main manufacturer until William Paley uncloaked the long-play vinyl record and the kinder, gentler tone arm.

After a quiet summer, Columbia released its first fourteen LPs in September 1948, keeping mostly to its classical Masterworks line because the decade's second musicians strike had paralyzed much of the popular music business since the beginning of the year. Twelve-inch LPs, limited at this point to classical works, retailed at $4.85, classical 10-inch LPs at $3.85, and popular music 10-inch LPs at $2.95. Columbia not only superceded the 78 album with this new long-play format, but also appropriated the name. An album is a book of pages, or sleeves, which is what the original record albums were, whereas the LP was a single vinyl record inside a cardboard jacket—hardly an album *per se*, but the public never questioned the misnomer.

To play this shiny new record, Philco, working in partnership with Columbia, introduced a $29.95 adapter unit—a motorized 33⅓ turntable with a featherweight tone arm in a shallow 15 x 14-inch box—that could plug into the speaker system of existing radios and record players. Philco also brought out a more expensive console model with a dual-arm changer that could play both LPs and 78s.

Meanwhile, RCA Victor was surreptitiously working to bring its own system online. On December 11, 1948, Jim Murray, a vice president at the company's Hollywood office, invited his recording artists to a special viewing of the new 45 player in his office. Rather than arrive as a group for a formal demonstration, they wandered in whenever their schedules allowed and Murray dazzled them with the new product. This, he told them one by one, is the most sensational innovation in the music industry since the introduction of electrical recording in 1925. In New York City, RCA unveiled the 45 for a gathering of hardware and record manufacturers.

But journalists were already on the case. "Some gossip that has come to our ears describes the imminent appearance . . . of a disc . . . which would revolve at a speed in the 40s," wrote Irving Kolodin in a November issue of the *Saturday Review of Literature*. Music columnist Joe Caida blew its cover a month later, in the December 4 issue of *Billboard*, proclaiming, "RCA Victor is not going to put on 33⅓. The company is going to put out a 45 r.p.m. record with no long-playing feature whatsoever . . . . So it boils down to this. No matter what anybody says or writes, the record business as of early spring 1949 will have three types of records available to consumers." RCA remained mum on the subject for fear of inhibiting Christmas shoppers from buying its current crop of 78s and 78 record players.

Not until the beginning of the new year did RCA Victor's general manager, Paul Barkmaier, officially release the full details. *Billboard*, in its January 8, 1949 edition, touted the imminent 45 in banner headlines: "Low Down On New RCA Disc." According to the subhead, "Changer is heart of new player unit." Quoting unnamed industry sources, *Billboard* said that RCA was "bringing out not only a new type, new speed record; but is introducing a completely new phonograph system" . . . . that "constitutes a combination of evolutionary steps in the industry.

Zenith touted a unique adapter system.

"The player, the heart of which is a new automatic changer mechanism, will be made available in an adapter unit, which may be hooked up to any present radio or phonograph, as well as in the form of a complete player unit, which merely needs to be plugged into any socket and in various combinations . . . . The spindle is actually the most revolutionary aspect of the mechanism. Unlike the present-day spindles, the RCA spindle measures about 1⅝ inches in diameter, and into this spindle is built the complete changer mechanism. About an inch below the head of the spindle two tiny prongs extend from each side of the spindle. The new platters actually rest on these prongs and drop onto the turntable in order, once the changer is activated."

RCA offered this new system in various combinations and prices. The cheapest self-contained player was a small black plastic unit—roughly nine inches square and less than five inches deep—with a three-tube amplifier, a four-inch speaker, and a golden spindle with matching golden tone arm. The format was also going to be included in many of RCA's upcoming radio and television consoles, including its top-of-the-line "ultra de lux" Berkshire model, a fancy piece of furniture that contained everything but the kitchen sink.

The *Billboard* article also verified rumors that the new disc would play at 45 rpm and measure 6⅞ inches in diameter. "The record," said *Billboard*, quoting an RCA's press release, "was developed . . . with the express objective of obtaining 100 per cent undistortion, or put another way, creating a record which is completely free of surface noises or distortion of any kind."

At the end of the article came an added piece of information that signaled a coming battle of the titans: "An important factor about the new RCA record, which must be borne in mind, is that it has no long-play feature, as such at all. Popular, hillbilly and such recorded items, for example, will play at their established length of approximately three minutes. Classical and other normal 12-inch items will play at the same length as usual, roughly five minutes. Whatever long-playing factor may be said to exist, exists in the fact that if nine of the new records, playing 5⅒ minutes each, were placed on the changer (the capacity will be billed at nine records, tho 10 or 12 may fit on it), the listener would get some 45 minutes of music, interrupted only by the split second between the time one record ends and another begins thru the operations of the changer mechanism."

The article added that except for the smallest portable unit, RCA's new record players would also accommodate 78s because of a two-speed mechanism and the detachability of the spindle. To further promote the new system, RCA was granting other manufacturers royalty-free use of its final working blueprints for the entire record player mechanism, as well as the Vinylite discs themselves.

Billboard noted that "the introduction of the new RCA player and platter in the spring will mark the beginning of a historic disc battle between the Camden characters and the Columbia gang from Bridgeport [Connecticut, home of Columbia's record lab]. In many ways the tussle is likely to turn out as fraught with significance and ultimate effect as the old battle between the cylinder and the first record." At the same time, the trade paper cautioned, "it is of prime importance that all factions contribute as little to the inherent confusion as possible and work as hard as they can to hold any confusion to a minimum."

Peter Goldsmith later admitted that Columbia Records executives were caught off guard by how quickly RCA Victor had arrived at a fully developed format of its own, not realizing that the company had been sitting on it since the late thirties. Suddenly Columbia's strategists had to change their promotional direction. Touting the advantages of the lustrous new LP over the aging, creaky 78 was one thing, but now they had a competitor that shared most of the LP's technical advantages and was more suitable for packaging pop songs. Columbia hastily joined forces with the Philadelphia-based Retail Record Dealers' Association—comprised of over a hundred record stores—in a campaign to convince pop consumers to stick with the reliable and time-tested 78. The dealers were natural allies because the 78 was their bread and butter. According to *Billboard*, "Since almost all [ninety-five percent] inventory of dealers is in 78, with the dealers enjoying greater return privileges for

78s, as well as sharing greater profits in 78 sales, [RRDA president David] Krantz said that it was to the best advantage of the dealers to promote 78s." The association estimated that with the right marketing, including a campaign to give a cheap record player away to anyone who bought eight or more 10-inch platters, the industry could bring perhaps another fifteen thousand new 78 buyers into the fold.

And yet, as Columbia was publicly stumping for the good old 78, it rushed into production a competing seven-inch single of its own, but at 33⅓ rpm instead of 45, with a small hole in the center and "the full fidelity and tonal qualities of the LP." In other words, it was just a small LP, but Goldsmith figured that its outward similarity to the 45 would thwart the as-yet-unreleased RCA format. In the opening days of 1949, Ed Wallerstein pronounced this new single "the logical step in the completion of the revolutionary technique established . . . when we introduced the microgroove system six months ago," as if the company had been planning it all along. Columbia went so far as to offer the retailers' trade association a tiny 33⅓ record player with prices in the $5.30 to $6.20 range. The first batch of 33⅓ pop discs, featuring Frankie Carle's and Xavier Cugat's orchestras, Frank Sinatra, Doris Day, Billie Holiday with Teddy Wilson, Harry Owens, and Dinah Shore, sold for sixty cents each, a nickel less than what the upcoming 45s were slated to sell for; the new Masterworks singles, including one by the New York Philharmonic, were ninety cents. However, with Columbia spending so much time and money on promoting the larger LPs, it treated the seven-inch microgroove disc like a stepchild and never completely got behind it. The slow single would last only a few years and never be anything but a fringe item.

This variety of sizes and speeds was a counterproductive way to sell music. *Billboard* writer Joe Caida described the growing problem in his January 15th column: "If you buy the Columbia 33⅓ player and records now, you cannot play RCA 45-rpm records on it. You can still buy any RCA artists or songs you like on 78-rpm records, to play on your 78-rpm mechanism, but they will not play on your 33⅓ unit. All your Columbia 33⅓ records will play on it, and any other record companies which put out 33⅓ records will play on it, but no 78 or 45 rpm records will play on it."

The consumer was being given three choices: invest in RCA's new format, invest in Columbia's recent format, or simply stick with your old 78s because both companies, along with the rest of the industry, were still pressing them. It was an awkward situation that pleased nobody. As one reader from Los Angeles complained to *Billboard* in February, "Now I don't mind having two record players—but I'll be damned if I buy three!"

Major phonograph manufacturers, however, were already working to solve this problem, or at least present a makeshift compromise. Since the LP's debut the previous June, most of these companies had been making at least one model with a two-speed motor that could play both 78s and LPs. Now, with yet another record system ready to hit the stores, several companies retooled again. One of them, VM Industries, designed both a three-speed player for new buyers and a "conversion kit" for the two-speed players it had already sold. In both cases the manufacturer supplied a round, flat, plastic adapter that snapped into the 45's hole to make it fit on the 33⅓ spindle, but the discs could only be played manually, one at a time. Emerson, which had avoided the LP in 1948, was now focusing on a radio-phono console with two separate turntables—one for 78s, the other for 45s—with separate tone arms.

Meanwhile, America's third largest record company, Decca, announced early that it would continue exclusively with the 10-inch 78 and stay out of the fray until the dust settled. To maintain the appearance that it was modernizing in step with RCA Victor and Columbia, however, Decca trumpeted its own new series of vinyl 78s capable of holding five minutes instead of the regular four.

That left the fourth largest company, Hollywood-based Capitol Records, as the tie breaker. In January 1949 both William Paley and Columbia Records president Frank White flew to the West Coast to plead with Capitol president Glenn Wallichs to jump on the 33⅓ bandwagon. But Wallichs was leaning toward what was by now being touted as the "big-spindle, rapid-change [45] platter" because Sarnoff had already offered him a deal: RCA Victor would press 45s for Capitol at its Camden plant until Capitol could set up its own production facility in Los Angeles. In early February, Capitol disclosed that it would join RCA with the 45's debut and market its own record players. Being a relatively new company with no backlog of symphonies, concertos, and suites, Capitol focused more on the day-to-day business of selling modern pop, country, R&B, and big band jazz that fit more naturally on smaller records. But Wallichs was quick to report to his record dealers that Capitol's choice of the 45 did not mean it was joining RCA Victor's ranks in a battle of speeds. He explained in a letter that he simply chose the better of the two innovations in disc reproduction and believed that "the small record is, for our type of business, most suitable because of advantages of weight, space, unbreakability, and sound reproduction." He told *Billboard* that he hoped his choice "will have a stabilizing effect on the industry," but added that the 78 would remain Capitol's primary format and that he "will use only those artists and selections that hold widest sales appeal for duplication [on 45]."

By now, RCA's engineers, executives, and publicity men were traveling around the country for meetings and demonstrations with their key distributors and record dealers to set up a merchandising and marketing program. The company also consolidated its deals with nearly a dozen record-player manufacturers, including Emerson, Scott, Teletone, Fad, Stromberg-Carlson, Motorola, and Admiral, and set up a temporary record manufacturers' clinic at an Indianapolis lab to show smaller record companies how to convert their pressing plants for the smaller disc. One indie label, Tempo Records

Admiral's changer played 'em all—automatically.

in Hollywood, best known as the label that produced the version of "Sweet Georgia Brown" embraced by the Harlem Globetrotters, took advantage of the publicity opportunity by announcing as early as February that it would be the first company to issue its records on all three speeds.

To allay retailers' fear of and resistance to the 45 novelty, RCA Victor promised a full exchange on all unsold records, so that dealers could, in the words of one New York distributor, "experiment on the factory's money."

Meanwhile, RCA and Columbia were suddenly destabilizing the overall retail market by dumping their older stocks of 78s, especially albums, before RCA's new system came out. Both companies offered incredible deals to key distributors around the country, slashing some of their classical stock as high as ninety percent. RCA designed this drastic housecleaning to send a message that shellac 78s were no longer worth as much as before—and would be worth even less when the cheaper 45s arrived in a few weeks. Columbia's impetus was to get rid of what was left of its classical and semi-classical 78s that had been superseded by the LP. In any event, the price slashing merely added to the turmoil within the record industry as it awaited the Battle of the Speeds.

CHAPTER 4

The Battle of the Speeds

•••

I n February 1949, Columbia board chairman Ed Wallerstein took a slap at RCA Victor by going public in a statement to the media, explaining that the confusion currently roiling the record industry and making buyers apprehensive had been caused by RCA Victor, not Columbia Records. The LP's unique features, he said, did not in themselves create a "record war" (Wallerstein's quotes), "but one major company—RCA—has chosen to ignore these developments. If it had done only that, there would be no need for comment. RCA has gone much further. It has indicated it will make no provisions of any kind, either in its equipment or records, for long-playing records; it has suggested that the long-playing records already in the homes of the American people would not be successful despite all the weight of evidence and the considered judgment of virtually all other manufacturers of equipment." He referred to RCA's format as a "small record playing at the unorthodox speed of 45 r.p.m.'s, on a special turntable which can take no other records, either of the conventional or long-playing type." He also took a parting shot at RCA by pointing out that its 1933 effort to manufacture a long-play system had failed, whereas Columbia's had succeeded.

Then Columbia launched its PR offensive against the coming 45 by running a full-page ad in the March 12, 1949, *Billboard* with the headline: "What's all this about a RECORD WAR?" Without mentioning the 45 configuration by name, Columbia soothed record dealers by assuring them of the LP's triumph during the eight months it had been on the market. "Columbia LP Microgroove Records Are Already an Established Success . . . and the Greatest Stimulus to the Record Business in Years!" the sub-headline proclaimed. The ad pointed out that 600,000 families had already bought LP record players and over two million albums—"the equivalent of more than 10 million conventional shellac records. And LP sales are rising every day." Columbia asserted that it had sold nearly as many musical works on microgroove as had been sold on 78s in all of 1948; that nearly every major manufacturer was producing phonographic equipment that could play both LPs and 78s; that radio stations around the country were installing microgroove players

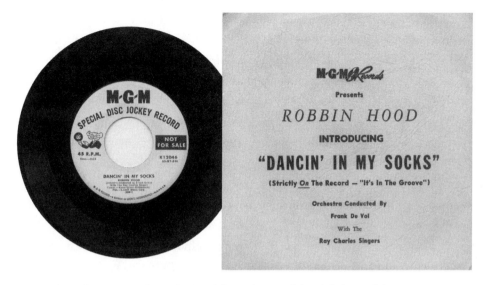

On early promotional records, MGM's lion cub (center left on label) touted the new 45 format. The sleeves were designed for radio stations only.

for airing LPs; and that the company was offering its system to other manufacturers. Mercury Records in Chicago had already signed on and would soon be releasing its own LPs.

Two weeks later, RCA countered with its own elaborate, four-page *Billboard* and *Cashbox* blitz to herald its bright new 45 disc. "After 10 million phonographs—After 1 billion records . . . comes the new RCA Victor system of recorded music!" the ad declared. One page was dedicated to PR puffery and assurances to the record industry, particularly those handling RCA's product: "This period is not one of revolution but one of transition. There will be plenty of time for all dealers to adjust their inventories in making way for this new, improved, more profitable product." The company proclaimed: "The product is ready . . . the public is ready!"

Another page focused on the 45 itself, extolling its "distortion-free playing surface," which RCA dubbed the "Quality Zone," and its easy storage. "More than 150 single records or 18 symphonies fit in one foot of bookshelf space." Furthermore, the "non-breakable" vinyl lasted ten times longer than shellac 78s, drastically cutting handling and storage damage, and its special "shoulder con-struction"—the thicker label area—protected the recording grooves.

But the selling point that RCA especially harped on, besides its array of RCA Victor record players, was "the world's fastest record changer," as if its "trigger-action speed" could make the listener forget the constant interruptions caused by the 45's scant playing time. Plus, it was a low-maintenance mechanism that could "play more than 50 minutes of music without the need of attention."

Though the original 1930s team of engineers had already designed the basic 45 playing system, RCA had substantially updated the new players. Clearly they were crucial to the success of the 45 record, so RCA offered something for everyone—a generous model line ranging from an outboard 9-JY player ($12.95) in a brown Bakelite case that could fit in the palm of one's hand, to the 9-W-125 radio-phonograph cabinet ($465.00) that could play both 45s and 78s. The tiny 9-JY had no amplifier, but it came with its own audio cable that could be plugged into most new American radios and phonographs. RCA initially sold it at cost simply to wean new buyers onto the 45 format—but later in the year raised the retail price to $29.95. The little portable's close cousin was the 9-EY-3, also tiny enough (10 x 10 inches) to fit anywhere, but self-contained, with its own amplifier. Like the 9-JY, the 9-EY-3 had a bright gold metal tone arm with a special pneumatic system that gently lowered the needle onto the record. The spindles were black with a bright red top.

Overall, these players were beautiful in their simplicity, though with eighty-five moving parts they could hardly be called uncomplicated. Adults and teenagers could buy a 9-EY-3 in a brown Bakelite case or in a tan or red leatherette case; kids could get one in a white Bakelite case with pictures of either Walt Disney characters or Roy Rogers and his horse Trigger. These players retailed at $54.95. The next step up, at $99.50, was the 9-W-50, which RCA boasted as the smallest automatic table-model phonograph and radio system it had ever made.

By now RCA was calling its new record a "45." *Billboard* had noted earlier, in January, "A tricky problem facing the RCA-ites is how to identify the new disc and player when it is finally introduced. Since Columbia has been doing an all-out job publicizing and promoting the 45-minute aspect of its long-playing microgrooved discs, the RCA gang, it was learned, want[s] to duck the confusion [that] would result from their introduction of a 45-revolutions-per-minute disc. Around Camden the project has long been referred to as 'Madame X,' but the feeling higher up is that this would hardly be in keeping with the company's dignity on a consumer level." With the introduction of the LP and now the slower-speed single, however, the trade papers and record business insiders were already beginning to refer to the vintage 10-inch platter as a 78, so RCA went with the 45's rpm designation. (Like "acoustic guitar" and "silent movie," the stand-alone number 78 denoting the older format was a retronym that hadn't existed until something new, like electric guitars or talkies or varying record speeds, came along that required comparison.)

RCA shipped custom window displays to record stores around the country. Each consisted of a rotating carousel, a 45-rpm turntable, and a light brown package of promotional copies of its first seven singles, along with a "Whirl-Away Demonstration Record" with snippets of music from the other 45s and a baritone voice that extolled the glories of the new system. The demo record was to be played over and over on the turntable, while the other seven rotated in the carousel. And what an eye-catching rainbow of plastic they were.

Thanks to a consumer products board at RCA Laboratories headed by industrial designer John Vassos, the company had come up with the idea of color-coding its 45s into seven "sparkling identifying colors"— psychologically appropriate vinyl hues to match the style of music in the grooves. Browsing in a store, a customer could zero in on his favorite music and ignore the rest at a single glance.

Because its prestigious Red Seal department had long associated scarlet with classical music in the public's mind, RCA carried the imprimatur over to 45 on "ruby red" plastic, with a dark red label. Semi-

RCA issued its first catalog of 45s at the end of 1949.

classical music, termed "popular classics"—George Gershwin's *Rhapsody in Blue*, for example—was released on midnight blue vinyl with a "rocket blue" label; children's music on "lemon drop yellow" vinyl (with a "Flemish blue" label); folk music, including hillbilly, on "grass green" plastic with a "quad green" label; black music—called *sepia* or *blues & rhythm* in those days just before *Billboard* and *Cashbox* codified the term *rhythm & blues*—on "cerise" (a word defined as light cherry red but, in RCA's spectrum, a bright orange) vinyl with a "slate gray" label; pop music on traditional black plastic with a "Persian peacock" label; and international music on "sky blue" vinyl with a black label.

RCA also devised a numbering system with new prefixes to differentiate not only 45s from 78s, but also the seven musical categories from each other. They were:

47-0000 children's music
47-2800 pop music
48-0000 folk (including country music, polkas, waltzes)

49-0000 classical

50-0000 blues and rhythm

51-0000 international

52-0000 pop classics

RCA Victor's 78s conspicuously carried the Victor logo, Nipper, at the top of the label, where it had resided for nearly fifty years. (One of Eldridge Johnson's first magazine advertisements for his Trademark Gram-O-Phone record player had featured a Francis Barraud painting of a fox terrier named Nipper gazing intently into the large horn of Johnson's gramophone invention, below the words "His Master's Voice," and after Johnson formed the Victor Talking Machine Company in 1901, he made Nipper his company symbol.) With the new 45, however, a much smaller Nipper was moved to the right side of the label to make room for the words "45 RPM" set in a box on the left side.

For its March 31, 1949, inaugural day, RCA dipped into its catalog and reissued material that had already been released on 78 over the previous three or four years. The plan was to encourage customers to opt for the durability and easier handling of the 45 without having to give up their favorite recordings. In all, RCA introduced seventy-six albums (box sets, really) and 104 singles, with the Red Seal series getting the lion's share: 30 albums and 65 singles. The rest of the albums were pop classics (25), children's music (15), pop music (3) and folk (3). As for singles, folk music was allotted a dozen and race music merely five.

Among the first green-vinyl releases in the folk 45 series were RCA's top country star Eddy Arnold's "Bouquet of Roses"/"Texarkana Baby" (48-0001) and "Anytime"/"What a Fool I Was" (48-0002), both of which had been big two-sided hits on the folk and pop charts the previous year on 78. The company also reissued country bandleader Pee Wee King's hugely successful 1948 hit, "Tennessee Waltz" (48-0003). These songs were such favorites that both country and pop fans would want to have them. (Eddy Arnold was so popular at the time that some of his 78s had been released with pop-prefix serial numbers that began with 20-, instead of the folk 21-.)

Interestingly, among the first titles in its race music series, RCA reissued only one previous hit, blues singer Arbee Stidham's "My Heart Belongs to You" (50-0003), which had topped the "sepia" charts the previous year. Most curious was the company's choice for the series' first two 45s: reissues of 1946 recordings by Arthur "Big Boy" Crudup, a Mississippi sharecropper who took a train north to Chicago every six months or so to record a batch of songs in a makeshift studio above a pawn shop. Crudup's specialty was old-time country blues with a beat, usually accompanied by a bassist and drummer to enhance his own syncopated guitar picking. RCA Victor and its Bluebird subsidiary had released about forty Crudup 78s since 1941, including several small hits, but the four sides being reissued on 45 had not sold all that well the first time around. The A-side of the first single (50-0000) was "That's All Right," which didn't sound all that different from several of Crudup's other songs, but its revival would turn out to have a far-reaching effect on RCA's fortunes—even though the single itself didn't sell much better as a 45 disc than it had done earlier on 78—because a Memphis kid, Elvis Presley, happened to pick up a copy and commit the song to memory, in preparation for his first recording session five years later.

Columbia hoped to thwart the 45 with its own 33⅓ single, which it introduced with a sleeve.

RCA also issued its first 45 albums, cataloging them under a separate system with lettered prefixes: Red Seal classical albums were WDM, as in WDM-1220 for Ravel's *Bolero*; light classical were prefixed WK, children's records were WY, and the rest were WP. Typically these packages contained three or four singles, but rather than combine them in the traditional 78 album book form, RCA presented them in a flat 7⅜ x 7⅜-inch box. Again, these were reissues of earlier albums, such as the Delta Rhythm Boys' 1947 *Dry Bones* (WP-193), but the discs inside, besides bearing their WP numbers, were sequentially numbered as RCA singles, so that they could also be sold individually, independent of the box. The singles (usually four of them) in the classical and theatrical albums also bore a third number to show the listener how to stack them in the proper order on the spindle to keep the music in sequence: Side 1 and Side 8 would be on opposite sides of the same record, Side 2 and Side 7 on the next one, and so on. RCA's mastering engineers tried to match the disconcerting gap caused by the periodic three-second record changes with musical pauses or breaks between movements.

RCA Victor spent lavishly to promote its new product, running ads in many of the most popular magazines, including *Time, Life, Colliers, Look, The Saturday Evening Post*, and big-city newspapers.

The company estimated that its ads reached a total magazine circulation of over seventeen million people, which means they'd actually be seen by two or three times that number. (In all, RCA allocated $2 million to get the 45 off the ground in the first six months.) In a March bulletin to distributors, RCA promised that "Enthusiasm for the 45 will be kept high on RCA Victor airings: [radio's] *Music America Loves Best, Music You Want* and TV's *Kukla, Fran and Ollie* show. DJ's will put on contests . . . publicity staffs work overtime. A whiz-bang teaser window, counter demonstrator, revolving merchandiser, wall chart, streamers, hangers, brochure, full-line folder, stuffer Q & A book, catalog sheets, clerk badges are among the other launching items." The company assured its distributors, "The new 45 system is going out with a repertoire that includes everything from a bebop bash to a minuet . . . all vital merchandise, best-by-test stuff. RCA Victor spent much time in carefully selecting the items to be included in its initial offering of 45 rpm recordings, and the results represent the choicest selections from the world's greatest catalog."

The sound of those 45s, according to another RCA company bulletin, could best be described in poetic terms, as if the new single had replaced not only the 78 but studio recording tape: "The [45] is like a magic ear. When the music starts playing in the studio, and the new record starts listening, the magic gets to work. Every tone given out, every shade of tone, is caught and held. Whether it is a vocal solo with piano accompaniment or an operatic chorus with full orchestra, this record hears all . . . . Whether it's the whisper of a violin in a Brahms lullaby, or all-out brass in a hot swing number, the record hears it, gets it down on wax—only now it's vinylite—and gives it to you." (By now, Union Carbide's Vinylite was becoming a generic, lower-case term and would soon be shortened to vinyl.)

Utilizing the lightweight advantage of the 45, which could be air-mailed at less cost than it took to send 78s first class, RCA also instituted what it called the Triple S Delivery System that promised "super speed shipments" of singles practically overnight. Delivery had always been a problem in the volatile and unpredictable world of hit records. In the past, if a single suddenly got hot in, say, Chicago and caught local distributors flat-footed, they'd have to wait several days to a week to get an adequate resupply of 78s, and then it might take another day for the platters to reach the stores—by which time the demand for that single might have cooled off. But with RCA's Triple S service, if the desired 45s weren't already in stock, extra record presses were standing by at the Camden plant to fill incoming orders that night, so that discs could be whisked by air the next day to the distributors or even to the individual stores.

With the exception of the Red Seal line, the general price of the 45 was 65 cents, compared with $1.25 for the average LP. (Red Seal classical singles were 95 cents). Prices for 45 albums varied according to music category and number of discs; the most expensive was the four-record Red Seal album at $4.30.

RCA Victor still had to release 10-inch platters to maintain its market among those eighteen million Americans still holding on to their old turntables, but even that was an opportunity to promote the smaller format by advertising individual 45 singles on 78 paper sleeves: "Ask to hear the latest RCA Victor '45' rpm records *today*," because "on '45' you get superior TONE, CLARITY, and LONGER LIFE!" as well as "All the hits."

The company even slanted its record sales reportage to the trade magazines in favor of the new 45. Eddy Arnold's "Don't Rob Another Man's Castle" had already gone to No.1 on *Billboard*'s Folk chart

When Columbia finally adopted the 45 format, it initially retained the traditional small hole.

on March 5—almost four weeks before the first 45s were issued—yet RCA listed it as being 48-0042 rather than the 78 designation, 21-0002, as if the 45s were already jumping off the shelves. (Incidentally, *Billboard* added the term Country & Western to the name of its Folk chart in late June 1949 to reflect the genre's growing importance.)

By mid-May, *Billboard* spot-checked 130 dealers around the country to see how the 45 was doing. Less than a quarter of them said "good" and almost twice that number said "disappointing." The rest, except for six dealers who weren't handling 45s at all, reported their sales as "satisfactory." Significantly, fifty dealers claimed that 45s were selling better than LPs, except in the classical market, where LPs, not surprisingly, were overtaking 78s as the main format. Otherwise, the 78 still held its own against the two microgroove newcomers. Overall, since *Billboard* didn't break down the distributors' responses according to cities or neighborhoods to give the buying patterns of various segments of the public, it was hard to tell from the polling exactly where the record market was heading.

CHAPTER 5

The Kiddie Discs

Within months after the 45's introduction, RCA Victor saw the emergence of at least one consumer group that it could depend on for the success of its new format: teenagers. In a November 14, 1949, bulletin to its distributors, the company announced, "The school set loves 'em, now that you can get those [big band] Bluebird hits on '45', and—from coast to coast—teenagers are lining up for bargain player attachments. The whole thing's on key with their allowances—neat little records they can slip in their pockets, with a first-class band playing their favorite hit—for 49 cents times are like the '30s, the early '40s again, when the youngsters made up the big biz in the pop market. They go for [Bluebird Records bandleader Ralph] Flanagan, they go for the lowest priced at the new speed, they go for the little disc that fits on the shelf beside their paper-backed novels, it's unbreakable, and has quality of tone that can't be matched. Sell 'em, sell 'em '45'."

As it turned out, RCA Victor was premature in thinking that teenagers would save the 45. If the disc was perfectly positioned to exploit a demographic and establish itself for many years to come, that market was kids who were waiting to be teenagers.

The recording disc itself had begun as a child's toy when German manufacturer Kammer & Reinhardt hired Emile Berliner to produce his first record and playback machine in 1888. Victor's first double-sided 7-inch record, released around 1900, was called "A Record for Children," with three nursery rhymes recited on each side. A year later the company released alphabet songs on both 7-inch platters and the new 10-inch 78s. Even after Victor discontinued the 7-inch plate in 1907, it occasionally revived the smaller format for children's releases, such as the popular "Bubble Books" albums in 1924 and, in the thirties, Winnie-the-Pooh picture discs. In the 1940s Victor and other companies began using colored wax to distinguish records for kids and switched over to unbreakable Vinylite that resisted the clumsy and destructive hands of tots. Illustrated picture sleeves began with children's records in the 1940s. In short, nearly every innovation in the history of recording had first come about in the production of children's records. And yet, though the major companies maintained separate divisions for children, such as RCA's Little Nipper series, they were slow in fully exploiting this market as a separate niche.

By mid-1948, the industry was in the doldrums. The Petrillo Ban—the decade's second musicians union strike led by AFM President James Petrillo—had depressed the availability of recordings by top pop talent, leaving the field open for small, independent companies to step in with non-union genres, such as hillbilly, rhythm & blues, and children's records, which the trade papers, in their inimitable argot, dubbed "kidiscs" and "tot-tallows." These records rarely made the charts, but they were a staple of the business. And now, with the nation's Depression- and war-deprived grown-ups hunkering down to raise the early beneficiaries of what would later be called the "postwar boom years," many storefront operations, being too small to compete in the expensive rough and tumble of making and marketing pop music,

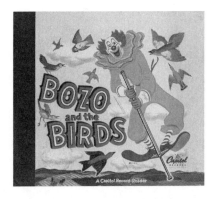

Bozo and the Birds *(Capitol 3033) was part of a popular Bozo the Clown record series in the late 1940s and early '50s. On 45,* Bozo and the Birds *was released on both an EP record and a two-single set, contained within a colorful 38-page book. Sound effects on the records told you when to turn the pages.*

saw the kidisc field as prime for innovation. In early 1948, *Billboard* announced that kids' records comprised thirty-five percent of the previous Christmas season market, and that overall they were now climbing from fifteen to twenty percent of total record sales. Industry prognosticators were guessing that fifty million kidiscs would be sold by the end of the year.

During the previous summer, Henry Lapidus, who owned the Synthetic Plastics Corporation in New York, had introduced a new label, Rocking Horse Records, whose 7-inch red and yellow plastic 78-rpm minidiscs retailed at a mere 35 cents—one-third the cost of most children's records. The little company that could, Rocking Horse shocked the record business by selling six million copies by June of 1948. Now Lapidus was ready to market 7-inch albums of three records each, accompanied by brightly colored pictures of nursery rhyme characters, for only $1.05. Furthermore, he had just launched a second label, Peter Pan Records, which was selling 6-inch discs directly to chain department stores to retail at 25 cents. Lapidus's profit margin was small, but his low overhead, high volume, and quick turnover made him both an overnight millionaire and a serious threat to the Big Six record companies, who found themselves stuck with unsold, expensive 10-inch children's platters. Granted, the sound quality of Lapidus' little plastic cheapies wasn't great, but kids weren't audiophiles and they played their records on tinny, tiny toy players anyway. Plus, they were hard on their stuff and generally needed replacements within a week or so after buying them.

Several other plastic companies moved in on the action. Sun Plastics in New Jersey set up production for an even cheaper 7-inch disc, pressed on both transparent and colored plastic, which sold for 20 cents and, according to company flacks, held up under 500 plays. The majors could no longer ignore what was happening. By the end of the summer, Columbia and RCA Victor rushed out 7-inch, 78-rpm vinyl records, mostly bright yellow, on their new respective kiddie lines, Playtime and Minidiscs, for 25 cents. RCA would later retain this yellow plastic when it introduced its new 45-rpm children's records. On May 28, 1949, *Billboard* would announce that sales were up 100 percent over 1948, and that "the idea of children having their own phonographs is also gaining acceptance." One manufacturer, Hudson Electronics, reported that its Junior Juke [record] player was selling twice as many units as in the previous year.

RCA in particular went all out to capture the children's market with elaborate record sets that the smaller, cheaper companies couldn't compete with. In fact, RCA's new Little Nipper 45 albums were more extravagant than anything it released in the adult market. Take for example *Johnny Appleseed* (WY 390), a full-color gatefold set of two yellow-vinyl 45s, narrated by Dennis Day, with a 6-page cartoon booklet inside—for $2.15. Or Kukla, Fran & Ollie's *At the Fair* (WY 2004), which included detachable puppet pieces and a 12-page coloring book—also for $2.15. Plus, the success of the latter record set, based on popular characters—actress Fran Allison and a cast of puppets—from a daily NBC-TV children's program, showed RCA Victor executives that along with their traditional kiddie fare, such as *Happy Mother Goose* (YW 423) and *Dragon Retreat* (YW 425), there was an entirely new children's world opening up in the expanding medium of television. In the years to come, TV shows and kiddie discs would prove to be a marriage made in heaven.

What all this meant, though few seemed fully aware of it at the time, was that children were becoming their own separate consumer demographic, catered to by mass production and mass marketing. Within six years the same thing would happen to the "teenage" segment of the population—in most cases the same kids. Rather than simply ease into the look and habits of their parents, these children would seek out their own clothing fashions and entertainment. The plastic 7-inch record was only the beginning.

And unlike the late-forties teenagers who went for Flanagan, the postwar kids would reap yet another belated benefit from the temporary pop vacuum created by the 1948 Petrillo musicians strike. When those dozens of feisty storefront hillbilly and R&B record labels stepped into the breach and got a steady foothold in the overall record market, the genie was out of the bottle and there was no squeezing it back inside again. Kids graduating into teen-hood in the 1950s would embrace their 45s because they had been weaned on little plastic records, but they would snub Ralph Flanagan, along with the big bands and crooners their parents listened to, and send the mainstream music business into a tailspin from which it would take years to recover.

CHAPTER 6

The Jukebox Saves the Day

A t the end of 1949 RCA released a 46-page, digest-sized catalog called *The World's Greatest Artists Are on RCA Victor 45 rpm Records*, listing its 7-inch releases by artists, composers, and the titles of all their albums, with musical compositions and songs. The number of recordings and variety of music was impressive. Besides a full complement of contemporary opera singers (including Marian Anderson and Robert Merrill), classical musicians (Jascha Heifetz, Vladimir Horowitz and Artur Rubinstein) and conductors (Arturo Toscanini), there were the bluesmen Arbee Stidham and Big Boy Crudup, yodeler Montana Slim & His Big Hole Bronco Busters, honking jazz saxophonist Illinois Jacquet, R&B bandleader Lucky Millinder, Ernie Benedict & His Polkateers, the irreverent Spike Jones & His City Slickers, the Glenn Miller and Tommy Dorsey big bands, crooners Vaughn Monroe and Perry Como, the jazz orchestras of Count Basie and Duke Ellington, cocktail blues combo Johnny Moore & His Three Blazers, jazz pioneer Benny Moten & His Kansas City Orchestra, gospel singer Freddie Evans, Irish tenor Dennis Day, the lush and easy listening of Percy Faith & His Orchestra, lightweight pop trio the Fontane Sisters (Perry Como's backup singers), the soulful Delta Rhythm Boys, Spade Cooley's country swing band, and singing cowboy Roy Rogers, as well as his wife Dale Evans and his former vocal group, the Sons of the Pioneers, to name a few.

But, the 45 output of most artists was limited. The hits of the company's recent top-selling talent, such as Eddy Arnold, had been made available on 45, but if you wanted to hear Perry Como's greatest hits going back to the early- to mid-1940s, you had to play them on 78. In fact, RCA generally avoided going into its vaults and did not include anything by its greatest recording artist, Italian opera sensation Enrico Caruso, who by simple fate had been trapped in the tinny, pre-1925 acoustic era, though that would soon change in 1950 with the release of the film *The Great Caruso*. (It would take another fifteen years before RCA's engineers figured out how to make Caruso's early twentieth-century recordings sound reasonably contemporary on modern equipment.)

Capitol and MGM Records also began releasing music on 45s, but without having a roster of classical artists, these companies concentrated on their current recording acts. On the other hand, the more traditional Decca Records' first 45s in late 1949 were box sets of mostly back-catalog albums by veterans like the Ink Spots, Al Jolson, and the Andrews Sisters.

Converting to the 45 was not necessarily beneficial to all record companies in those early days. On July 30, 1949, *Billboard* announced that the first significant independent label was signing on: "Leon Rene, president of Exclusive Records, plans to release Herb Jeffries's *Magenta Moods* album . . . in doughnut disc form within the next 90 days. This will mark the label's first step into the low-speed ranks." Rene, a Louisiana Creole bandleader and songwriter who relocated to Los Angeles in the late 1920s, had begun Exclusive in the mid-forties as a means of recording his own songs, which included "When the Swallows Come Back to Capistrano" and "I Sold My Heart to the Junk Man." In just a couple of years, Exclusive became the country's top black-owned record label, thanks in part to the 1948 musicians strike that hobbled the major companies. However, the 45 experiment proved costly to small operations like his because of the smaller profit margins. As Rene would later tell writer Arnold Shaw, "Competition with the majors forced the independent labels to use the 7-inch 45-rpm records, and [we] had to reduce the price of R&B records from a dollar-five to seventy-five cents, retail. This forced many independent labels out of business."

Already losing 78 sales to East Coast mobster bootleggers, Leon Rene declared bankruptcy in late 1949, before he could release his first 45.

Still, record presses at plants around the county were stamping out a million 45 discs a month by the end of the year, prompting RCA Victor President Frank Folsom to announce to the media that the 45 was in good shape and "here to stay." In a gesture of peace, archrival Columbia Records signed on in time to release some of its Christmas singles on 45. More dramatically, David Sarnoff reciprocated by abandoning his obstinacy and agreeing to start pressing albums on LP, after losing a million dollars in sales over the previous year and a half. (Columbia earned $3 million from the sale of vinyl albums from mid-1948 through 1949.)

What primarily prompted Sarnoff's capitulation was that RCA Victor's prestigious Red Seal label lost critical sales because classical music buyers were opting for the long-play album over the short-play 45. Columbia's assault on RCA's traditional dominance of the classical field throughout the 1940s had been one of the reasons Sarnoff was angry with William Paley in the first place, and now the situation had gone even further awry. RCA's classical artists and conductors, including Heifetz, Rubinstein, and Leopold Stokowski, were complaining that the company's rejection of the LP had diminished their recording careers. Opera basso Ezio Pinza, the star of Broadway's *South Pacific*, jumped ship for Columbia as soon as his RCA contract expired. (Columbia's *South Pacific* cast album was the first hit record on LP.) Finally, Toscanini, a close friend of Sarnoff's, convinced him to relent and adopt the LP before the hemorrhaging got any worse. On January 4, 1950, Sarnoff announced that he was making available RCA Victor's "great artists and unsurpassed classical library on new and improved Long Play (33 rpm) records." The battle of the speeds was over.

When Mercury Records in Chicago began pressing 45s later in the month, all of the Big Six were on board. In the opening weeks of 1950, the Ames Brothers' pop cover of country star Johnnie Lee Wills's "Rag Mop" turned out to be the last No. 1 single released exclusively on 78 by a major label. Even small companies catering mostly to black and hillbilly consumers were dipping their toes in the water. According to a February item in *Billboard*, "A new flock of indie labels this week got set to release their wares on one or both of the new speed systems."

Among these companies was Savoy, located in Camden, New Jersey, not far from RCA's factory. It was an important label in the jazz and R&B fields, with a combined roster that included bebop tenor saxists Charlie Parker and Dexter Gordon, pianist Erroll Garner, and bandleaders Paul Williams and Johnny Otis. At first Savoy issued only instrumental standards and light classical music on a limited number of 45s, but as orders started coming in from distributors around the company, it expanded to include blues and R&B singles.

On the West Coast, Los Angeles's biggest indie, Modern Records, also joined the fray. "Plattery said it would issue 16 single releases on 45, retailing at 79 cents," *Billboard* announced in mid-February. "Artists will include Hadda Brooks, Kay Starr, Erroll Garner, Andre Previn and Nappy Lamare. Modern originally planned to emphasize 33⅓ but decided against the slow speed due to lack of enough album material to justify LP issue. Diskery will release only singles on 45 for the present." Across town, the Aladdin and Specialty labels, both important in rhythm & blues, also began adding small runs of 45s of their more successful singles.

Over the next few months, hardy little labels around the country hurried to convert part of their new inventory to 45. Freedom Records in Houston, Texas, took the opportunity to expand beyond R&B to hillbilly and pop. In Philadelphia, Gotham Records bought 45 presses for its plant and set up its own printing department to produce labels and promotional material. In New York, Jubilee and Apollo released limited runs of R&B 45s on their cross-over artists like the Orioles and saxophonist Arnett Cobb. Either black consumers were making the conversion to the new format, or else these records were selling to more white listeners than anyone realized.

Also in early 1950, Capitol Records issued what was most likely the first major record pressed on all three formats: Arranger and bandleader Les Baxter's *Music Out of the Moon*, an album of British composer Harry Revel's mood pieces featuring Dr. Samuel Hoffmann on an electronic instrument called the theremin, a 1919 Russian invention whose eerie whine—called "music from the ether"—was controlled by hand manipulations within an electrical field. Originally released on a triple-78 album (CC-47) in 1948 with a provocative full-color cover photograph of a partially clothed woman lying on a bed whose red and silver sheets were shaded to resemble the moon's surface, *Music Out of the Moon*'s reissue on a 10-inch LP (CCF-2000) and in a 45 box set (CCF-2000), both using the 78 album's cover art, was the beginning of fifties space-age pop music. Baxter's use of the otherworldly theremin would thereafter associate it with science fiction. This album most likely inspired the theremin's presence on the soundtracks of such films as *The Day the Earth Stood Still* (1951) and the 3-D enhanced *It Came from Outer Space* (1954). *Music Out of the Moon* also established the career of Baxter, who went on to pioneer a niche of album pop music called "exotica" that blended African, South American, and Polynesian instruments and rhythms.

Though the battle between RCA Victor and Columbia seemed to be over, the 45 was still struggling against the workhorse 78. True, the public increasingly accepted the new format, but the summer of 1950 brought bad news. The United States found itself embroiled in a ground war against communist troops in Korea that put immediate demands on the nation's supply of vinyl.

The July 29 issue of Billboard summed up the problem: "The rise in the cost of virgin vinyl this week, the first effect of the Korean War on the disc business, has added to the woes of indie diskers who were already complaining about the poor summertime service they were getting from pressing plants . . . . The vital vinyl, an essential war product, meanwhile rose 2½ to 3 cents per pound in a week." Making matters worse, there was a strike within the chlorine industry. "Chlorine is an important ingredient in [vinyl] and the strike virtually paralyzed its production," said Billboard. Even after the strike was over, manufacturers found it difficult to stock up again because chlorine was needed by defense industries.

On RCA's plus side, the rise in vinyl prices hurt Columbia's LP more than it did the 45. "One plant, noting a 1-cent increase in its own cost of producing an LP disc, raised its pressing price 2 cents," *Billboard* reported. "One plant operator feels he may be forced to emphasize 45s, since they use less material. Ten 45s can be made from a pound of vinyl, while only two or three 12-inch discs can be made from the same amount." On the other hand, 78s were untouched by the new war rationing because, thanks to vinyl, shellac was no longer important in the manufacture of electrical insulation.

By November rumors abounded that a vinyl shortage would curtail 45 production altogether, unless manufacturers used substitutes like styrene, which were inferior. RCA Victor rejected this alternative, however, and streamlined its 45 production by recycling the scrap vinyl, called *chips*, left over when holes were cut in the discs. This kept a steady flow of 45s going out the factory door, but at a significant cost: Because of the impurity of used vinyl, RCA had to eliminate its brightly colored 45s and confine itself to pressing black records. From then on, red, green, and blue 45s would be specialty items only, pressed in very limited runs. Only yellow children's records would be spared.

As it turned out, the 45 had a special friend that was more powerful than the Korean War and all the chlorine workers combined. It was the jukebox.

The jukebox has its roots in nineteenth-century coin-operated player pianos and a large 1890s Edison cylinder machine, a kind of audio Nickelodeon, that had several listening tubes attached. In 1906 the John Gabel Company introduced a coin-operated record player called the Automatic Entertainer that was wound up like a music box. But not until the introduction of electrical recording in 1925, with its microphones and amplification system, could record machine makers create the modern jukebox, with its music cabinets with big speakers and full sound. By the end of the Depression, four manufacturers— Wurlitzer, Seeburg, Rock-Ola (founded by a Canadian named David Rockola), and AMi—controlled most of the business, but Wurlitzer was the undisputed king. By that time the word "jukebox" had attached to the machines because of their popularity in roadside "juke joints," or dance clubs, and thanks to the availability of new plastics they were gaudy contraptions of light and color, glowing in otherworldly greens, yellows, and reds.

In 1948 Seeburg, a Chicago manufacturer, unveiled an innovation it had been working on in secret. Where the other companies merely updated their models periodically with different cabinet designs, Seeburg re-engineered the jukebox's basic gears and guts and came up with the M100A, featuring a playing mechanism—called Select-O-Matic—that allowed the selector-player to move horizontally along a fixed row of vertical 78s instead of waiting for a revolving cylinder to bring platters to it. This reconfiguration allowed the jukebox to hold more records, fifty in all, giving café, restaurant, honky-tonk, and nightclub customers one hundred selections to choose from. The selector also snatched the records and played them vertically instead of flipping them onto a turntable and then taking them back off again a couple of minutes later—thus saving precious seconds between plays. The M100A turned out to be such a huge success that Seeburg surpassed Wurlitzer in overall jukebox sales and rentals. Then, two years later, in 1950, Seeburg modified its M100A into the M100B, the first 45 jukebox, also capable of holding fifty singles. "Everybody followed Seeburg with their M100B," said Warren Rowe, an El Monte, California, jukebox operator who worked in the trade for fifty years. "Seeburg saw the writing on the wall, the better fidelity [of 45s]. The others played catch-up after that."

A September 1950 *Cashbox* item noted, "Altho the jukebox industry has not yet taken to 45-rpms to any great degree, indications are that the adopted speed will make fast inroads with music ops who have converted. To say nothing of the tremendous savings the platter makes for phono ops" because of size, durability, weight, and ease of handling.

The jukebox was a godsend for the 45 in its competition against the LP. Here was a realm the 45 had to itself. There have been many jukebox configurations over the years, but none of them ever played vinyl albums. The LP was, in effect, a stay-at-home at a time when, according to *Cashbox* in early 1952, the jukebox industry was using fifty million platters a year. "Some diskeries claim that at least 15 percent of their single records are sold for coin machine use," said *Cashbox*. Columbia Records claimed that it sold 150,000 of the first 200,000 copies of Tony Bennett's "Because of You" (39362), 1951's biggest hit, to jukebox operators. Most of them were 78s, but enough were 45s to keep the format healthy, and their number was growing monthly.

In fact, by spring of 1952, with the Korean War settling down into a stalemate and vinyl producers overcoming their initial shortages, the jukebox industry announced that over the coming year it would be phasing out 78s in favor of the easier-to-handle 45. According to *Billboard* writer Norman Weiser, "More than 15,000,000 45 rpm records will be channeled into the jukebox field this year . . . and barring an all-out war which would halt production, this figure will be more than doubled in 1953." By now the record companies had worked out their production kinks so that they could more efficiently get 45s to distributors and jukebox operators around the country. "[B]oth 45 and 78 rpm sides are now being released simultaneously, compared with a two-to-three-week lag in 45 rpm output last year."

"According to estimates from the various [jukebox] manufacturers," said another *Billboard* writer, "there are currently about 35,000 45 rpm machines on location thruout the country, and this figure will be expanded considerably before the end of the year, with the best guesses now calling for at least twice that figure to be in use within the next 12-month period."

But most of this activity came from the major record companies selling pop music. Jukebox operators in the South and Southwest who specialized in down-home music resisted the change. "Hillbilly and r&b etchings are still coming thru in small quantities, and operators depending on this type of music for their machines are holding to the 78 rpm speed," said *Billboard*. Though every rhythm & blues independent label had gone into 45 production by mid-1951, they were still pressing up far greater numbers of 78s because their audience, mostly poor and working-class regardless of race, ignored the 45 record, mostly for economic reasons. Even when MGM Records launched an R&B line in December 1952, it released only 78s and said it would disregard 45s unless "the demand materialize[s] in that direction."

Yet record companies and jukebox operators alike knew that it was only a matter of time. "[T]he estimate now is that within three years the jukebox field will be using more than 50,000,000 45 rpm records a year, and if the production picture brightens shortly, this figure may be reached much sooner than anticipated."

CHAPTER 7

The 45 Takes Over!

O n May 1, 1954, the Record Industry Association of America (RIAA) declared the good news that the previous year's record sales had hit an all-time high of $205 million, up $16 million from 1952. Within these tidings, the trade organization took special notice that the 78 platter—which had kept the music playing for over fifty years—was steadily losing ground. The 78 accounted for only fifty-two percent of total sales in 1953. The biggest bite from its market share came from the 45, now responsible for slightly more than one-fourth of all records sold—a long way up from its mere four percent in 1949. (Long-play albums were responsible for twenty percent of sales.) At RCA Victor the figures were even more impressive. General Manager Manny Sachs claimed that the 45 was already accounting for "more than fifty percent of all [RCA] single pop record sales" and that the 78 comprised only twenty-three percent of the company's business.

Two weeks later, the Big Six—RCA Victor, Columbia, Decca, Capitol, MGM, and Mercury—announced jointly to the nation's radio stations that they would begin shipping 45 promotional singles instead of 78s, effective in mid-July. The switch had been a long time coming. RCA and Columbia had wanted to convert to 45s two years earlier, but there had been too much resistance from station owners claiming they needed time to buy multispeed turntables and other equipment. At one point the two companies floated the idea of creating an interim format—a 7-inch 78—but station managers shot it down, insisting they didn't need to add a fourth format to the already confusing situation. But now, in the late spring of 1954, with the 45 gaining in popularity, radio could no longer resist. According to Sachs, "[C]onversion of the disc jockey service at this time anticipates the day when the 45 system will completely replace the 78 speed."

Jocks themselves generally welcomed the 45 because it was sturdier and took up less room. According to Los Angeles deejay Dick "Huggy Boy" Hugg, who launched the Penguins' "Earth Angel" and several other early R&B hits, "We'd get these boxes of 78s, they were bulky and heavy. You'd open 'em up and maybe one or two would be cracked. You had to be careful with [78s], treat 'em like babies. You were handling 'em all the time, moving 'em around, and they'd break on you, so the companies would send a couple of backups 'cause they didn't want to lose any airtime if a record got broken. But 45s didn't break. You could toss 'em around like Frisbees. You could pick up a box of 45s without getting a hernia. The sound wasn't as good, I don't think, but they made our job easier, that's for sure."

Another early Los Angeles disc jockey, Art Laboe, who is credited with coining the term "oldies but goodies," concurred. "It was a matter of economics," Laboe told Oliver Wang. "The 45 was a whole lot cheaper. The 78 platter was expensive to make and to ship. Also, it was like a mirror—if you dropped it, it would shatter."

The main thing holding back full-scale use of 45s was the reluctance of consumers still loyal to their 78 collections. As far as the record companies were concerned, economics was on the side of the 45. By *Billboard*'s reckoning, the majors could save up to $250,000 a year by shipping the little vinyl donuts instead of the heavy shellac.

As it turned out, the changeover from one listening format to another was the lesser of the Big Six's worries in 1954. The more urgent problem was that their virtual monopoly of the record market had come under attack. As early as May 1953, a *Billboard* headline blared: "Explosive Growth of R.& B. Labels Seen As Industry Phenomenon." The proliferation of new, independent storefront companies during the previous twelve months had been "one of the most sensational developments in the field in over a decade." Rhythm and blues comprised only 5.7 percent of all record sales in mid-1953, but as *Billboard* noted, "Still, this market now consists of close to 100 active labels." Among them were Chess and its Checker subsidiary, Aladdin, King/Federal, Duke/Peacock, Modern, Gotham, Specialty, Jubilee, Imperial, Atlantic, and many others that would soon become important players in the music industry.

The response of the majors to this shift in America's musical taste had been tepid. Decca's Brunswick subsidiary and Columbia's Okeh were essentially regenerated blues labels from the 1920s and their management, answering to corporate bosses in New York, had no real grasp of what was happening on the streets. RCA's new Groove label was doing a slightly better job of recruiting black talent, but the company didn't know how to effectively promote or distribute R&B.

And so, in 1954, the R&B market was breaking wide open without them. "Teen-Agers Going For 'Music With a Beat' As Industry Reaps a Financial Harvest," *Billboard* announced with a flourish in April. "Once limited in sales appeal to the relatively small Negro market, rhythm and blues has now blossomed, with disc sales last year reaching an all-time record of $15,000.000." The article noted that 700 deejays across the country were airing R&B exclusively, while many pop jocks were "following the change in listener tastes by including rhythm and blues selections with their regular pop offerings." Jukebox owners, closer to the action and more attuned to public preferences, were already replacing pop records with R&B wherever young people hung out and danced. The operative word here was *young*. As *Billboard* pointed out, "Teen-agers are instigating the current trend towards r&b and are largely responsible for keeping its sales mounting. The teen-age tide has swept down the old barriers which kept this music restricted to [the black] segment of the population."

What may have inspired the urgency of this article were two R&B records exploding on the national airwaves. The first was "Shake, Rattle, and Roll" by veteran blues singer Big Joe Turner; the second was "Sh-Boom" by a young Bronx vocal group called the Chords. Both singles came from Atlantic Records, though "Sh-Boom" had been released on a subsidiary, Cat Records, whose name and jitterbugging-stick-figures logo had been designed to appeal to white teenagers. Both songs floated many boats that year. Besides topping the Harlem Hit Parade, the two singles raced neck and neck up the pop charts, and their inevitable white cover versions—by Bill Haley and His Comets and the Crew-Cuts, respectively—fared even better. "Sh-Boom" turned out to be the year's best-selling song, with four different recordings in the Top 25. The Crew-Cuts' rendition spent nine weeks at No. 1, and the Chords' rougher-edged original reached No. 5.

The teenager—hyphenated "teen-ager" at the time because of its recent coinage—was a product of America's postwar prosperity and vague discontent. Before World War II, society had expected kids to grow up, put away childish things, learn a trade, and in many cases take a full-time job as soon as they entered adolescence. But the generation of the 1950s had grown up as their fathers were off fighting the war and their mothers were distracted by work on the home front. When America emerged as an industrial superpower in the late 1940s, parents were anxious to get jobs in the new production sectors, buy a spanking new house in the bright new suburbs and subdivisions, and spoil their children.

As noted in Chapter 4, RCA Victor had recognized these pampered little consumers as early as 1949 when, as part of the introduction of its new 45-rpm format, it released a line of children's records at only twenty-five cents apiece, along with portable, toy-sized phonographs on which to play them. Other companies like Peter Pan, Teddy Bear, and Simon & Schuster's Little Golden Records also adopted the durable plastic 45. Sales doubled almost overnight and phonograph companies rushed out kiddie-sized players, such as Hudston Electronics' Junior Juke, to meet the demand. As *Billboard* had stated so presciently in May 1949, "Apparently the idea of children having their own phonographs is . . . gaining acceptance."

Weaned on golden little discs, fifties teenagers became a separate target for record merchandisers. Graduating from yellow to black plastic was as natural to them as being promoted into the next grade at school. But beyond the 45's familiarity, they considered it more space-age, more hip. It also didn't bear the onus of being associated with that boring old music their parents listened to.

These youngsters also expected to maintain the privilege of having their own players. The old Victrolas and the cabinet-sized consoles of the forties and fifties were stationary pieces of furniture, strategically placed in the family living room and controlled by the parents. But with RCA and other companies selling cheap portable players to accommodate the smaller 45s, kids and teens for the first time had the option of playing their own music in another part of the house. For them, the vinyl single meant freedom to buy and listen to what they wanted to hear. Furthermore, they had no emotional or financial investment in 78s, no shelves sagging with collections of cherished platters that would gather dust if the old record machine got tossed in the trash. This generation had arrived to kill off the aging 78 and, for a time, frighten the major record companies with their fickle musical tastes.

By the end of 1954, RCA Victor, anxious to sell its ever-changing new line of phonograph models —as well as deal with the higher costs of producing smaller runs of 10-inch records—dealt the 78 another blow by reducing the prices of all of its 45s and raising the price of the heavier platters to 98 cents—an increase of a dime. Columbia immediately followed suit, leaving the other majors to agonize for a couple of weeks before they too had to hike prices.

Within two months *Billboard* was delivering the news that 78 sales were plummeting, especially with new pop records that tended to sell to a younger crowd. "Standard sales pattern over the last year has been as follows," wrote staffer Israel Horowitz. "Initial sales of a new pop entry favored 45 strongly. Until sales topped the 50,000 mark 45s might lead 78s by as much as sixty-five to thirty-five percent. As the record gained popularity and sales reached about 200,000, the 45 majority tapered to about fifty-five percent. Then with heavy sales rolling in, and sometime record buyers contributing to the total, 78s caught up to wind up the over-all sales at roughly half and half.

"The pattern that has shown itself during the past two months, however, has 45s building up a lead that 78s can't overtake, even on top-selling wax." When RCA Victor tracked its five top-selling singles, said Horowitz, it found that 45s comprised fifty-eight percent of the initial sales, then went as high as sixty-five percent on reorders.

If any record tipped the scales, it was an unlikely hit single from a black-owned, Texas-based indie label called Duke Records. Released in December 1954, "Pledging My Love" was sung by 25-year-old Johnny Ace (née John Alexander Jr.), the son of a Memphis preacher. Ace had been crooning haunting, melancholic R&B ballads since 1952, but his sales had been mostly limited to black audiences. Then, on Christmas Eve, Ace accidentally shot himself backstage at the Houston Civic Auditorium, just before he was scheduled to perform to a packed house. The press played up his death as a game of Russian roulette gone horribly wrong, though in truth Ace had simply been waving around what he thought was an unloaded .22 pistol. Women wrote suicidal poems to magazines and newspapers, demanding *why, why, Johnny?* and proclaiming their everlasting devotion. A high school student reportedly shot himself during a reenactment of Johnny's last gamble. And as often happens after the death of a young entertainer, grieving fans and the merely curious went looking for the last single.

"Pledging My Love" entered the R&B charts on January 22, 1955, but the morbid publicity also prompted pop stations to override their segregated playlists and give the record a spin. By

February 19, when "Pledging My Love" penetrated the national Top 40, it was clear that Johnny Ace had crossed over to the white market. Eventually his funereal ballad got as high as No. 17 on the national pop charts, despite being covered by popular white artists Teresa Brewer and the Four Lads.

Irving Marcus, co-owner of Duke Records' parent company, was the first to notice that Ace's posthumous hit was attracting a new audience, simply by looking at the orders coming into his office from around the country. Up until Ace's death, Duke's biggest fan base had been young black adults, so the initial pressings—and sales—of "Pledging My Love" were predictably 78s. But then

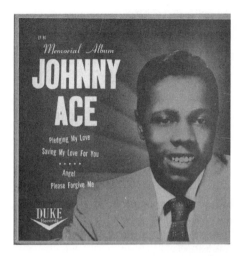

Johnny Ace, rock 'n' roll's first casualty, also had the first "45 hit."

distributors and jukebox operators began clamoring for 45s. "For the first time jukebox operators have been calling me direct on this disc, as they are having troubles filling their machines through the distributor," Marcus said at the time. "This is because the deck has taken off so fast we are temporarily behind in deliveries. In almost every case the demand from the operators is for 45s." The single was spreading to a whiter, more affluent audience. By all best estimates, it was the first black record to sell more 45s than 78s. It was only a matter of time before the coming rock 'n' roll craze, fueled mainly by the 45 single, would consign the 78 to the dustbin of history.

As if to commemorate the event, Capitol Records began construction on its new corporate headquarters building on Vine Street in Hollywood, California. Conceived by an architectural graduate student named Lou Naidorf and built by Welton Becket & Associates, the 13-story, circular Capitol Tower was designed to resemble a stack of 45 records on a turntable. The glass and steel building became an instant Hollywood landmark that continues to dominate the city's skyline fifty years later.

Today one can trace the growing popularity of 45s in the 1950s by the prices that collectors are willing to pay for rock 'n' roll and R&B singles. Up until 1955, record companies pressed more 78s, so the 45 versions tend to be several times more valuable. But as the industry phased out the bigger platters, their subsequent value increased. According to *Goldmine* magazine, a 1959 RCA 78 of Elvis Presley's "Wear My Ring Around Your Neck," pressed in minimal quantity, is worth up to ten times as much as a common 45, because by then the 78 was dead in this country. The United Kingdom stayed with it a little longer, and in far-flung places like India and South Africa, there were 78s being pressed as late as 1963, including the Beatles' first single, "Love Me Do," on Parlophone Records.

CHAPTER 8

The EP

···

RCA Victor introduced the *extended-play* 45 in late 1951 to get more music on the regular 45, but within a few months the format evolved into yet another consumer option, a mini-album, which became known by the initials EP. An EP typically contained two songs on each side and came with a stiff cardboard cover that made it look like a smaller version of an LP. At the time, 10-inch LPs with four songs on each side were the standard for pop music, so the 7-inch EP became half an album, and a two-EP set in a gatefold cover was essentially a full album in a different package. But as the 12-inch, 12-song LP became the standard format in the mid-1950s, the EP figuratively got smaller—a one-third equivalent of the LP instead of half. Some companies briefly, and unsuccessfully, issued three-EP sets to correspond to certain LPs, but found it was better to issue the three EPs separately, usually with a title and covers similar to the album but sold individually. The EP flourished through the rest of the decade and into the mid-sixties, thanks to rock 'n' roll in general and Elvis Presley in particular.

The format came about when RCA's engineers began looking for ways of extending the 45's playing time beyond five minutes. Its microgrooves could already hold much more music per radial inch than the 78, but that still wasn't enough to accommodate a movement from a classical or semi-classical piece, not to mention some jazz recordings, that ran for six or seven minutes. The problem first came up when RCA wanted to reissue Benny Goodman's famous, electrifying 1936 performance of "Sing Sing Sing," an eight-and-a-half-minute showcase for drummer Gene Krupa, on one side of a 45. For the original 78, the company had split the song in half, parts one and two, but now, if the 45 was going to compete with the LP, wouldn't it be better to contain the uninterrupted performance on one side without breaking the spell?

RCA's lab engineers discovered that if they reduced the angle of the record groove walls from a vertical ninety degrees to a slanting seventy degrees, they could actually crowd more one-millimeter grooves into the 45's one-inch-wide "quality zone." Further, if the recording engineer reduced the modulation level—in effect, flattening the music by getting rid of peaks and lows—they could squeeze even more music onto the record, up to nearly eight minutes, which wouldn't quite accommodate the full length of "Sing Sing Sing," but could hold enough that, with a little editing or fading, would satisfy Gene Krupa fans. But ultimately the value of this extended-play 45 would be that it could hold two full, normal-length songs with plenty of room to spare. A song on an EP wouldn't have the same volume or brightness as it would on a single, but the fidelity was good enough that most people, especially the ones with portable players, wouldn't notice the difference.

In late 1951 RCA launched its EP with high hopes, judging from the dizzying array of numerical codes and series pre-

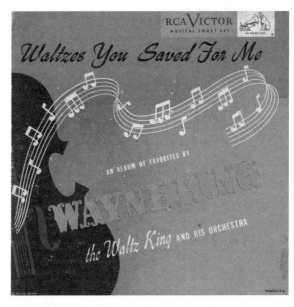

Wayne King's Waltzes You Saved for Me *was released as both an EP and an album box, with the same cover and numerical designation.*

fixes. Each EP was given a three-letter designation, beginning with E ("extended play"), then a second letter for musical style (Y for youth, R for Red Seal classical, P for pop, J for jazz, etc.) and a third denoting the number of discs in the package (A for one, B for two in a gatefold, and so on, up to eight discs in a box). Thus the prefix EYA meant that the record was a single EP in the children's series, which cost $1.13. The prefix ERG meant that the package was a classical box consisting of seven EP 45s ($10.90), since G is the seventh letter in the alphabet. In the latter case, the box was essentially a 45 album, but some or all of the individual singles inside were EPs because of their groove density.

RCA's first jazz EP was *Hot Mallets* (EJB 1000) by Lionel Hampton. (There were no jazz EPs in this series with only one disc, so no EJA existed.) The first pop EP spotlighted radio lampoon vocalist *Beatrice Kay with Hugo Winterhalter's Orchestra* (EPB-3000). A four-digit number meant the EP had no LP counterpart. Those that did were part of the LP numerical series. For example, a two-single album box by bandleader Wayne King called *Waltzes You Saved for M*e (WP-70) was also released as a one-disc EP (EPA-70).

To repackage older recordings from its catalog, RCA came up with a collectors series marked by a T at the end of the prefix. For example, the first EP in this series was *Muggsy Spanier* (EPBT-1000)—pop music (even though Spanier, a cornetist, played ragtime jazz), two 45s, a collector's

Capitol hired surrealist painter Salvador Dali to design its series of Jackie Gleason's orchestra's Lonesome Echo *EPs (EAP-1/2/3-627).*

edition. On the other hand, the company also issued a second EPBT series of EPs that corresponded with current 10-inch LPs, beginning with *Johnny Hodges & His Alto Sax* (EPBT-3000), a smaller variation of his album of the same name (LPT 3000). All these EPs were released in 1952.

Columbia Records was among the first to use extended-play 45 box sets to reissue old 78 albums. In 1951 it repackaged Frank Sinatra's 1948 eight-song *Christmas Songs By Sinatra* album on two 45 EPs (Columbia 5-1322/23) within a box (B-167), then later released them again as individual EPs called *Christmas Dreaming* (B10321/22). Columbia also introduced Sinatra's newest recordings on stand-alone EPs as part of a sales strategy to sell a series of musical tributes called *Frank Sinatra Sings*, including *Frank Sinatra Sings Irving Berlin* (B-1524) and *Frank Sinatra Sings Hits from* South Pacific *and* Oklahoma (B-1608). These EPs, which had no LP counterparts, sold well enough to keep the series going until 1954, after Sinatra had left Columbia to join Capitol Records. Columbia also liberally packaged its other top artists, such as Doris Day and Duke Ellington, on EPs.

Capitol Records became the first of the majors to realize the value of good graphic design, especially for their cool jazz and pop EPs, to create the mood of the music inside. Their dreamy and sophisticated covers, usually blue, black, and white illustrations, on such EPs as Les Baxter's *Blue Tango* (EAP-1-447) and Frank Sinatra's bluesy *In the Wee Small Hours* (EAP-1-581), became instantly recognizable. The company even commissioned surrealist Salvador Dali to illustrate the jackets for a set of three Jackie Gleason orchestral EPs called *Lonesome Echo* (EAP-1/2/3-627).

MGM Records began issuing EPs in conjunction with its LPs, using similar covers for each format, from the same photo sessions. Its first release was the soundtrack of MGM Studio's *Till the Clouds Roll By*, performed by Lennie Hayton and his orchestra (X-1). But the company also exploited the popular Alabama hillbilly artist it had picked up in 1947, singer-songwriter Hank Williams, by releasing a couple of EPs, including *Crazy Heart* (X1014, in 1952), which contained an alternate take of the title song (11054), a hit from the year before. After Williams's death on New Year's Day of 1953. MGM issued a gatefold EP called *Moanin' the Blues* (168) with two 45s (X-4041/42) containing some of his most popular recordings.

When Decca Records adopted the EP belatedly in late 1952, it led with its most solid-selling singer: *Bing Crosby Vol. 1* (Decca 2000). For its third EP, Decca released Guy Lombardo & His Royal Canadians, everybody's favorite New Year's Eve musicians, playing *Auld Lang Syne* (2002) in time for ringing in 1953.

By the end of 1952, Eli Oberstein, a former RCA Victor producer who specialized in budget labels that sold in department chain stores like Woolworth's, cashed in on the cachet of the new EP format by setting up the Record Corporation of America

Early jazz album covers were often on the arty side, but Prestige Records' 1952 Wardell Gray EP (1345) had nothing but a no-frills photo of the bebop saxophonist in action, the same as the shot on his two Prestige 10-inch albums that year.

in Union, New Jersey (which to the hurried eye could be confused with the Radio Corporation of America in Camden, New Jersey). Oberstein's "RCA" rushed 150 budget mini-albums—mostly easy-listening, nondescript orchestral offerings from favorite symphonies, operas and classical pieces—into the nation's department stores on the Royale label in time for the Christmas holidays and made himself a lot of money, enough to issue several hundred more of these bargain basement discs over the next few years.

Oberstein inspired an exploitation industry for the EP as a budget format. Several companies, including Tops, popped up to issue such timeless EP classics as *Organ Favorites* (E502) and *Polka Party* (E503), but they found their real calling in 1954 and '55 in response to the growing popularity of rhythm and blues. Along with fly-by-nighters like Dig This Record, Big 4 Hits and Prom, Tops began covering hits like "Earth Angel," "Sh-Boom," and "Church Bells May Ring" with nameless artists and putting them on low-priced EPs packaged in sleeves, not jackets, and sold in department stores. Tops boasted "4 Top Hits on Every Record." Never mind that they were pale imitations of the real hits.

Independent R&B labels generally eschewed the EP at first, except when it came to marketing saxophonists, who were thought to be crossovers into the jazz field where EPs were more common. For example, in Los Angeles, among the eight or nine EPs Aladdin Records released, most were by Illinois Jacquet, Lester Young, and Lynn Hope—all saxophonists—while Modern Records issued only two EPs, one of which was tenor sax honker Joe Houston's *All Nite Long* (200). Houston and fellow wild-blowing, exhibitionist sax man Chuck Higgins similarly accounted for three of the five EPs released by another tiny L.A. label, Combo Records. Dot Records in Tennessee issued three EPs by screaming tenor man Rusty Bryant. And Federal Records, a subsidiary of King Records in Cincinnati, promoted an acrobatic Los Angeles tenor player named Big Jay McNeely by releasing the sixteen tracks he recorded for the label on four EPs, from 1952 to 1954.

Much of this attention to the saxophone (graphically depicted on many gaudy covers as the letter J) probably had something to do with the extraordinary success of Earl Bostic, an alto saxophonist from the black bands of the forties whose velvety tones provided King Records with a seductive cross between R&B and easy listening. There may have been more American EPs by Bostic than any artist except Elvis Presley. Though Bostic had only one major hit, "Flamingo" (King 4475, in 1951), King Records cranked out his EPs and LPs with amazing frequency, generally with theme covers that avoided tipping the listener to the fact that Bostic was black, fortyish, and not very sexy. One series of EPs alone was called Earl Bostic & His Alto Sax, which went from Volume 1 (EP 200) to Volume 8 (EP 207).

In fact, among all the major R&B independent labels, King was the only company that exploited the EP market from the start, partly because it controlled everything—from recording to printing labels and jackets to pressing 45s—within the walls of its own plant. Artists like Roy Brown, Wynonie Harris, Ivory Joe Hunter, and the Midnighters may have been minor players in the overall scheme of things in the early fifties, but they nonetheless were available on EP.

The other most important R&B indie, Atlantic Records, resisted the EP until late 1955, when president Ahmet Ertegun realized, as he told one trade paper, that it would be "a smart item for the juke operators." Atlantic by then was having regular No. 1 R&B hits, breaking through to the pop market and defining the coming rock 'n' roll revolution with records by Joe Turner, Ruth Brown, Ray Charles, and LaVern Baker. Even its two main vocal groups, the Clovers and Clyde McPhatter & the Drifters, though unable to cross over to the pop charts in those early days, were selling hundreds of thousands of records and attracting legions of white kids. Accordingly, Atlantic began issuing EPs regularly during the next several years.

The problem was that since EPs had no purpose in the day-to-day business of hustling up hit records on the radio, small independent companies were loathe to put them out unless the artists had already proved themselves and could sell to a solid fan base. As *Billboard* pointed out as early as January 1956, "Some R&B lines with large catalogs and contracted talent find they have to make some EP packages available as an accommodation to a few distributors and the artists themselves. But even an EP by a top name is unlikely to sell more than thirty to a distributor on an initial order,

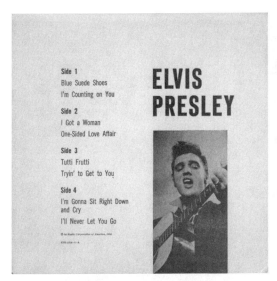

Side 1
Blue Suede Shoes
I'm Counting on You

Side 2
I Got a Woman
One-Sided Love Affair

Side 3
Tutti Frutti
Tryin' to Get to You

Side 4
I'm Gonna Sit Right Down
and Cry
I'll Never Let You Go

ELVIS PRESLEY

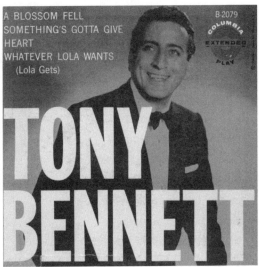

A BLOSSOM FELL
SOMETHING'S GOTTA GIVE
HEART
WHATEVER LOLA WANTS
(Lola Gets)

B-2079

TONY BENNETT

This two-pocket Elvis Presley set of singles was a giveaway in 1956 with the purchase of an RCA player.

Tony Bennett was one of Columbia's most popular artists in the 1950s, and he remains an all-generational favorite even today.

with reorders a long time coming. Several companies have issued instrumental rock & roll packages for dancers. There is no indication as yet that these are paying their way."

What changed the market and turned the musical landscape upside down, of course, was the arrival of rock 'n' roll. The LP was always a luxury in the early teen market, but the EP was a perfect fit. Kids were hooked on 45s, so selling them EPs that showed what their musical heroes looked like was a natural. The guy who set the standard—and changed everything—was Elvis Presley, whom RCA Victor bought from tiny Sun Records in November 1955 and turned into a national sensation. Along with his first LP, *Elvis Presley*, RCA issued a matching *Elvis Presley* EP (EPA-747), which looked exactly like the album, only smaller, and dutifully shipped it to disc jockeys. Hungry for anything Elvis, they started playing "Blue Suede Shoes" off the EP and turned the song into his third hit (No. 20) in the spring of 1956, even though it hadn't been released on a single. The original version by Carl Perkins on Sun (234) was the larger hit, but Elvis took away enough sales to keep Perkins from going to No. 1. Presley also overshadowed his former label mate to the point where he, not Perkins, was labeled in the press as "Mr. Blue Suede Shoes." Presley later apologized to Perkins and insisted that his performance wasn't meant to be released on 45. In fact, RCA Victor didn't get around to issuing an Elvis single of "Blue Suede Shoes" (47-6636) until several months later, after the song had run its course.

(Incidentally, a first pressing of the *Elvis Presley* EP had an incorrect label that listed a third song on the A-side, "I'm Gonna Sit Right Down and Cry Over You," that didn't exist on the record. RCA quickly corrected the mistake so that only a few of the misprints survive today, each worth about $200 mint, according to *Goldmine* magazine).

Presley was so hot by then that RCA Victor pressed up a series of three non-commercial EPs as giveaways to whoever bought its new line of Victrola record players. All three were titled *Elvis Presley* (SPD-22, SPD-23, and SPD-24).

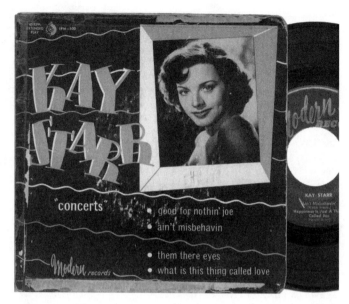

Before white songstress Kay Starr became a hitmaker for RCA Victor in 1955, she recorded for several indie companies, including R&B and jazz label Modern Records.

Because Elvis's first movie, *Love Me Tender*, contained only four songs, the EP was its perfect soundtrack album. RCA Victor, besides releasing the title song on what turned out to be a No. 1 single (47-6643), included all four selections on the *Love Me Tender* EP (EPA-4006). One of the EP's songs, "Poor Boy," reached No. 24 on the singles charts in early 1957. Another song, "Love Me," from yet another EP called *Elvis* (EPA-992) went to No. 2 at about the same time, and a second song from the EP, "When My Blue Moon Turns to Gold Again," slipped into the Top 20—even though neither was released on a single. During the Elvis Presley hysteria of 1956, fans were clamoring to hear everything he recorded, so RCA, instead of rushing out singles to cover the accidental EP hits, released different singles altogether, resulting in Presley having at least half a dozen hits in the Top 40 at any moment. (In 1956 alone, RCA commercially released two Elvis Presley LPs, eleven singles and nine EPs, two of which—992 and 993—had exactly the same title and cover.)

In 1957 Elvis's EPs broke yet more new ground. When RCA issued four religious songs under the title *Peace in the Valley* (EPA-4054), the EP, despite being a mere 45, rose to No. 3 on *Billboard*'s album chart. (The title song also ascended to No. 25 on the singles chart.) Shortly afterward, with the release of Elvis's second film, *Loving You*, RCA included the soundtrack's seven songs both on a No. 1 LP called *Loving You* (fleshed out with five non-soundtrack fillers) and on a double EP package, *Loving You, Volume I* (EPA-1-1515) and *Loving You, Volume II* (EPA-2-1515). As soon as *Volume II* charted as an album, RCA reissued *Volume I* under a new title, *Just For You* (EPA 4041), and likewise sent it into the LP Top 40, along with a reissue of the *Love Me Tender* EP. Elvis made the format so viable that RCA began reissuing its older catalog artists, including long-dead Jimmie Rodgers, Fats Waller, and Caruso, on EP. It even awarded the very much alive Perry Como a full box set (SPD-27) of ten EP 45s.

Though Presley's EP chartings as singles and albums seemed arbitrary, the problem was that the music trade papers had neither a clear method of tabulating them (airplay was a big factor in isolating specific tracks) nor a place to put them, until October 7, 1957, when *Billboard* finally got around to inaugurating a Top 10 EP chart. It ran for three years, almost to the day. Over those years the chart included 131 EPs by a total of fifty artists, plus three stage/soundtrack compilations. Unlike the album charts, where top sellers tended to be Broadway shows and adult entertainers, the EP Top 10 favored rock 'n' roll because the mini-album was easier on teenage budgets. Elvis Presley and Ricky Nelson, the only rock 'n' roll acts to have No. 1 albums in the fifties, also led in No. 1 EPs. Elvis's *King Creole Vol. 1* (RCA 4319), which spent fifty-five weeks on the chart, thirty of them at No. 1, was the best-selling EP during that time. His *Jailhouse Rock* EP (4114) was second,

Jubilee Records originally released calypso singer Harry Belafonte's 1954 Ballads by Belafonte *EP (5006) with a cover that hid, or at least played down, his racial identity, but as soon as he became a sensation on RCA, Jubilee happily reissued the record with a photo to exploit Belafonte's famously photogenic face. Record companies in the 1950s and early '60s routinely concealed their black artists behind generic LP and EP covers.*

charting for fifty weeks, twenty-eight of them on top. (In all, Presley had six No. 1 EPs and Ricky Nelson had four.) The third and fourth most popular rockers on EP were guitarist Duane Eddy and the Everly Brothers, who not coincidentally were also poster boys on most of their singles' picture sleeves. Among country artists during this period, Marty Robbins's *Gunfighter Ballads Vol. 1* (Columbia 13491), Jim Reeves's *He'll Have to Go* (RCA 4357) and *The Unforgettable Hank Williams Vol. 1* (MGM 1637) were the best sellers. Pat Boone, Johnny Mathis, Frank Sinatra, Mitch Miller, Nat King Cole, Perry Como, Mario Lanza, and the Kingston Trio were also popular on the EP chart.

American companies seemed to have no formal strategy for issuing their artists on EPs. There was no clear plan like the one that England's Columbia Records (a subsidiary of EMI there) developed a few years later, in 1961–62, to market a husky-voiced, fifteen-year-old singer named Helen Shapiro. She recorded a string of well-crafted hit singles written expressly for her: jazz tunes and standards for a couple of EPs, and for albums she recorded covers of American hits. None of Shapiro's hit singles appeared on her EPs or LPs until later. In essence, Columbia-EMI used the three formats to sell three different sides of their teenage protégé.

In the U.S., probably the most common tactic for companies to market popular rock 'n' roll acts was to issue an EP whose tracks were taken from a current LP, with at least one hit song enclosed. Usually the cover was similar but slightly different from the LP, as with Buddy Holly's 1958 Coral EP, *Listen to Me* (EC-811169), which used an orange-hued picture of Holly without his trademark glasses taken from his *Buddy Holly* LP photo session. On the other hand, Brunswick Records released Holly's other recording identity, as an anonymous member of the Crickets, on both an LP and an EP with almost the same title—*The Chirpin' Crickets* (EB-71036) on EP, *The Chirping Crickets* on LP—and the identical photograph. Whether these EPs spurred sales of the LPs or cut into them is unclear, but since rock 'n' roll acts were generally not big LP sellers, the record companies were probably happy to take what they could get in EP sales. Interestingly, the bright red cover artwork of Bill Haley and His Comets' 1956 *Rock Around the Clock* 12-inch album (DL-8225), dominated by a cartoon clock face, was used on an EP called *Rock 'N Roll* (ED 2322) that didn't include any of the songs from the *Clock* LP, because Decca had already included "Rock Around the Clock" on an earlier, 1955 *Shake, Rattle & Roll* EP (ED-2168) whose cover was taken from the 1954 original 10-inch *Shake, Rattle & Roll album* (DL-5560), which had contained "Rock Around the Clock" before anybody knew how big it was going to be a year later. Confused? Well, the British *Rock Around the Clock* EP (Brunswick 9250) did use the 12-inch LP's red cover. Companies also occasionally released three EPs as a companion for, or a reissue of, an LP. For example, Imperial Records, Ricky Nelson's label, essentially repackaged its 1957 *Ricky* LP (9048) on three Ricky EPs (153/154/155) almost a year later, and likewise issued four series of Fats Domino EPs in groups of three to match

LPs of the same title. Specialty Records put out two sets of three Little Richard EPs, each set with the same black-and-white photo, with only the background color changed, prompting RCA Victor to cover him by releasing two EPs of his earlier, non–rock 'n' roll tracks on its RCA Camden budget line, using the same black-and-white photo on both but tinted different colors. Capitol Records released four series of Gene Vincent EPs, each in groups of three, between 1957 and '59, even though he had only two modest Top 40 singles during that time. Chess

Music for Sleepwalkers *(Key 511) was an early example of ambient music, designed to be an aural tranquilizer.*

Records' first EP, Chuck Berry's *After School Session* (EP 5118), was an abridged issue of his 1957 Chess LP of the same name, and the next two, *Rock & Roll Music* (EP 5119) and *Sweet Little Sixteen* (EP 512), were taken from his *One Dozen Berries* LP. And Decca, very generous with Bill Haley and His Comets' EPs, sold several of them in groups of twos or threes.

Only now and then did EPs seem to have a concept behind them. In 1957 Gee Records released back-to-back EPs by Frankie Lymon & the Teenagers: One was a collection of jump tunes called *The Teenagers Go Rockin'* (GEP 601), which contained the group's debut hit, "Why Do Fools Fall in Love," while its companion, *The Teenagers Go Romantic* (GP-602), contained only love ballads. (This was a variation on the way rock 'n' roll companies typically put an uptempo song on one side of a 45 single and a ballad on the other.)

As rock 'n' roll cooled down around 1959, the R&B labels discontinued their extended-play lines, except to press up small-hole, 33⅓ jukebox EPs. The majors generally turned away from rock 'n' roll, leaving a handful of indies to sell a new generation of white (though mostly ethnic) pinup boys like Frankie Avalon, Fabian, Paul Anka, Bobby Vee, Bobby Rydell, and Jimmy Clanton. Whereas earlier EP covers were often funny (with head shots placed on cartoon bodies) and amateurish, companies selling teen idols took their lead from the Elvis and Ricky covers, directly selling smiling or pensive faces to the young female buyers looking for fuzzy niceness and candy cuteness.

But by 1964, when Beatlemania came screaming across the Atlantic into the American heartland, the dearth of American Beatles EPs was a sure sign that the market was drying up in the U.S.

Vee-Jay released one called *Souvenir of Their Visit to America* (1-903), Polydor exploited its tapes of singer Tony Sheridan accompanied by the Beatles with *Backbeat* (PRO 1113-7), and Capitol issued only two commercial EPs, *4 By the Beatles* (R-6365, in 1964) and *4 By 4* (EPR-5365, in 1965). Capitol did release a couple of other Beatles EPs, but they were six-song, 33⅓ discs issued to jukebox operators. Considering that Parlophone released fourteen Beatles EPs—fifteen if you count the stereo and mono versions of the six-song, two-disc *Magical Mystery Tour* (MMT-1 and SMMT-1) EP—in the U.K. during the time the Beatles were together, and that hundreds of EPs were issued all around the world, from Israel to Japan to Mexico, the fact that Capitol released only two in the U.S. proves convincingly that the 45 EP was no longer a significant marketing niche. Even the Monkees, TV's photogenic poster boys capitalizing on the Beatles' mystique, had just two U.S. EPs—and both were for jukeboxes only, not for commercial release. The reason for this is that by the mid-sixties, the LP was becoming America's dominant format and the record companies realized that EPs took away the more lucrative album sales. The 45 single served merely to launch hits on the radio and to give teenage girls their pinup fix with picture sleeves. The 45 EP simply got caught in the squeeze, and by 1969 it was dead.

But after the 12-inch single took over in the early 1980s, a new niche opened up for a very different kind of EP, often referred to as a Maxi-EP. A 12-inch record is by its size alone already an extended-play format, and record companies found it a good vehicle for packaging extra tracks, live performances, demos, alternate takes and remixes that didn't fit in on any album, or to introduce new talent (the Bangles, Great White, Dwight Yoakam, and many other artists got their start on six-song EPs), or to satisfy hardcore fans of established artists with a few musical odds and ends while they waited for the laborious album project that was months or years behind schedule.

The EP has even carried over to CD, though calling the eighty-minute-plus format an "extended play" seems superfluous. Recently EMI reissued Parlophone's original fifteen 1960s Beatles EPs in a CD box set, using the original track listing and jacket art for each of the corresponding CDs. The songs from all the EPs combined—including separate mono and stereo mixes of *Magical Mystery Tour*—would easily have fit on a couple of CDs, but for the sake of "authenticity" (and profits), EMI opted to duplicate all fifteen of the 45-rpm 7-inch originals (in 5-inch CD packages) as nostalgia items.

CHAPTER 9

The Record Sleeve

··

R ecord companies had typically used photographs and graphics on the stiff cardboard covers of their 78 albums and, after 1948, microgroove LPs. But not until they began manufacturing little 7-inch albums, or EP 45s, in late 1951 did they make cover art a crucial element in selling 45 singles.

In the parlance of the industry, a *sleeve* (called a *sheath* in England) is the flat paper envelope that holds a disc. Most likely the sleeve was invented with the first commercial record to protect it from dust, nicks, and oily finger smudges. (Even nineteenth-century cylinders had their own tube-shaped sleeves.) Though records have always been round, sleeves were always square—but they shared roughly the same dimensions so that the records would nestle snugly inside. With 10-inch 78s, the 10¼ x 10¼-inch sleeve was nearly always "center cut," which means a round, three-inch-diameter hole was punched out in the center to reveal the large, often colorful label of the platter inside. Thus the record advertised itself and the sleeve merely served as a utilitarian envelope. However, since it added to the overall cost of the record, the major companies had always taken advantage of its advertising possibilities by printing their own sleeves with prominent logos. Sometimes there was a list of the company's popular releases on the reverse, but they were confined to back-issue hits that wouldn't have to be updated often, so that one design, printed in quantity at a cheaper price, could service the widest range of records. Smaller companies mostly used blank green or beige sleeves.

As with so many other innovations in the recording industry, the *picture sleeve*, initially called an *illustrated envelope*, began as an enticement for children. In the late 1940s kiddie discs were gift-wrapped in whimsical, eye-catching gatefold and fold-over sleeves that would have seemed frivolous in the packaging of adult music. One of the first 45 records with a full, four-color picture sleeve was a recitation of "The Night Before Christmas" (47-0141) by Clement C. Moore, with music by Milton Cross & the RCA Salon Orchestra. The record had not only a sleeve with an aerial shot

The following is the text inside the image:

RADIO CORPORATION
OF AMERICA
RCA VICTOR DIVISION
CAMDEN, N. J., U. S. A.

This is your preview of . . .

THE NEW RCA VICTOR 45 R.P.M. RECORD LINE!

There are seven different colors, representing seven different musical categories
as follows:

RECORD	LABEL	CATEGORY
Red	Red	Red Seal Music
Black	Persian Peacock	Popular Music
Midnight Blue	Rocket Blue	Popular Classics
Green	Quad Green	Country and Western Music
Cerise	Slate Gray	Blues and Rhythm
Sky-blue	Black	International Music
Yellow	Flemish Blue	Children's Entertainment

Use these seven records as samples between now and March 31st,
and for use with the forthcoming window and counter displays.
You may wish to hold them as collector's items—the first production run of a record that will set the pace for the entire industry!

To introduce its new 45 format, RCA shipped the first singles in a sleeve that explained the color code.

of Santa Claus and his flying reindeer, but also a fold-over flap with another full-color illustration of angelic, caroling children. It was issued as part of RCA Victor's Youth Series in 1949.

Another original way that RCA presented children's records in 1949 was the gatefold album format, used for example with *Johnny Appleseed* (WY 390), two 45s (47-0198/99) in a 7 x 14-inch fold-out paper sleeve, with four extra pages inside. That same year, Capitol Records put out *Little Johnny Strikeout*, a gatefold set of two 45s (30126/27), with cartoon illustrations inside and out, of Johnny getting tips from New York Yankee outfielder Joe DiMaggio. These records were similarly packaged as 78s. Decca's earliest 45 picture sleeve, though issued in its main series instead of as a children's record, was nonetheless a nursery novelty by comedian Danny Kaye called "The Little White Duck" (27350), in 1951.

Christmas singles and picture sleeves, it turned out, went together like knick-knacks and chimney stockings. Companies even took the opportunity to market their adult stars to kids, sometimes releasing the same record under two different numbers, putting one in a picture sleeve but not the other. For example, Columbia Records repackaged many of singing cowboy Gene Autry's Christmas and novelty hits: "Rudolph the Red Nosed Reindeer" was both a 1949 Columbia Junior single (6-375) with a center-cut cartoon picture sleeve, and a 1950 standard release (38610) in a generic company sleeve. Decca likewise issued Bing Crosby's 45 remake of "Rudolph the Red Nosed Reindeer" in late 1950 as both a black-vinyl, company-sleeved pop single (27159) and as a yellow-vinyl, picture-sleeved children's record (88050). RCA routinely did the same thing with Perry Como's Yuletide 45s. Even Jubilee Records, a tiny New York independent label, decked out two holiday 45s by a popular black vocal group, the Orioles—"What Are You Doing New Year's Eve" (5017) and "O Holy Night" (5045)— making them the first R&B singles with non-center-cut picture sleeves. Both singles featured separate black-and-white head shots of the quintet, each one inside an illustrated Christmas ornament. Those two sleeves are very rare today and could finance your next elaborate Christmas if you had them.

RCA Victor packaged its 45s in generic sleeves for the first year or so, then introduced a couple of series of solid sleeves designed for limited numbers of singles. The first was a buff sleeve with a prominent brownish-purple banner touting "One of the 101 Best Sellers," using a 45 disc as the zero in 101. This series included 45s by Spike Jones, Tommy Dorsey, Perry Como, Mario Lanza, Eddy Arnold, Jeanette MacDonald & Nelson Eddy, and other leading RCA acts. Each of the 101 singles had its own sleeve with the name of the artist(s) and, in smaller typeface, the songs and the issue number, but otherwise the sleeves were alike.

This was the first full 45 picture sleeve, issued by RCA Victor in 1949 as hit 78s were being raised on the new format.

Then came a custom sleeve with a red and black cover advertising "Music Made Famous by 'The Great Caruso,'" taking advantage of MGM's new film biography of Enrico Caruso, starring Mario Lanza. Caruso had been Victor's first major star at the beginning of the century, and Lanza, a light-opera singer with a sob and a throb in his voice, was currently on the RCA Victor roster, so the company cleverly designed the sleeve to sell 45s by both artists—four red vinyl Lanza singles and eight remastered Carusos on black vinyl, including a reissue of his first big seller from 1907, "Vesti la Giubba (On with the Play)" (49-3228) from *Pagliacci*. These Caruso singles were the first pre-electrical recordings (*i.e.*, acoustic, performed into a horn instead of a microphone and based on sonic vibrations instead of electrical representations of sound) pressed on 45.

Next, RCA came out with a center-cut sleeve touting "The Singers' Single Record Series," featuring "9 Top Singers * 9 Top Song Writers" and "54 Tin Pan Alley Greats by 'The Stars Who Make the Hits.'" On one side of every sleeve were black-and-white head shots of nine vocalists, including Perry Como, Eddie Fisher, Mindy Carson, Don Cornell, Dinah Shore, and Tony Martin; on the other side was a list of the titles and issue numbers of three 45s by each artist. Thus the sleeve could be used for any of the twenty-seven releases.

But not until mid-1952 did RCA Victor issue its first adult picture sleeve record, a center-cut, 78-only package touting Eddie Fisher's "Wish You Were Here" (20-4830), the title song from a then-popular Broadway musical. Though Fisher's records sound unremarkable today, he was RCA's Elvis before Elvis then, a handsome curly-haired kid in his early twenties whose hammy, Al Jolson–style baritone created screaming pandemonium wherever he sang, even after he was drafted into the Army. Fisher enjoyed a long string of schmaltzy hits, most of them in the Top 10, which seemed to arrive at stores every month or so even though he was off doing benefits and bond-raisers around the world or entertaining his fellow G.I.s in Korea. When "Wish You Were Here" became his first No. 1 record, someone in the executive suites made the connection between the 10-inch single's runaway sales and the black-and-white photo of Fisher's shy yet beckoning smile on the sleeve. By the end of the year RCA Victor picked Eddie Fisher's "Even Now" (47-5106), his twenty-third chart entry, to be its first non-kiddie 45 with a picture sleeve.

In 1953 Fisher represented another milestone when RCA designed its first full-color (though center-cut) 45 picture sleeve, "Eddie Fisher Sings . . . star of *Coke Time* on TV and radio," with a hand-tinted photo of Fisher on the right side, issued to promote his new Friday night television program on NBC, and available on all of his subsequent singles. It was the first time that record executives recognized the natural synergy between the two visual mediums of the 45 picture sleeve and adult television shows.

This sleeve, designed to accompany Eddie Fisher's many hit singles, was RCA's first four-color 45 picture sleeve.

By late 1955, when RCA Victor paid more money than it had ever spent before to acquire young Elvis Presley from tiny Sun Records, the company was occasionally issuing pop 45s with black-and-white picture sleeves, yet it slotted none of them for their bonus baby's first seven releases, not even Elvis's first two No. 1 hits, "Heartbreak Hotel" (47-6420) and "I Want You, I Need You, I Love You" (47-6540). However, an early promo 45 was sent to disc jockeys with a special "This

Is His Life" four-panel cartoon sleeve humorously describing how Presley got to where he was. This sleeve was never issued for the general public, and there's still some confusion among collectors and archivists whether it accompanied RCA's first Presley 45, "Mystery Train" (47-6357), or the later "I Want You, I Need You, I Love You." In any event, RCA's lack of foresight gave the Singing Dogs' "Hot Dog Rock and Roll" (47-6432) the honor of being its first so-called rock 'n' roll 45 with a picture sleeve, a coup that perhaps Nipper had orchestrated.

This thin cardboard 45 sleeve was used for record store display only, and not sold with the record.

RCA finally got around to giving Presley his own picture sleeve—in black and white—after he began appearing on national TV shows. The photo showed him singing to a droopy-faced, tuxedoed basset hound on *The Steve Allen Show*, because the record inside was "Hound Dog" (47-6604), Presley's raucous remake of a 1953 Big Mama Thornton blues song. But despite the visual focus on "Hound Dog," RCA Victor actually designated the flipside, "Don't Be Cruel," as the A-track and gave it larger billing on the sleeve. When "Hound Dog" turned out to be the bigger hit (both sides reached No. 1 and the single sat at the top of the charts for eleven weeks), RCA reversed the order and type size of the titles on the sleeve. Nowadays, the earlier sleeve with "Don't Be Cruel" on top is worth at least twice as much to collectors.

In November 1956, Elvis's "Love Me Tender" (47-6643) replaced "Hound Dog" at the top of the charts, and this time RCA issued four different picture sleeves, all using the same photo of Elvis sitting on the set of the film *Love Me Tender* with his guitar, but each one had a different color. The original (and rarest) was black and white; the other three were tinted light pink, dark pink, or green.

From then on, however, Elvis's extraordinary popularity dictated that he be given the full-color pinup treatment, because by now millions of fans were mesmerized by his image, no matter what object it was attached to. The sleeve for his next single, "Playing For Keeps"/"Too Much" (47-6800), not only gave both songs equal billing but splashed Elvis in bright dynamic colors,

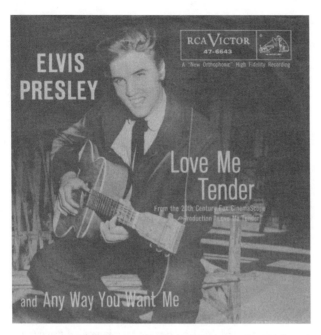

RCA released Elvis's "Love Me Tender" 45 (47-6643) with a black-and-white photo sleeve with three separate color washes.

dominated by his blood-red shirt. For the rest of his life, right up until "Pledging My Love" (10998) in August 1977—and beyond—RCA Victor never put out a new Elvis Presley 45 (as opposed to a reissue) without an available full-color picture sleeve showing his iconic visage.

But Elvis Presley was not RCA's first artist to get the full-sleeve, full-color treatment. Just a few weeks earlier the company had released the photogenic black calypso star, Harry Belafonte, on two singles, "John Henry" (47-6780) and "Danny Boy" (47-6790), using the same photo on both. On the other hand, each Presley picture sleeve from then on was a separate pinup shot. RCA Victor thereafter led the field in full-color picture sleeves well into the 1960s.

Generally there seemed to be no rhyme or reason for why a record was issued with a picture sleeve and the next one wasn't. It was just one of many marketing decisions a company had to make after it settled on what songs by which artists to put out. What would be the 78/45 ratio of the initial release? Would the pressing be only black vinyl, or would there be a limited release in red? Would the sleeve be center cut or a full graphic? Would it be in color or black and white? Could it be tied in with a TV show, a movie, or a tour?

Often the decision to use a picture sleeve was predicated not only on the popularity of the artists' recent recordings, but on who was buying them. Teenage girls, the 45's most ardent demographic, had to be taken into account. For example, Epic Records in the late 1950s released a slew of forgettable 45s by teenage Hollywood heartthrob Sal Mineo with picture sleeves, but awarded its most prolific artist, black baritone Roy Hamilton, only one—after he had already given the label eleven hits.

Besides Christmas, children's, and teen idol records, the 45s most likely to have picture sleeves were connected in some way with TV shows. In the 1950s and sixties, over ninety percent of American homes had a TV set, but there were only three networks, assuring that any Top 10 program was a shared national experience. One of the major TV hits of the fifties, Walt Disney's *Davy Crockett*, which ran from December 1954 to January '55 on ABC-TV, was probably responsible for more hit records—and more pictures sleeves—than any other TV program. When actor Fess Parker, who played the early nineteenth-century pioneer, recorded "The Ballad of Davy Crockett," Columbia Records released it both on its children's imprimatur (242, complete with picture sleeve) and as part of the company's pop series (40449, without a sleeve). Disney also issued the recording on its Little Golden Record series (D127), with a sleeve of course, followed by Parker's "Be Sure You're Right" (Davy's TV catchphrase) and "Bang Goes Old Betsy" (D213), this time with a rugged illustration of Parker in full Crockett regalia, including the indispensable coonskin cap. (Old Betsy was Davy's flintlock rifle, by the way, not some frontier floozy.) Cricket Records cashed in with "The Davy Crockett March" and "Old Betsy" (C-52), with a crudely illustrated sleeve that looked like the company owner's kid did it in junior high school art class.

The Sons of the Pioneers recorded several RCA singles connected to popular TV Westerns, including "Cheyenne" (46), "Jesse James" (59), "Tales of the Texas Rangers" (63), "Wagon Train" (68), "Broken Arrow" (69), "The Restless Gun" (71) and "Sugarfoot" (105), generally with sleeves featuring color shots of the stars, such as *The Restless Gun*'s John Payne.

Broadway plays have always been a source of popular songs, and even if an artist were simply covering a tune from a current smash, record companies used picture sleeves to create an immediate connection. Kapp Records, for example, in the early 1960s released pianist Roger Williams's instrumental version of *West Side Story*'s "Maria" (437) and Louis Armstrong No. 1 reworking of "Hello, Dolly!" (573) with bright sleeves.

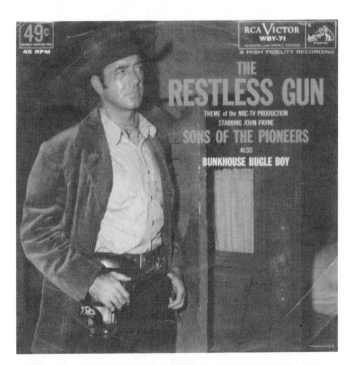

Popular TV shows like NBC's The Restless Gun *(1957-59) were good promotions for singles.*

The sleeve for the orchestral themes (Columbia 40754) from two of James Dean's Warner Bros. films showed only the image of the recently deceased actor.

The picture sleeve was also ideal for movie themes. Record labels, especially those connected with film studios, were happy to rework a film's poster art into a picture sleeve, such as the ones for Richard Maltby's "The Man With the Golden Arm" (Vik 0196), and Percy Faith's "Theme From a Summer Place" (Columbia 41490). When Warner Bros. launched a label in late 1958 to sell its young stars to the record-buying public, naturally it packaged singles by photogenic actors like Tab Hunter and Edd "Kookie" Byrnes in picture sleeves.

In 1955 the coming rock 'n' roll revolution's first icon was actor James Dean, even though in real life he was a bebop jazz fan and probably would have scorned Elvis Presley, who was a relative unknown touring through Texas with a *Louisiana Hayride* road show on the night Dean was killed in a car accident. Ray Heindorf & the Warner Bros. Orchestra recorded "Theme From Rebel Without a Cause" b/w "Theme From East of Eden" on Columbia (40754), released in a sleeve adorned with images of the recently deceased screen idol. (It's the earliest known picture sleeve in the Columbia pop 40000 series.) When Mantovani, known for his lush orchestral arrangements, also hopped on the James Dean bandwagon with "Let Me Be Loved" (London 1761), the theme from the 1961 documentary *The James Dean Story*, the sleeve featured a stark pencil or chalk drawing of Dean's face on an off-white sleeve.

Trying to correlate 45 picture sleeves with the importance of rock 'n' roll stars or certain milestone recordings is fruitless. Though Elvis Presley and Ricky Nelson 45s were released with picture sleeves almost as a matter of course, most of what are now considered the most legendary rock 'n' roll artists of the 1950s were generally overlooked by their record companies when it came time to gild their singles. Decca Records' Bill Haley and His Comets, who jump-started rock 'n' roll in 1954–55 with "Rock Around the Clock" and a string of other hits, didn't rate a 45 picture sleeve until 1957, after the group had become irrelevant. The 1950s hits of Chuck Berry, certainly one of early rock 'n' roll's greatest artists, were all sleeveless. So were all of the fifties' 45s by Johnny Burnette's Rock & Roll Trio, the Coasters, Frankie Lymon & the Teenagers, the Crests, Buddy Knox, James Brown, Ray Charles, the Platters, Sam Cooke, the Drifters, Danny & the Juniors, Conway Twitty, Clyde McPhatter, and the Crew Cuts (though a special sleeve was issued with a 7-inch 78 record of their "Sh Boom"). None of the three stars killed in a fabled 1959

Groove, RCA Victor's R&B subsidiary, did not issue any picture sleeves in the 1950s—not even for hitmakers Mickey and Sylvia—but did put out an EP.

plane crash—Buddy Holly, the Big Bopper, and Ritchie Valens—rated a picture sleeve during their lifetimes, and the singles of another legendary rock casualty, Eddie Cochran, were sleeveless before his fatal 1960 car wreck, except for the fairly obscure "Mean When I'm Mad" (Liberty 55070).

Likewise, Capitol Records gave the ill-fated king of rockabilly, Gene Vincent, only one photo sleeve in the 1950s, and that was with a little-known 45, "The Night Is So Lonely" (4237). The Diamonds had many hits, including "Little Darlin'," but only one modest seller, "High Sign" (Mercury 71291), had a picture sleeve. Bo Diddley didn't have a picture-sleeved 45 until "Say Man" (Checker 939) in 1959. Atlantic Records, one of the most important R&B and rock 'n' roll labels of the 1950s, had a policy of never releasing singles with picture sleeves, until its subsidiary label, Atco, began aiming Italian-American rock crooner Bobby Darin at the teen market. King Records, another trend-setting R&B indie, never issued a picture sleeve in the fifties. Sun Records in Memphis, Tennessee, released only three 45s with picture sleeves during the decade, and all had black-and-white photos: Jerry Lee Lewis's "Great Balls of Fire" (281) and "High School Confidential" (296), and Johnny Cash's "Guess Things Happen That Way" (295). Carl Perkins of "Blue Suede Shoes" fame didn't get a picture sleeve until he left Sun to sign with Columbia in 1958. That same year, Robin Luke's original release of "Susie Darlin'" (International 206) on a small Hawaiian indie had a picture sleeve, but when Dot

The Miller Brewing Company sent this 45 to radio stations. Various popular artists, singing in different styles, extolled the sparkling taste of Miller High Life beer.

Records in Los Angeles leased the master and turned it into a Top 5 single (15781), the sleeve was gone. (Because International initially over-printed the sleeves before turning the recording over to Dot, many more of them are available today than the 45s.)

Besides Elvis Presley and Ricky Nelson, the only important fifties rock 'n' roll artists routinely given picture sleeves were Brenda Lee, guitarist Duane Eddy (a total of twenty, nearly all in color), the Everly Brothers, Little Richard, and Fats Domino (though the latter two artists' photo sleeves were limited to black and white).

Just as MTV videos twenty-five years later would skew pop music toward visual appeal, record companies mostly used picture sleeves to push singers with teen idol faces. Del-Fi Records, which had sold Mexican-American rocker Ritchie Valens without picture sleeves, adorned its 45s by TV child actor Johnny Crawford in Technicolor splendor to tease his adolescent female fans. More notably, the Chancellor, Cameo, and Swan labels in Philadelphia, infamous for packaging Italian-

Dora Hall, the Pia Zadora and Angelyne of the 1960s, was married to a paper-cup magnate who financed her career, complete with TV specials and various fan club 45s, all free with a coupon.

American pinup boys for Dick Clark's *American Bandstand*, hawked Frankie Avalon, Fabian, Bobby Rydell, and Freddie Cannon 45s in full-color dreaminess.

The queen of picture sleeves was Annette Funicello, a child star who grew into voluptuous adolescence on Walt Disney's *Mickey Mouse Club* and other TV shows. When Disney formed its Disneyland and Buena Vista labels for marketing its young stars, Annette's innocent sex appeal was put on full display. Most of her 45s were graced by brightly colored sleeves that are collector's items today.

The print run for sleeves was always smaller than the vinyl press run. Los Angeles record collector Gerry Diez, who worked at a major singles retailer in the San Fernando Valley from 1958 to 1970, recalls that picture sleeves were "pretty much a hit and miss proposition. RCA Victor knew that Elvis was a good-looking kid, so they would always put out a picture sleeve. The fans expected it and [RCA] wanted to carry on with that tradition." The number of sleeves sent to each store "would all depend on the whim of the distributor," says Diez. "Say you order a hundred copies of the new Elvis record.

If [you're] a good singles account they do business with, the distributor would make sure you got as many copies as you wanted with a picture on it, especially if it's a teen idol like Elvis, Frankie, or Fabian. With Elvis we would always get the picture sleeve with the record. After the first month [of sales], we'd start to get more copies with fewer sleeves. Records would have a shelf life."

With a second-tier artist like Ray Peterson, "the first shipment of 'Corrina Corrina' [Dunes 2002, 1960] I got twenty copies with picture sleeves and twenty to thirty copies in plain sleeves. The picture sleeve stuff would sell first to people who really wanted the record. We sold 200 and 300 copies of that record. It's a lot more expensive to put out a picture sleeve. Since the main buyers of 45s were teenaged girls, if the label thought a kid was good-looking, like Rod Lauren on 'If I Had a Girl' [RCA 47-7645], it was put in a picture sleeve."

By the 1960s, picture sleeves became more common, but each record company gave them different priorities. Columbia Records issued picture sleeves in genre markets, such as country & western and folk music, even though visual image was supposedly not as important. Decca Records and MGM Records, on the other hand, favored only a few artists with picture sleeves and paid scant attention to graphic design quality. Most surprising was Berry Gordy Jr.'s Motown Records, a singles-driven company that went to elaborate lengths to master 45s to have an impact coming through the speakers of small radios, but slapped together picture sleeves as an afterthought. (Motown's earliest picture-sleeve 45 was Mary Wells's "Bye Bye Baby" (1003) in January 1961, but as with her many subsequent sleeves, its photo was black and white and the artwork was amateurish. Even the Supremes, with nine intermittent picture sleeves scattered between 1962 and '66, were given shoddy pink and blue sleeves with fuzzy photos.)

Regardless of how frequently a company depended on picture sleeves, it wouldn't waste the added expense on an unproven act, especially if that act had no distinctive identity. For example, when the Swan label got the rights to the Beatles' "She Loves You" (4152) in 1963, the group was still unknown in America, so the single was issued with a generic center-cut sleeve. Not until the early reports of Beatlemania in England began reaching the U.S. did Swan repackage the single in a picture sleeve.

When Atco discovered that it had the rights to an early Beatles recording of "Ain't She Sweet" (6302), it hastily threw together a crude two-color (black-and-blue) sleeve with drawings of four mop-top haircuts. Likewise, Vee-Jay, a black-owned label in Chicago, got the rights early to an album's worth of Beatles recordings from EMI in England, after EMI's American company, Capitol, turned them down. Vee-Jay gave the records the standard treatment until early 1964, when it realized it was sitting on a gold mine. Suddenly "Please Please Me" (VJ 581) was being reissued in a special sleeve sent to disc jockeys proclaiming "The Record That Started Beatlemania." The commercial single's sleeve had a black-and-white photo. Also, Vee-Jay's Tollie subsidiary corrected its original decision to release "Love Me Do" (9008) without a sleeve by quickly coming up with an ugly graphic using a bluish-tinted painting of the four Beatles sitting in empty air.

By the time Capitol Records belatedly took control of the American rights to the Beatles' catalog, it released all their singles with picture sleeves—starting with "I Want to Hold Your Hand" (5112) in December 1963—because the group's hysterical young fans were the ultimate in impulse buyers, scrambling to grab anything with a photo of the Fab Four on it. But even Capitol, which was already lavishing picture sleeves on the Beach Boys, beginning with their first major single, "Surfin' Safari" [4777] in 1962, must have been unprepared for Beatlemania's intensity, because it used the same black-and-white photo from the "I Want to Hold Your Hand" sleeve for both the follow-up single, "Can't Buy Me Love" (5150), and the fifth single, "I'll Cry Instead" (5234), as well as on several pieces of sheet music. When a few parents objected to the photo because Paul McCartney was holding a cigarette in the fingers of his right hand, the offending fag was airbrushed out on at least one batch of "I Want to Hold Your Hand" sleeves.

Capitol did not issue any singles from the Beatles' most famous album, *Sgt. Pepper's Lonely Heart's Club Band*, but the following year (1967) it did release "All You Need Is Love" (5964) from the *Magical Mystery Tour* LP with individual color photos of John, Paul, George, and Ringo dressed in their Sgt. Pepper uniforms.

Columbia Records used the same photo of singer Johnnie Ray on its single of "You Don't Owe Me a Thing" (40803) and the corresponding EP (B-2123). As it turned out, the single was a two-sided hit in 1957.

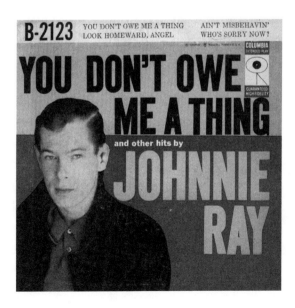

Even more than with Elvis Presley's 45s, Beatles' picture sleeves took on a life of their own. In the forty years since the first singles, there have been more than fifty Beatles sleeves issued in the United States alone, and many times that in countries around the world. Today, collectors pay hundreds, even thousands of dollars for near-pristine sleeves of rare releases.

Thanks to the Beatles, sixties rockers tarted themselves up in pure cuteness, with coy or puppy-dog eyes peering out from under shaggy haircuts. Where would Donovan, the Dave Clark Five, Ian Whitcomb, Peter & Gordon, Steppenwolf, the Peanut Butter Conspiracy, and the Lovin' Spoonful be without their 45 picture sleeves? Canned Heat and the Turtles proved that even plug-uglies could sell singles as long as they had the right haircuts. Even folk acts, if they were photogenic, were being sold on picture sleeves, including Bob Dylan and Peter, Paul & Mary.

But the purest example of marketing mop-top pop in the 1960s was the Monkees, dubbed "the pre-fab(ricated) four" because they were hired to portray a beat group of Beatles clones in a TV show based on the kinetic Beatles film, *A Hard Day's Night*. Colgems Records wouldn't have thought of releasing a Monkees 45 without a fetching sleeve to lure the girls. Oftentimes the records seemed to be included simply to sell the sleeves. The Monkees were a promotion-driven machine, and Colgems/Arista took every opportunity to push their happy faces down the throats of teenagers from all over the world, including Turkey, Israel, and Iran. Naturally, 45 picture sleeves were part of the equation, not only in the 1960s but well into the eighties. In Japan alone, there were twenty-eight different colorful Monkees sleeves, four more than were issued in the United States. Mexico had fourteen. One extravagant Japanese 45 of "Daydream Believer" (Bell Records 207) was pressed on gold vinyl and sheathed in a wraparound gold foil picture sleeve, with lyrics printed on the back.

By the late 1960s, new recording artists were turning away from frivolous fifties-style music. The term rock 'n' roll soured into a pejorative because it conjured up teen pop about cars, blue suede shoes, and puppy love. Now the music was simply "rock," and it was serious stuff that reflected the social confusion brought on by the Vietnam War, the civil rights movement, and the escape of what seemed like an entire generation of white suburban kids into psychedelic love fests. In this atmosphere, many new acts like the Doors, the Jefferson Airplane, Cat Stevens, and Jimi Hendrix outwardly disdained the trappings of fame, sudden wealth, and teen adulation. Their musical palette was the LP, not the single, and their airwaves venue was free-form FM radio instead of the highly regimented and commercialized AM, because they needed more room to stretch out and make their case without the interruptions of advertisers.

If a record company needed to promote an album by punching up and editing down a two-and-a-half-minute, Top 40–friendly performance on a 45, the artists grudgingly went along with it.

But with the exception of Hendrix —whose first single, "Hey Joe" (Reprise 0572), was the only one issued with his picture during his brief career—these artists appeared on the front sleeves of their 45s in pinup photos, only now they had to look sullen, as if under protest against the materialistic corporate machine. Still, there were some acts, such as the Mothers of Invention, who were so out of the mainstream that their companies didn't use their faces to adorn their 45s. Likewise, Janis Joplin, first as the lead singer of Big Brother & the Holding Company and then as a solo artist, never had a picture sleeve on her singles.

Veteran Los Angeles country artist and promoter Cliffie Stone produced several early Capitol polka singles with their own sleeves.

With the album, cover art had to be more than simple studio poses of the artists staring back at the consumer. Record companies stopped using in-house art departments and went looking for respected artists, graphic and otherwise, such as R. Crumb, Andy Warhol, and Peter Max. Record artists expected their single sleeves to have this same level of sophistication. So as time went on, into the 1970s, '80s, and '90s, sleeves reflected what was happening in the culture, from kitsch and pulp to postmodernism. More established recording artists, such as the Rolling Stones and KISS, had corporate logos that became the centerpieces of their cover art. As music became more stylized, so did the graphics, oftentimes expressing a mood or some idea rather than a photo opportunity for the artist, until it seemed that the sleeve was an independent entity that existed separately from the vinyl within.

CHAPTER 10

Hot Biscuits (How to Make a 45)

· ·

L et's stop for a moment and talk about how a record, in this case a 45 single, is made. Up until the late 1940s, studio sessions were recorded directly from the microphone to a lathe that carved the music into 16-inch blank lacquer platters, but just about the time RCA launched the 45, the entire industry was changing over to quarter-inch recording tape, which was cheaper, easier to use, and more malleable in post-production.

The artist, let's say Perry Como, backed by the Fontane Sisters and an orchestra, goes into the studio and cuts four songs in three hours, the standard session for major record companies. (The term *cut*—meaning to record—dates from the time when lathes in the studio control rooms actually cut the grooves into large recording discs.) Since Como and company are recording live, they'll perform each song at least a couple of times until the producer feels he's got a usable take. Later, after the session, the producer will go back, listen to all the takes, pick the best ones and edit them out of the studio tape, so that they can be *leadered*—a blank white leader tape is spliced on either end of each performance—and spooled onto their own reels. Then the company decides which of the songs has the most hit potential, and which of the remaining songs would be a good B-side.

The B-side's job is to complement the A-side. For example, if the A-side is a serious ballad, the B-side will be lighter and more uptempo. The B-side can also be a pay-off to a songwriter or music publisher, because if the A-side becomes popular, the B-side "takes a free ride" along with it up the charts and earns for its publisher and songwriter exactly the same royalties as the hit side. That's why, whenever an A-side fizzles and the B-side starts getting airplay instead (which often happened when disc jockeys had more power to play what they wanted—see Chapter 13), the company will sometimes remove the old A-side from subsequent pressings and slap on a song it controls.

Okay, so now we've got a tape reel with two Perry Como songs on it. The tape is sent to the mastering lab, where the mastering engineer is sitting at his record lathe. Off to his side, connected to the lathe, is a control board and tape machine, where he spools the reel-to-reel tape through the recording heads. Before he does anything else, the engineer, usually with the producer at his side, plays the tape several times, electronically equalizing and compressing the music to eliminate the red-zone peaks that might later blast the stylus off the finished record. He also wants to make sure there's not too much bass—or *bottom end*—because that would put too much information into the grooves and widen them to the point where the small recording area of the 45 master lacquer will fill up before the taped song is over. (The louder or fuller the music, the wider the grooves.) On the other hand, if the bass or drums are too light, he might amplify the bottom end to give the song some oomph. He might also add a little echo to liven up the performance. And in some cases, if the music seems to drag a little, he might even speed the tape up half a step to make the rhythm more exciting. The art of the mastering engineer can be the difference between a hit and a miss.

For the first song on the tape, the engineer places an eight-inch blank lacquer master disc— simply called a *lacquer*—onto the turntable of his lathe. He lowers an overhead cutting mechanism, a recording head with a sapphire cutting stylus, onto the surface of the lacquer, setting down about one inch in from the edge. He speeds up the lead screw of the cutting stylus for just a second to create a silent lead-in groove. Then he'll start the tape. As the music is being transferred to the lacquer, the fixed stylus moves inward, like a phonograph playing a record, but in this case there are no grooves to follow because the engineer is himself the pioneer, plowing a circular, spiraling path across the shiny, virgin surface that countless others will follow later. As the stylus works its way toward the center, it cuts the grooves precisely even, each one adjacent to the last, maintaining the same depth. As the spiral tightens and gets smaller, the mechanism automatically slows down the plowing needle's progress, so that the song won't start speeding up like water swirling down a drain on the finished recording. All the while, the engineer is removing the thin lacquer filings the stylus is grinding out of the surface, curling up like the peel of an apple as it's being pared.

Since the microgrooves are only about two mils (two thousandths of an inch) deep, the engineer's recording system has an attached calibrated microscope that the engineer can swing over the lacquer at any time while it's being cut and make certain the grooves are smooth and have the correct depth. He constantly checks to make sure he's not slicing the parallel grooves so tightly together that they'll impede upon each other. A groove without a firm wall separating it from the next will give ghostly premonitions of what's going to be heard a moment later when the final record is played.

Now that he's started, the engineer can't stop his cutting stylus without ruining the whole lacquer. Just one little mistake and he'll have to scrap it and start again with a new one. He keeps checking the running time to make sure that the disc's inch-wide recording area won't run out of space before the music is over.

At the end of the recording, after the stylus makes about two blank revolutions, the engineer creates the spiral lead-out groove by speeding up the lathe's lead screw. The master is now done, except that he must visually examine it very closely under the microscope for flaws. Under no circumstances can this lacquer be played. If the engineer wants to hear what the record sounds like, he'll have to play part of the tape back and make a brief groove test in the outer one-inch blankness of the lacquer's recording area. If the sound is too low, too high or distorted, he'll have to throw it away and cut another disc. If everything sounds good, he'll usually scratch a symbol or number into the dead wax on the inner edge of the recording. This could be a studio number, a pressing plant number, or perhaps his initials. He may also designate which song is side A and which is side B. These markings become part of the master and will appear on every disc made from it.

After the engineer has finished with the two single-sided lacquer masters that will be the sides of the 45, he bolts them by their small center holes into a protective Styrofoam box designed for that purpose, so that the two delicate surfaces, though facing each other, can't touch. The lacquer is so sensitive that even a slight nick can ruin it.

The box is sent to the plating plant, an industrial building or area where each lacquer will be carefully unbolted, removed from the box, and silver-plated. Since a lacquer would melt if it came face to face with even moderate heat, the plant worker coats it delicately at first with the slightest mist of silver nitrate from a spray gun. Then he dips the lacquer into a stannous chloride solution and washes it off with a water spray, leaving an ultra-thin coating. He sprays another silver nitrate solution on the disc for a few seconds until it turns perfect silver in color, then dips the disc into another wash. Now that the surface of the recording—the soft lacquer grooves—has been de-sensitized and protected by the coating, the factory worker can add more liquid metal to the disc, building it thicker with each new dip in solution and a zap of electricity to bind the molecules together into a solid plate. He'll first use a very fine-grained copper or nickel—called *pre-plating*—so that small chunks of silver won't slip into the grooves and distort them. Then on subsequent layers he can put a heavier coating, until finally there's enough metal attached to create a rigid support.

After he's built up a desired thickness, the worker gives the metal surface a quick blow with a special rubber mallet and pries it off gently with an inserting tool to break the entire silver-copper mold free from the lacquer, which is usually damaged by now and can no longer be used. Not to worry, though, because with a swish of the mold into chromic acid he removes the original micro-thin silver coating from the metal underneath, leaving a hardened negative of the recording, a mirror-image of the original grooves. This is called a *matrix*.

If need be, the metal matrix itself could be used to stamp out records, but since it's now the only existing copy of the original lacquer, it's used instead as a mold to produce a positive metal record—called a *mother*—that could be played for testing purposes, but again it's best not to. The factory worker hand-plates the mother pretty much the way he did the lacquer, with the result being another metal negative called a *stamper*. Unlike the lacquer, the mother can be replated again and again, producing as many stampers as the pressing plant needs—each one identical. It will be kept on file to make even more stampers in the future, because the heating-cooling process required to make vinyl records causes them to expand and contract and wears them out after about a thousand pressings. Plus, as many mothers as needed can be made from the original metal matrix to be sent to other pressing plants all over the country or the world to make stampers that can turn out huge quantities of records with exactly the same level of quality.

Okay, so now the worker is at the fourth generation: lacquer to matrix to mother to stamper. He's ready to produce the fifth and final generation, the 45 vinyl record itself, called a *release pressing*. But first he must plate the stamper with a hard, ultra-thin chrome surface to prevent it from wearing out too soon. Then he has to shave down the stamper's rear side to a flat surface so that it will fit on the press, and trim its outside edge to size.

More problematic, he has to punch a small hole exactly in the middle, which is not as easy to determine as you might think. On the original lacquer, the spiral of grooves led to the hole in the exact center, but since that hole has been spread and stretched during the plating process, he can't depend on it. He must make a new hole, and he must make it perfect, because the slightest deviation will sour the final recorded music. Part of it is intuition. He plays the grooves with a special needle and watches how the tone arm wobbles back and forth. He also has a device that reads the arm's motion on a dial. When the dial tells him that the tone arm's wobbles are reasonably uniform, he brings down a punch and cuts the hole in the middle. It may take him a couple of tries before he gets it right. Every 45 stamper goes through this trial-and-error search for the perfect hole. Then, as soon as he finds it, he has to bring down another punch to knock out an even bigger hole around it, to fit the center of the press.

Finally we arrive at the pressing of the single itself. The process, called *compression molding*, is similar to making a waffle. Two stamper discs—one for the A-side and one for the B-side—are fastened onto the press, one above, one below, facing each other. The person operating this machine (who is wearing a mask because steaming vinyl is a carcinogen) has within arm's reach a hot plate holding a dozen or so *biscuits*—rectangular, pre-measured blocks of vinyl—that have been heated to the consistency of mush. When he opens the press, he places a label face down on the lower stamper, scoops up a biscuit and puts it on top of the label, then places another label face up on the biscuit. Naturally he matches the labels with the proper stampers (although occasionally the labels end up on the wrong sides). Now he pulls the lever to lower the top stamper against the bottom one like a waffle iron, as a system of valves and hoses automatically blasts steam at 300 degrees Fahrenheit into the pressers and melts the vinyl into a liquid that flows into every groove. Seconds later another hose cools everything off with a rush of cold water, instantly hardening the vinyl. The presser opens his machine and lifts out the record, with the labels bonded to the vinyl. Other machines will still have to trim down any ragged edges and punch the final big hole in the center, but basically the process is over.

An inspector now looks at the finished 45 and either pronounces it ready to go or tosses it into the reject bin, so that the vinyl can be ground up into powder (called *re-grind*), mixed in with new vinyl and turned into another biscuit. This re-grind must be used sparingly, however, because when vinyl is reheated and recooled, it doesn't harden into a smooth, glossy surface. Too much re-grind will make even a brand new record sound grainy and noisy.

There is an alternate, cheaper process, called *injection molding* that was added in the 1950s by Columbia Records and a few smaller companies, using styrene (actually polystyrene), a hard, relatively inflexible plastic, instead of vinyl. The styrene is heated into liquid rather than softened into a biscuit, and squirted or injected into the closed stampers in the press. The labels must then be glued or painted on after the disc leaves the press. The company saves money because there's no heating-cooling cycle to wear out the stampers, but the result is a record that wears out quickly.

So there you have it, the making of a 45, from the recording studio to the flexible, unbreakable plastic product that eventually ends up on your record player.

CHAPTER 11

"Stormy Weather": The Most Legendary 45

espite the nearly eternal shelf life of its plastic composition, the 45 record was considered as disposable as the pop music in its grooves, without longtime merit or significance. After its introduction in 1949, many years passed before anyone besides children took the donut disc seriously enough to consider it as a collectible worthy of lifetime dedication. Not until the late sixties would you see a grown man reverently slide a shiny mint 45 out of a fading buff sleeve and whisper, "Look, fifties dust!"

In 1952 the American Record Collectors Exchange in New York compiled the first *Price Guide to Collectors' Records*, listing the value of all cylinders and discs issued in the acoustic era, before 1925, including a 1903 Columbia platter by opera basso Edouard DeReszke worth $150, quite a sum in those days. But the first genre to capture the obsessive hearts of a significant number of high-rolling collectors was jazz, particularly the jazz of the late 1920s and early thirties, confined to 78s. A second wave of anal-retentive music aficionados focused on early blues, likewise within the exclusive purview of the 78.

Then, in the 1950s, came the first 45s that would later intrigue musical pack rats. These singles belonged to a niche within rock 'n' roll that had its roots in jazz, pop, gospel, and blues. Though its contemporary fans called this music R&B, a later generation, circa 1969, would give it the name "doo-wop"—taken from a background chant on several records, including a 1955 hit by the Turbans called "When You Dance" (Herald 458). Doo-wop artists were generally urban black kids who had grown up listening to the Ink Spots and the Mills Brothers. Singing a cappella in schoolyards, or in public bathrooms and hallways where their voices would echo off the tile walls, they made up in creativity what they lacked in musical education.

The recording that launched this trend in do-it-yourself vocal group music was "It's Too Soon to Know," a plaintive ballad by a Baltimore quintet who named themselves the Orioles after the Maryland state bird. Though written by an inexperienced teenage white girl and released on a small independent label, the Orioles' first single was so distinctive and mesmerizing that it reached No. 13 on the national pop charts in late 1948, just a few months before the advent of the 45 record. (As pointed out earlier, the year 1948 spawned a great number of indie hits because the major record companies were bogged down in a yearlong musicians union strike that precluded them from recording their acts.) Suddenly every black kid in New York and most other Eastern cities wanted to sing like Sonny Til, the Orioles' charismatic lead singer.

Early doo-wop, roughly from 1949 to 1953, was recorded almost exclusively by storefront record companies, often under primitive conditions, and sold to young, urban black consumers who were likely to have older 78 record players. Outside of a few hipsters in the Irish, Italian, or Jewish neighborhoods that abutted the nation's ghettos, whites were unaware of this musical demimonde of jivey vocal rhythms and plangent paeans to unrequited love. Though many of the indie labels were quick to join the 45 revolution, their press runs were mostly in 78s. Consequently, as street-corner music gained popularity in the years ahead, collectors had a difficult time finding 45s of the earliest records, and thus a new collectible was born: the pre–rock 'n' roll doo-wop 45. The single that many consider the most fabled of all is the Five Sharps' "Stormy Weather," released on Jubilee (5104, in 1952).

The story began when five young men from the Jamaica housing projects in Queens, New York, after several months of performing at local functions, were spotted by a producer and taken into a studio to record two songs, their own "Sleepy Cowboy" and a Harold Arlen standard, "Stormy Weather," a major hit for Ethel Waters, Duke Ellington, and others in 1933, though today people are more familiar with Lena Horne's note-for-note imitation of Waters's version in the 1943 film, *Stormy Weather*. The session took most of the day and the quintet (which included a pianist) was paid in hot dogs and soda pop. First tenor Bobby Ward later told writer John Johnson of the *Los Angeles Times* that they heard their recording of "Stormy Weather" twice on the radio, but that sales were so bad that he and the other members had to buy their own copies. Without returning to the studio, the group broke up and three members left music altogether. However, the other two, Clarence Bassett and lead singer Ronald Cuffey, went on to record a small 1958 hit, "Trickle Trickle" (Casino 102), with a group called the Videos. Bassett then joined Shep & the Limelites and sang background on "Daddy's Home" (Hull 740), a doo-wop classic.

The legend began in 1961 in a dingy music shop in a subway tunnel under Manhattan's 42nd Street. The store, Times Square Records, was owned by Irv "Slim" Rose, a cadaverous and gloomy man who bought radio time on local station WHBI to play and promote his inventory of 1950s R&B. Slim by all accounts was the first to see the value of doo-wop records, particularly 45s. The wall behind his counter—called the Rare Wall—contained hundreds of obscure R&B records, many of them commanding as much as $10, a veritable fortune in those days.

One Saturday, as a group of collectors was hanging around the shop, a man walked in to get an appraisal of his 78-rpm copy of a recording of "Stormy Weather" by an obscure group called the Five Sharps. When Slim played it on the store record player, the collectors all heard it for the first time. The song moved at a funereal pace and was crudely harmonized and recorded. It even had the corny sound effects of clapping thunder.

Though some of the gathered collectors pronounced this version one of the worst records they'd ever heard, Slim Rose liked it so much that he borrowed the 78 to play on his radio show. Unfortunately, either Slim or his pet raccoon, Teddy, broke it, which wasn't surprising since 78s were prone to snap and crack without much provocation. Profusely apologetic, Slim assured his customer that he would replace the broken platter. He put up a sign in his store offering $25 in credit for a 78 of the song and $50 for a 45. When weeks went by without any takers on his offer, Slim raised the rewards. Finally he went to the Jubilee Records warehouse on Tenth Avenue and discovered that the master for "Stormy Weather" had been destroyed in a fire several years earlier.

Since Jubilee in 1952 had been releasing singles on both formats, collectors assumed that there must be a 45 somewhere (for even then, collectors valued doo-wop 45s much more than 78s). But nothing ever turned up. As the legend of the Five Sharps' "Stormy Weather" grew, the original record company cut a new version in 1964 with another group altogether, and released it on a 45 single, Jubilee 5478, as by the Five Sharps, but this record was (and remains) nearly worthless to collectors.

Later on, after Slim's Record Shop went out of business, collectors managed to find three 78s of "Stormy Weather." One was in mint condition but had a hairline crack from the center hole to the edge, one had a half-inch chip, and the third, discovered in a junkyard, was in good condition. The latter copy was put on the auction block in 1977 and sold for $3,866 to two California men, David Hall and Gordon Wrubel. A mint copy would have gone for much higher.

The cracked record, which had been found in the original Jubilee sleeve in 1972, was purchased by two collectors, Bob Galgano and Ralph Newman, and both sides were transferred to tape by recording engineer Ralph Berliner, the grandson of recording technology pioneer Emile Berliner. According to Newman, "We worked for weeks to edit out 78 clicks per minute on close to five minutes of program material. In some cases, we had to do 'lifts' or 'grafts' from elsewhere in the song to fill in holes created by the edits in piano notes, etc." After obtaining permission from Jubilee Records, Galgano and Newman mastered a new 45 of the Five Sharps' "Stormy Weather" on the Bim Bam Boom label

(103). "We pressed up only a couple of thousand to keep it scarce, including several on red and multi-colored plastic, some of which I still have," said Newman. "We sold the record for two dollars." An enterprising bootlegger got hold of a couple hundred of these remakes, printed up fake Jubilee labels with the original serial number, pasted them over the Bim Bam Boom labels, and sold the records for much more than two dollars apiece. This same collector also pressed up a handful of these bootlegs on both red and green vinyl, the latter drawing a recent offer of more than one hundred dollars.

Though worthless to collectors, the Bim Bam Boom single's true value was that it allowed regular doo-wop fans to hear the recording and decide for themselves whether "Stormy Weather" deserved its cult status. The reissue also led to all five original Sharps getting together in 1975 to perform at the Academy of Music in New York with several other classic vocal groups, and then to sing at a series of smaller shows around the city until the novelty wore off and sent them back into obscurity. Since then, all have died except for Ward and Bassett.

So the question remains, how valuable would a real 1952 Jubilee 45 of "Stormy Weather" be if it suddenly turned up? According to the aforementioned David Hall, who co-owned Good Rockin' Tonight, a now defunct appraisal service and auction house, "If a 45 was found, I have no doubt it would bring $5,000." He admitted that most likely it would considerably depress the value of his 78.

If $5,000 sounds like a high figure, consider that Jerry Osborne, who publishes books for music collectors, was offering that much for "Stormy Weather" in 1980. While the value of other doo-wop singles has skyrocketed since then (Good Rockin' Tonight in 1999 auctioned off for $18,000 a copy of the Hornets' "I Can't Believe" on States 127, which in 1980 was appraised by Osborne at only $180), the price tag on "Stormy Weather" has remained the same.

And yet, claimed Hall, at least one buyer offered $25,000 for his 78. Was Hall just trying to perpetuate the legend of "Stormy Weather" and inflate the worth of his prize record? Maybe. But he and his business partner keep their precious platter locked away in a bank vault and take it out only once every five years, to give it a celebratory spin.

At least one collector, the late Dave Antrell, a Los Angeles medical doctor who owned the world's second largest cache of doo-wop 45s, doubted that a vinyl version ever existed in the first place. "Don't hold your breath for a 45 of it," he said in 1990, "because Jubilee didn't press up 45s in those days except for records by the Orioles and others that looked like they were breaking out."

Whether there was a 45 or not, the ultimate importance of the Five Sharps' "Stormy Weather," say many collectors, is that it was the Holy Grail that got them hooked on rare doo-wop 45s in the first place. It was the ghostly inspiration that turned record collecting into a passionate profession and sent an army of almost exclusively white guys scurrying into junk shops and Salvation Army stores looking for used singles.

Recorded only in the distortion-free *quality zone*, music "comes alive" on RCA Victor 45-rpm records.

What **magic number** *makes music mirror-clear?*

Now, for more than a year, music-lovers have had—and acclaimed—RCA Victor's remarkable 45-rpm record-playing system. Already, millions know "45" as the magic number that makes music mirror-clear.

As the American Society of Industrial Engineers said when presenting RCA Victor with its 1950 Merit Award, "We are moved to admiration by your bold departure from past practices in developing a completely integrated record and record-player system."

Research leading to "45"—confirmed at RCA Laboratories—covered 11 years . . . and resulted in small, non-breakable records which can be stored by hundreds in ordinary bookshelves, yet play as long as conventional 12-inch records. The automatic record-changer, fastest ever built, changes records in less than 3 seconds—plays up to 50 minutes of glorious music at the touch of a button! Every advantage of convenience, compactness and cost, marks "45" as the ideal record-playing system!

See the latest wonders of radio, television, and electronics at RCA Exhibition Hall, 36 West 49th St., New York. Admission is free. Radio Corporation of America, Radio City, New York 20, N. Y.

Fully automatic RCA Victor 45-rpm record player and records—small enough to hold in one hand . . . inexpensive enough for any purse.

 RADIO CORPORATION of AMERICA
World Leader in Radio — First in Television

A 1950 full-page ad stressed RCA's color-coding system.

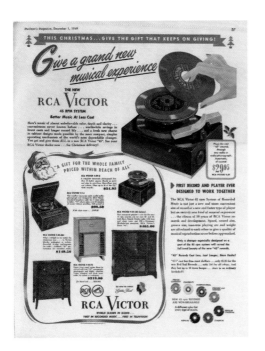

RCA advertised its new system in many major magazines.

Big Boy Crudup's "That's All Right" was the first R&B 45.

"Grass green" was RCA Victor's attempt to associate the color of a countryside with country music.

Children's records like Johnny Appleseed *(WY390) introduced the first extravagant 45 packages.*

RCA's "Greater Variety for Greater Sales" ad.

Companies had their own ideas about marketing specialty music. Capitol treated its country music box sets with more dignity than Columbia, which illustrated its covers with bumpkins.

This early Elvis Presley EP (EPB 1254) used the same cover art as Presley's then-current LP.

Although jazz musician Shorty Rogers had nothing to do with The Wild One's soundtrack, RCA created the impression that this EP (EPA-535) was connected with the popular film.

The Crickets' first LP and EP (71036) had the same photo and nearly identical title. The EP's four songs were the A- and B-sides of the group's first two hit singles, and all four were also available on the album. The cover was notable for the futuristic 1955 sunburst Fender Stratocaster that Buddy Holly (second from right) cradled in his arm. The Beatles' George Harrison spoke for many musicians when he later said, "I'd seen Buddy Holly's Strat, I think, on the cover of the Chirpin' Crickets album, and tried to find one, but in Liverpool in those days the only thing I could find resembling a Strat was a Hofner Futurama."

Though the Chess/Checker label's Bo Diddley LPs had colorful covers, it printed his only EP, Bo Diddley (Chess 5125), with a plain black-and-white cover.

EPs were often used to reinforce surprise hits—such as the Falcons' "You're So Fine"—and promote the artists' next release, which in this case happened to be "The Teacher."

EP covers for R&B artists, such as honking sax man Big Jay McNeely (Federal 301) and blues shouter Wynonie Harris (King 260), were often crudely and colorfully designed to reflect the raw, spontaneous music inside. These EPs can sell for hundreds of dollars today.

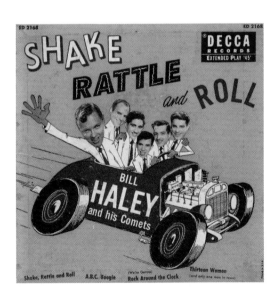

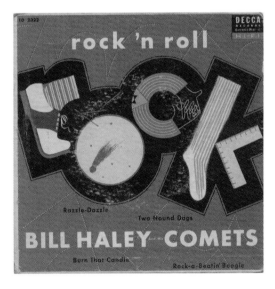

In 1954, Bill Haley's first Decca EP, Shake, Rattle, and Roll (ED 2168), shared the same cover as his first 10-inch LP of the same name. A year later, after the success of the single "Rock Around the Clock," the LP's jacket was redesigned, but the EP's cartoonish jacket remained the same. Only later, in 1956, did Decca use the Rock Around the Clock *album artwork—but for an altogether different EP, called* Rock 'N Roll *(ED 2322). In England, however, the* Shake, Rattle and Roll *EP was issued as* Rock Around the Clock *(Brunswick 9250), using* Rock 'N Roll's *pink graphics.*

Budget lablels like Tops (above) and Prom (below) marketed EPs with cheap cover versions of hit records.

RCA Victor began issuing specialty sleeves in color in 1950.

Hipster deejays like Jazzbo Collins and Huggy Boy (misspelled "Huggie Boy" on the blue label) were popular enough to rate their own singles.

Disney executives were among the first to see the possibilities of using movie and TV characters to sell 45s.

Chess Records used the same photo and layout on all four of its Chuck Berry picture sleeves.

Despite Bob Dylan's spectacular early success, Columbia released only two of his 1960s singles with picture sleeves.

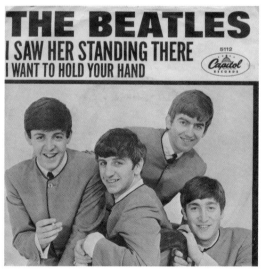

The Beach Boys' "Surfin' Safari" (4777) was Capitol's first full-color picture sleeve, in 1962. However, Capitol issued the Beatles' earliest No. 1 American hit, nearly two years later, with a black-and-white photo. Paul McCartney's cigarette was later airbrushed out.

This copy of the Five Sharps' "Stormy Weather" (Jubilee 5104) is a bootleg. An authentic 45 may never have been pressed— but it remains the doo-wop collector's Holy Grail.

Glad Music
1096 B M I

Vocal
Time 2:30

BALLAD OF DONNA AND PEGGY SUE
(A Tribute To Ritchie Valens And Buddy Holly)
(Jerry Green - Ray Campi)

RAY CAMPI
1047

D Records in Texas released only 45s, at least a couple of hundred of them, including Ray Campi's "Ballad of Donna and Peggy Sue" (1047), the first record to commemorate the 1959 plane crash that killed Buddy Holly, Ritchie Valens, and the Big Bopper, who got his start on D Records. Campi wrote the song on the way to the Houston studio and recorded it with the Big Bopper's band, just days after the tragedy. The B-side memorialized the Big Bopper.

Music publishers routinely sent demo 45s of their songs to artists and their record companies to spur further remakes. This disc featured six versions of Burt Bacharach's 1968 hit, "The Look of Love."

Early doo-wop records on red vinyl, like the Flamingos' "That's My Desire" (Chance 1140) from 1953, are worth upwards of $1,000 if they're in near-mint condition.

Times Square Records, a store in the subway below New York's Times Square, spearheaded an early 1960s doo-wop revival, issuing 45s that resembled the design of the earlier Chance label out of Chicago.

The Penguins' "Earth Angel" (Dootone 348) took off so quickly that the tiny pressing plant ran out of shiny red labels, forcing it to turn to other colors, including blue.

By the 1970s, British companies, which used the smaller hole and therefore had extra room, began issuing picture discs on 45s, such as NEP's 1982 Black Sabbath single (1) with two early 1970s hits back to back.

At least one British label, Columbia-Emi, used EPs to promote certain artists' side projects that weren't issued on singles on LPs, such as pop star Helen Shapiro's jazz and blues recordings.

London's Virgin Records picked up the Sex Pistols' 1977 recording of "God Save the Queen" (181) when the punk rock group's antics prompted A&M Records to drop them. Virgin sent the 45 to the top of the U.K. charts. The unissued A&M 45 of "God Save the Queen" is now worth $6,000 in near-mint condition, but this one would garner only a few bucks.

Los Angeles-based Faro Records promoted its artists on the label of its 45s.

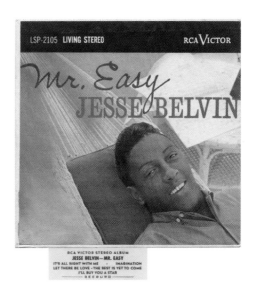

Jesse Belvin's posthumous Mr. Easy EP (LSP-2105), taken from his 1960 RCA LP of the same name, was released only for jukeboxes. The backside was blank.

The Suburban Lawns were a quirky New Wave band from Downey, near Los Angeles, whose "Gidget Goes to Hell" on their tiny Suburban Industrial label (no number) became an underground radio hit in 1979. Their do-it-yourself approach to making and promoting 45 singles became the standard for edgy, hip artists.

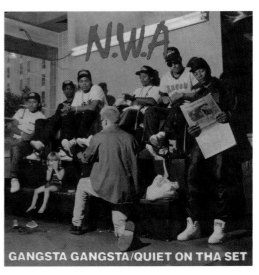

South Central L.A.'s Niggaz With Attitude pioneered gangsta rap with at least five 45 singles, even though rap's main format was the 12-inch.

All of Elvis Presley's early Sun 45s are worth thousands of dollars in mint condition. On Arthur Gunter's "Baby, Let's Play House," the Pentacostal-raised Elvis replaced Gunter's line, "you may get religion," with the now famous "you may drive a pink Cadillac."

One popular 45 on roadhouse and honky-tonk jukeboxes was Peppermint Harris's drinking classic, "I Got Loaded" (Aladdin 3097), from 1951. The record's green vinyl increases its value considerably.

CHAPTER 12

A-Sides, Free Rides & Killers B's

The inexpensive little 45 was the perfect record for the freewheeling rock 'n' roll era, serving with distinction the one-hit wonders and two-bit independent labels that were the backbone of the music. According to Bob Keene, who produced Ritchie Valens in the 1950s and the Bobby Fuller Four in the 1960s, "The 45 was the big thing then, and a hit record was like an oil gusher." Everybody was looking for a hot single. A few kids could go into a cheap studio—or set up a tape recorder in a garage or living room—and record their one song that always got the best response at clubs, sock hops, and supermarket openings around town. As long as they could come up with a throwaway song for the other side of the record, they were ready to go. In at least one case, a 1966 novelty song called "They're Coming to Take Me Away, Ha-Haaa!" (Warner Bros. 5831) by a supposed asylum inmate named Napoleon XIV, a second song wasn't even needed; they simply put the A-side on the B-side, but backwards, titled "!Aaah-Ah, Yawa Em Ekat ot Gnimoc Er'yeht."

As often happened in the 1950s and '60s, a one- or two-man record company, working with a local or regional distributor, would press up a few hundred 45s and take half of them around to the radio stations in the area. (In many cases it was the distributor who dispensed the promotional records, since they had an ongoing relationship with the disc jockeys.) If a single caught the ear of a few jocks, got slotted on the local charts (most stations had their own Top 10 or Top 30 singles of the week), and built up enough momentum, the regional distributor could make a few deals with its counterparts in other parts of the country, who in turn had their own local hits they were anxious to spread around. Sometimes a national record company like Dot, Chess, or Mercury would step in, lease a promising single, and reissue it under its own imprimatur.

Since pressing up a few hundred 45s was relatively cheap, the main expense of getting a record off the ground was promotion. You ran ads in trade papers. You took care of the right people at the distribution company, to make sure your single took precedence on their priority list. You slipped a few bucks to important disc jockeys, or you loaned them your artists to appear free at special events. Bob Keene, for example, promoted Ritchie Valens's first single in Los Angeles by having the young singer deliver pizzas to winners of call-in contests at the city's hottest radio station. "The key in those days was to get with the jocks," said Keene. "We took care of them, made friends with them. I took Ritchie out on hops for free. That way, the jocks could charge a head charge and make some dough, then they'd turn around and play our records."

Beyond the local markets, distributors and deejays around the country had to be courted and cobbled into a network ready to push your single. They all wanted to be in on the ground floor of a hit record, but they had to be convinced that they were betting on the right horse. Bob Rolontz, who worked for Groove Records, an R&B subsidiary of RCA Victor, told writer Arnold Shaw that whenever he was releasing a new 45, he had to go on the road. "There was a northern tier [of distributors and deejays] you covered, which included Philadelphia, Pittsburgh, Cleveland, Detroit, and Chicago. Also Baltimore-Washington, D.C. In Baltimore you brought your records to [deejay] Hot Rod Hulbert. You went to see him at midnight with sandwiches and coffee, and you stayed until three and four o'clock in the morning. In New York you saw Alan Freed, of course, and other guys . . . . In the South, Atlanta was very important. You could break records on WAOK because of Zenas Sears, partly because there was a hot distributor in the area. Atlanta was to the South what Cleveland was to the North . . . . In those days you took a record right to the disc jockey. If they liked it, they played it. If they didn't, they threw you out. You waited and sweated your time out to see the jockey. But he was the determining factor. At times you brought the artist with you."

Once a single took off, it could make a lot of money for the record company, the distributor, the music publisher, and the songwriters. Occasionally the artists even made a few bucks if they had a contract with a larger company, but generally they were the last to see any money, because the standard recording contract allowed that all promotional expenses came out of their cut. That meant their royalties paid for everything from phone calls to postage stamps to hookers for the jocks—in other words, the company's day-to-day expenses. Recording artists were expected to make their money doing live shows, and the records were there to promote them.

At the other end of the food chain were the music publishers, the industry's 800-pound gorillas, who got their pound of flesh out of every 45 in the form of "mechanical" rights: a royalty of four cents *per song* in the 1950s and '60s. Out of that four cents the publisher put two in its own considerable pocket and ostensibly passed along the other two pennies to the songwriter(s)—the name(s) in brackets under the title of the song on the label. The same deal applied to either side of the single, whether it was the hit song or the one getting a free ride on the "bottom." Having your name under a hit song (or on its B-side) was money in the bank, a windfall, a share of a skyrocketing stock or that oil gusher. Furthermore, every time a song played on the radio, the publisher and songwriter

Record promoter George Sherlock, whom the Rolling Stones enshrined in song as "The Under-Assistant West Coast Promotion Man" on the flipside of "Satisfaction" (London 9766), was so taken by a demo of Ian Whitcomb's "Turn On Song" that he wanted to deliver 8-inch test pressings of the raw studio recording, complete with the thump of an ashtray falling off Whitcomb's piano, to his disc jockey friends. As soon as the song started getting airplay, Whitcomb overdubbed a tambourine onto the original track to make it more exciting, and Tower trimmed the song down from its three-minute length to make a more radio-friendly release — at 2:42. Retitled "You Turn Me On" (Tower 134), the single became a 1965 Top 10 hit.

made a couple of pennies in "performance" royalties, collected by two companies, Broadcast Music Inc (BMI) and the more established American Society of Composers, Artists and Publishers (ASCAP).

Under those conditions, songs were like nuggets of gold in an otherwise tenuous landscape, and stealing credit for them in order to collect the royalties was not uncommon. It had been going on for years. In the 1920s the world's most popular singer, Al Jolson, recorded an original song only if the publisher made him a cowriter. During the swing era of the late thirties and forties, bandleaders commonly "cut in"—or cut themselves in—on anything composed or improvised by their musicians, and if they were major names like Goodman or Hampton they might even cut themselves in on songs that were brought to them. However, with the rise of rhythm & blues, rock 'n' roll, and the rough and tumble world of hit 45s, taking both the songwriting credits *and* the publishing became almost an industry standard. Artists who wrote their own songs usually had to sign them away as a precondition to recording them. Most had little knowledge of music's property value, and the record companies made no effort to wise them up.

Take blues great B. B. King, for example. His early fifties recordings were mostly composed by King himself, but he shared his writing credits with Ling, Taub, or Josea—all code names for the three brothers who owned his record company. The brothers also owned all of B. B. King's song publishing. And even though his songwriter royalties were supposed to be separate from his artist royalties and therefore not subject to promotional costs, that's not how things worked in the independent record industry. It was general knowledge, accepted by most blues, R&B, hillbilly and rock 'n' roll musicians, that the only money they would ever get from making a recording was whatever the company paid them at the studio session.

Chuck Berry's first single, "Maybellene" (Chess 1604), in 1955, offers a good example of how the business worked. The song's publisher was ARC Corporation, and the songwriters were listed on the original 45 as Berry-Fratto-Freed. ARC was owned by the same brothers—Phil and Leonard Chess—who owned Chess Records, so on top of everything else they were getting the publisher's two cents for every copy of "Maybellene" that sold and another penny or so from BMI whenever the song played on the radio. The Chess brothers also owned the publishing for "Wee Wee Hours" on the B-side of the single—another two cents for every single sold. To appreciate the windfall these men received, consider that they really weren't publishers. The original music publishers from Tin Pan Alley paid their songwriters a salary and hired "pluggers" to go out and hustle their songs to bandleaders, record company A&R (artists & repertoire) men, radio show producers, and anyone else who could get a song started, whereas record company owners like the Chess brothers simply took the publishing rights as part of doing business and generally made no effort to push the songs to other artists beyond the hope that someone at a larger company would decide to record lucrative cover versions using "legitimate" pop stars.

Since Chuck Berry at this point was an unknown, the Chess brothers needed help in assuring his exposure, so they offered New York disc jockey Alan Freed a third of the writing credit for "Maybellene," so that he could make a fraction of a penny in payola every time the song played on the radio or sold at a record store. (Freed also owned half the songwriting credit on an earlier Chess Records hit, "Sincerely," by the Moonglows, which became a huge cover hit for the McGuire Sisters.) Never mind that Freed's co-ownership created a conflict of interest every time he played the single on his program. The other "writer," Russ Fratto, was the landlord of the building where Chess Records was headquartered, and he also ran a print shop next door that printed the distinctive blue Chess labels, so his inclusion was a pay-off of some kind.

Similarly, Little Richard's first hit, "Tutti Frutti" (Specialty 561), was published by Venice Music and credited to Penniman-LaBostrie-Lubin. Venice Music was owned by Art Rupe, the president of Specialty Records. Penniman was Richard Penniman, Little Richard himself, who had fashioned "Tutti Frutti" out of a late-1930s song recorded by Slim Gaillard. LaBostrie was Dorothy LaBostrie, a New Orleans songwriter who changed some of Little Richard's raunchy lyrics at the last minute before the song could be recorded. And Lubin was Joe Lubin, a Hollywood songwriter who was nowhere near New Orleans when Little Richard recorded "Tutti Frutti." Art Rupe had added Lubin's name simply as a favor or a payback of some kind. (In an interview with one of the authors, Lubin said that he received writer credit in exchange for cleaning up and rewriting the lyrics for Pat Boone's cover.) But Little Richard couldn't complain too loudly, because his name later ended up on songs he didn't write either, including "Keep A-Knockin'" (Specialty 611), for which he was credited as a composer even though the song was first recorded in the 1930s when he was a toddler.

Little Bobby Ray's "Rockin' 'J' Bells (Original Sound 08) was issued in both mono and stereo in 1959. Since stereo 45s were so rare, the company touted it all over the label.

Black songwriter Otis Blackwell had to give up fifty percent of "Don't Be Cruel" (RCA 47-6604) and "All Shook Up" (RCA 47-6870) as the price for having Elvis Presley record his songs. Elvis also got a third of the writer credit for "Heartbreak Hotel" (RCA 47-6420), even though the song was brought to him fully formed on a demo and even vocalized in his own distinctive style by Tommy Durden, so that Elvis was spared any heavy lifting. Elvis's name was even added to "Love Me Tender" (RCA 47-6643), whose melody came from a Civil War song called "Aura Lee." The other composer of "Love Me Tender" was Vera Matson, the wife of *Love Me Tender*'s music director, Ken Darby. Since Darby was signed to ASCAP and Elvis was a member of BMI, they weren't allowed to share writing credit, so Darby registered his wife with BMI and put her name on the song instead.

American Bandstand host Dick Clark was a music mogul who co-owned an artist management company, a record pressing plant, a label printing shop, at least two record companies (Swan and Jamie), a record distributor, a couple of music publishing firms, and a TV production company. It was no secret that turning over part of a song's publishing to Clark's Sea-Lark Enterprises or January Music could assure major exposure on his national TV show. For example, Clark played the Crests' "Sixteen Candles" (Coed 506) on his show only four times over a period of ten weeks, but when January Music received part ownership of the song, it became an *American Bandstand* staple over the next three months—and a No. 2 hit in early 1959.

Clark's producer and right hand man, Tony Mamarella of Chancellor Records, also received a piece of several songs under the name Anthony September, usually on the B-sides where nobody would notice. One song assigned to September was "Ninety-Nine Ways," probably written by Bernie

Lowe and Kal Mann, the owners of Cameo Records in Philadelphia. But since Lowe and Mann were also the writers of a song called "Butterfly," recorded by Charlie Gracie (Cameo 105), giving "Ninety-Nine Ways" to Mamarella and putting it on the B-side of the Gracie 45 was a small price to pay for Dick Clark's considerable help in pushing the single to the top of the charts in 1957. When Dot Records covered "Ninety-Nine Ways" with Hollywood pretty boy Tab Hunter (15548), Dick Clark played that version on *American Bandstand* too. The single nearly cracked the national Top 10 and funneled a good deal of money to both Mamarella and Clark, thus assuring their promotion of Cameo's next single.

When rock journalist Todd Everett asked Ed Cobb of the Four Preps how "It's You"—a song from Meredith Willson's *The Music Man*—ended up on the flipside of their biggest hit, "26 Miles (Santa Catalina)" (Capitol F3845), Cobb answered that Capitol Records, in order to get the rights to *The Music Man* Broadway cast recording, had to guarantee that a certain number of Willson's songs would be covered by Capitol artists. (That's why a straight version of Willson's "Trouble" was inappropriately included on a 1959 Capitol album of song parodies called *Stan Freberg With The Original Cast*. On the other hand, another Capitol act, the Beatles, recorded "Till There Was You" from *The Music Man* simply because Paul McCartney liked the song.)

The B-side also became important to rock 'n' roll music beyond its intrinsic financial value. If anyone needs an example of the inability of record executives to recognize hits, not to mention the wisdom of giving disc jockeys some freedom in picking their own play lists, look no further than the B-sides that, through one twist or another, became A-sides. The one thing that "Gee" by the Crows (Rama 5), "Earth Angel" by the Penguins (Dootone 348), "16 Candles" by the Crests (Coed 506), "Get a Job" by the Silhouettes (Ember 1029), "Silhouettes" by the Rays (Cameo 117), "The Twist" by Hank Ballard & the Midnighters (King 5171), "Louie Louie" by Richard Berry (Flip 321), "You Send Me" by Sam Cooke (Keen 34013), "Tweedle Dee" by LaVern Baker (Atlantic 1047), "Rockin' Robin" by Bobby Day (Class 229), "Hushabye" by the Mystics (Laurie 3028), "I'm Sorry" by Brenda Lee (Decca 31093), "The Wanderer" by Dion (Laurie 3115), "The Lion Sleeps Tonight" by the Tokens (RCA Victor 47-7954), "What's Your Name" by Don & Juan (Big Top 3079), "Save the Last Dance for Me" by the Drifters (Atlantic 2071), "Tears on My Pillow" by Little Anthony & the Imperials (Gone 1027), "Surfin' Safari" by the Beach Boys (Capitol 4777) , "To Sir With Love" by Lulu (Epic 10187), "Incense and Peppermint" by the Strawberry Alarm Clock (Uni 55018), "Signs" by the Five Man Electrical Band (Lionel 3213) and "Na Na Hey Hey Kiss Him Goodbye" by Steam (Fontana 1667) all have in common is that they began life as the intended B-sides of other songs slated to be the hits, and many of these stepchildren ended up at No. 1 on the charts. Without a few influential disc jockeys playing what *they* felt should've been the hit sides, rock 'n' roll as we know it wouldn't have happened.

Saxophonist Danny Flores remembers it all very well. Back in 1958 he was working as a session man for Challenge Records at Gold Star Studios on the corner of Vine Street and Santa Monica Boulevard in Hollywood. "We were just laying down instrumental tracks for Jerry Wallace [of "Primrose Lane" fame], so he could overdub his voice on them later," Flores said a few years ago. Working with Flores on this album project were guitarist Dave Burgess, who was also the A&R man for cowboy star Gene Autry's new Challenge label, and a three-man rhythm section. Flores recalled that whenever they had a little studio time left over, Burgess worked on his own project, an instrumental called "Train to Nowhere." Since he had already recorded a

Capitol sent a series of Mystery Artist promos to radio stations to pique the interest of program directors and disc jockeys in the early '60s. This 45 is by Nancy Wilson.

couple of flop singles for Challenge under the name Dave Dupre, Burgess wanted to release "Train to Nowhere" using a new group name. But he needed a flipside, some throwaway jam or jive, anything would do, because who cared what was on the bottom of a single?

"I had this little riff I'd picked up down in Tijuana," Flores said. "I used it before I'd take intermission at this club I was playing in. You know, we'd be playing it and I'd say, 'We'll be right back, we're taking a pause for the cause.' So we said, 'Let's use that.' " In the limited studio time they had, Flores ran the tune down for the other musicians, they worked up a quick arrangement and taped it. Stan Ross, the studio engineer, recalled, "It was sort of a demo, a balance thing. I pointed everybody in individually [at the song's beginning] because I wanted to hear every instrument." Flores tagged the end of each instrumental chorus by moaning "Tequila." When the session ended, everybody but Flores and Dave Burgess considered the tune such a toss-off that they left without even listening to the playback.

For the group's name Burgess came up with the Champions, after their boss Gene Autry's horse. By the time the labels were printed up, the name had been shortened to a snappier Champs. Challenge released "Train to Nowhere" (1016) in late December 1957, and the record went exactly nowhere . . . until a few disc jockeys started turning it over and playing the catchy B-side. When distributors called Challenge asking for more copies of "Tequila" instead of "Train to Nowhere,"

Autry hastily called his other distributors around the country and told them to turn the record over. As if to make the point even clearer, a cover of "Tequila" (ABC-Paramount 9899) by Eddie Platt was beginning to chart at the same time. In mid-March "Tequila" settled in for a five-week run at the top of the pop charts. And despite the fact that none of the Champs was black, the record won Best R&B Performance honors at the first annual Grammy Award ceremonies, held that year.

Al Silver, who ran Herald Records, a successful New York R&B label in the 1950s, told Arnold Shaw how he created a hit after a 45 called "The Jones Girl" was brought to him in 1956 by a distributor in Hartford, Connecticut. "He called me up one day and said a local company had a record by a group on which he had sold about eight thousand. He wanted me to take it over for national distribution; otherwise, he'd lose it if he took it to some other company.

"When he sent me the record," Silver continued, "I found its quality extremely poor. It was recorded in a church basement with home equipment. But who was I to argue against a local sale of eight thousand copies? We took the record over, making a deal with the people who had it. Standord, with an *o*, was their label. We put it out on our Ember label (1005). When we were ready to release it, we called the Hartford distributor to ask how many he wanted. He replied that the record had dropped dead and he didn't want any. We released it anyway. And about two weeks later, it started to click in Cincinnati. Then, it began to sell in another area. We had 'The Jones Girl' marked as the A-side, which was the way the Standord people marked it, but the disc jockeys and the public thought differently . . . . They picked 'In the Still of the Nite,' the other side."

The Five Satins' "In the Still of the Nite," pressed initially as "I'll Remember (In the Still of the Nite)" to forestall legal action from authors of the Tin Pan Alley standard "In the Still of the Night," reached No. 24 on the national charts, but more importantly, it eventually became one of the most popular doo-wop records of all time. Today the original Standord 45 is extremely valuable, and even various early versions of the Ember reissue are quite rare and expensive.

Murray the K (Kaufman), a deejay on WINS in New York, helped create a No. 1 record in 1961 by getting hold of a test pressing and playing it without the permission of the record company. Colpix, a subsidiary of Columbia Pictures in Hollywood, had just signed a black Pittsburgh group called the Marcels and wanted their first release to be a remake of a Chantels song called "Goodbye to Love." But Murray the K liked the other side, a doo-wop send-up of Rodgers and Hart's "Blue Moon," which the group had learned in the studio at the last minute because the producer had rejected one of their other songs. "[Murray] started playing it on his station without permission," said the group's bass singer, Fred Johnson. "And the response was spectacular." The sudden popularity of "Blue Moon" (Colpix 186) forced the company to call its distributors around the country and tell them to hype it to the local jocks instead of the intended A-side, and within weeks "Blue Moon" had swept its way to the top of the charts in both the U.S. and the United Kingdom.

The story of "Sh-Boom" (Cat 104) is a lesson in how companies manipulated the B-sides of their singles. When Atlantic Records in New York formed a subsidiary label called Cat Records in 1954, it signed a black Bronx quintet named the Chords with the idea of using them to cover Patti Page's massive pop hit, "Cross Over the Bridge" (Mercury 70302), for the R&B market, "to catch some of the spillover," as record producer Jerry Wexler put it. In those days the typical recording session was three hours, during which the artists were expected to lay down four songs. So

Les Elgart's 1954 recording of "Bandstand Boogie" (Columbia 40180) didn't make the charts, but it became famous after Dick Clark used it as his theme song on his Philadelphia TV show, American Bandstand, *in 1957.*

the group also recorded a couple of their own numbers, including a piece of street nonsense called "Sh-Boom." According to Wexler, "We thought it was just ineffable nonsense akin to 'Three Little Fishes'." But since Atlantic Records' publishing arm owned everything the group wrote, it slapped "Sh-Boom" on the B-side of "Cross Over the Bridge" in order to collect the royalties as a free ride if the single sold well. When disc jockeys got the promo, several of them flipped it over. As distributors around the country began calling to order more copies, they asked for "Sh-Boom," not "Cross Over the Bridge." Wexler immediately designated "Sh-Boom" as the hit side, pulled the "Cross Over the Bridge" stamper out of the 45 pressing machines, and replaced it with a new B-side, "Little Maiden," which was also owned by Atlantic, so that Atlantic could collect publishing royalties from both sides of the single instead of giving away half to another music publisher.

But Patti Page's label, Mercury, wasn't out of the picture. It issued a cover of "Sh-Boom" by the Crew-Cuts (70404), which reached No. 1 in 1954.

Perhaps the most historic record deal that almost didn't happen was Decca Records signing Bill Haley and His Comets in early 1954. Like nearly all major labels that acquired rock 'n' roll acts in the years to follow, Decca found itself with Haley only because one independent-minded

Reprise Records, co-owned by Frank Sinatra, briefly issued singles on a label named after Sinatra's ill-fated Cal-Neva casino; Nevada refused to issue him a gaming license because of his mob ties.

producer with clout, Milt Gabler, wanted him over the objections of everyone else in the company. Haley had already recorded a freak hit, "Crazy, Man, Crazy" (Essex 321), for a tiny Philadelphia label, and Gabler felt perhaps he could turn Haley's band into a white version of Louis Jordan and His Tympany Five, which had been Decca's top-selling black act throughout the 1940s. Since Jordan had specialized in clever novelties, Gabler gave his new protégés an obscure R&B song called "Thirteen Women and One Man" to record for their first single. For the record's B-side, Gabler agreed to let Haley record a song owned by his manager, Jimmy Myers, as a way of thanking Myers for bringing Haley to Decca. Myers's song was called "Rock Around the Clock."

When "Thirteen Women" (Decca 29124) by Bill Haley and His Comets was released in May 1954, it failed to rouse anyone. But as soon as a few disc jockeys played the other side, the single got some action. Unfortunately, Decca failed to put its weight behind "Rock Around the Clock" and let it die after the record briefly climbed halfway up the pop charts to No. 23. Luckily, it caught the ear of a young MGM screenwriter in Hollywood, who fought to get the song into his next movie, *Blackboard Jungle*, a year later. Decca reissued "Rock Around the Clock" and turned it into the world's No. 1 rock 'n' roll record.

Today's multinational conglomerates would not have recorded "Tequila" or "Sh-Boom," and under their guardianship "Rock Around the Clock" would most likely have languished. Except for certain "urban" black markets, the B-side no longer exists. The rock 'n' roll B-side began to disappear in the late 1970s, and the last surprise B-side hit was KISS's "Beth" (Casablanca 863) in 1976. The tag-along side was more often an inconvenience for record companies, who were forced to pay, begrudgingly, a second mechanical royalty. The B-side was also troublesome if it competed with the hit side.

Perhaps the first producer to see the freewheeling disc jockey as a counterproductive force was

Phil Spector, who spent almost as much time doting on his 45-rpm teen dramas as classical composers did on symphonies. Spector had definite ideas about which of his studio creations were hits and which were merely backsides. He knew that in order for a single—particularly one on a small indie label like his own Philles Records—to pick up the needed momentum to become a hit, it required steady airplay, and if a few jocks turned the single over to test out the other side, the play was wasted and the hit side was denied valuable airtime. This dilution was common enough that industry insiders had a term for it: "split play."

The tri-center was an option on some singles, especially in the U.K. There were also several companies that manufactured lead and plastic adapters that could be snapped into the 45's big hole in case the listener didn't have a 45 spindle. This Capitol single is from 1952.

Spector's first designated hit on his label was the Crystals' "Oh Yeah, Maybe Baby" (Philles 100), but when disc jockeys started passing it over for its flipside, "There's No Other (Like My Baby)," which only reached No. 20 on the charts in early 1962, he was livid. After split-play slowed down a couple more of his singles, Spector, always the perfectionist, realized that part of the problem was that he lavished the same care on his B-sides as he did on the A-sides. So he came up with the perfect antidote: Following the example of his mentor Lew Bedell at the Dore label, who released retitled throwaway instrumental B-sides well into the seventies, Spector purposely made lousy B-sides. He'd tape his studio musicians as they warmed up, then he'd put these unfocused jams on the bottom of his records and give them inside-joke titles like "Flip & Nitty" (Philles 107), "Dr. Kaplan's Office" (110), "Harry (From West Virginia) and Milt" (119) and "Irving (Jaggered Sixteenths)" (122). No jock in his right mind would have played these recordings. As an added bonus for Spector, he didn't have to pay composer royalties to the musicians because they were working for hire. He alone was the publisher and "composer" of these flipsides and entitled to take a free ride and receive full mechanical royalties. One of these useless B-sides alone could net him $40,000 (in 1960s money) if the record reached the million mark, as many of Spector's singles did.

Sometimes split play created two-sided hits that frustrated record companies because they'd "given away" an A-side. Probably the greatest example of a 45 with two A-sides was Elvis Presley's "Don't Be Cruel"/"Hound Dog" (RCA 47-6604), released in the summer of 1956 when Presley was the hottest act in showbiz. Presley's previous single, a No. 1 hit called "I Want You, I Need You, I Love You" (RCA 47-6540), had already gotten enough split play from disc jockeys to push the flipside, "My Baby Left Me," into the Top 40 for a couple of weeks, but nobody expected both "Don't Be Cruel" and "Hound Dog" to shoot to No. 1 on the national charts and stay there for eleven weeks. The single also topped the R&B and country charts. RCA executives could only regret not having released the two songs separately and making twice as much money.

New York gangster and music man Morris Levy didn't make the same mistake when he leased a single (Triple-D 798) by a white group called the Rhythm Orchids from a label in Dumas, Texas, where it was already a hit. Levy or his A&R man saw potential in both sides of the record, and since each song had been sung by a different member of the group, he reissued them on different singles to launch his new label, Roulette Records. The first, "I'm Stickin' With You" (4001), was credited to Jimmy Bowen & the Rhythm Orchids, while the other, "Party Doll" (4002), was credited to Buddy Knox & the Rhythm Orchids. "Party Doll" went to No. 1 in 1957 and "I'm Stickin' With You" reached No. 14.

Bob Keene wishes he could have done the same thing after his company released Ritchie Valens's "Donna"/"La Bamba" (Del-Fi 4110) in late 1958. When both sides began getting heavy airplay in Los Angeles, he wanted to rush Valens back into the studio to record another B-side, but the 45 took off so quickly that he didn't have time to split up the songs. "Donna" charted at No. 2 and "La Bamba" at No. 22 in early 1959, and were both popular when Valens was killed.

In the 1970s record companies began neutralizing the disc jockey by sending out promo 45s with the designated hit song on both sides, sometimes one in mono, the other in stereo. Sometimes one side would be longer than the other and designated the "dance side." In the case of Don McLean's monster 1971 hit, "American Pie" (United Artists 50856), the deejay 45 was not only mono/stereo but also a radio edit that trimmed the lengthy two-part song down to three-plus minutes, so that it could play from start to finish without taking up as much valuable advertising time. (No matter, the song, with its cryptic lyrics, became such a media sensation that most stations played the uninterrupted 8½-minute version straight off the LP.)

By the early 1980s the B-side was used primarily as a gimmick to market singles to a public interested mainly in LPs. Using a 1960s strategy common with the Beatles, the Who, and Bob Dylan, record companies began putting songs on the B-sides that were not available anywhere else. The B-side of Bruce Springsteen's "Born in the U.S.A." (Columbia 04680), for example, was "Shut Out the Light," which wasn't available on his latest album. His "Pink Cadillac" (04463) was likewise not on LP, nor

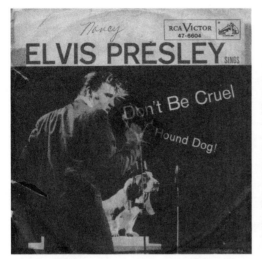 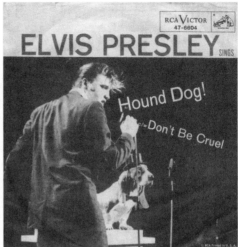

RCA Victor first issued "Don't Be Cruel" (47-6604) as the A-side, but when the flipside, "Hound Dog," took off, the company changed the sleeve. The photo was taken as Elvis sang to a basset hound on NBC TV's The Steve Allen Show.

was Prince's "Erotic City" (Warner Bros. 29216), so if fans wanted these songs they had to buy the 45. Writer Craig Rosen, in December 1984, noted in the *Los Angeles Times* that seventeen of *Billboard*'s current Top 40 singles (including those by Madonna, R.E.M., and the Bangles) had non-album B-sides, often an instrumental version or remix of the A-side. Warner Bros. released so many such singles that it was able to pool non-LP sides by Prince, Madonna, the Pretenders, and Talking Heads onto two good-selling albums, *Attack of the Killer B's* and *Revenge of the Killer B's*.

By the 1990s, with the increasing conglomeration and centralization of both the record and radio industries, the basic cost of pushing a single (mostly CDs at this point) into the pop charts increased to $150,000. With money like that at stake, the B-side was a monkey wrench that nobody wanted to throw into the works, except to sell odd tracks to die-hard fans. The disc jockey had but one job: Play exactly what he was told to play and say what he was told to say by the program director, who in turn was under strict orders from some distant headquarters. To make sure everything was done by the book and by the clock, stations began loading their playlist songs into computers—and the computers "spun" the hits, leaving the deejays to simply kill random moments of dead air with mindless patter. As far as the record conglomerates were concerned, the business was strictly an A-side operation.

CHAPTER 13

The 7-Inch Alternatives

··

Nothing went together so inextricably like rock 'n' roll and the sleek, chrome-gilded automobile of the 1950s, preferably with fins bigger than a great white shark's. Both offered freedom to young people of the era, and part of their experience of cruising drive-ins or racing down highways with the wind in their hair was listening to music cranked up full blast on the car radio. The only drawback was that you couldn't always hear the songs you wanted. If only cars had a record player accessory. But nobody seriously considered transposing the 45 record player into an automobile for a couple of good reasons. First, the thing would skip like crazy every time the car hit the slightest bump. Secondly, the driver would have to stack 45s on the spindle and tinker with the dials every so often, not a wise decision at sixty miles an hour. Thirdly, where would you put the damn thing? Clearly the idea was impractical.

But Dr. Peter Goldmark, who had spearheaded CBS Electronics Labs' development of the LP in the late forties, considered the car record player a challenge worth his considerable talents. "I started to wonder how much information one can put on a small record for use in a car without a changer," Goldmark wrote in his 1973 memoirs. "The answer, it turned out, is easy to figure. To give us forty-five minutes of playing time on a side, as much content as both sides of an LP, and to give us a record small enough to fit with its mechanism inside the glove compartment, the record would have to be seven inches in diameter and would have to revolve at 16⅔ rpm, one-half of the LP speed." In addition this record required 550 grooves per inch, twice the number of grooves on an LP.

Based on his earlier work with microgroove recording, Goldmark and his engineers in just six months developed an ultra-microgroove that was one-third the width of a human hair. "The fidelity was superb," he said. But when he took his new project to his boss William Paley, the old man turned him down flat. "He . . . felt that record players installed in cars might cause drivers to turn off the radio to listen to records, and thus CBS would lose listeners."

So Goldmark installed his automobile player into his own Chrysler and asked the Chrysler Corporation's chief electrical engineer to drive it through the company's test range of cobblestones, potholes, sharp curves, washboard roads, and other jolting irregularities designed to make sure new cars were tightly built. Goldmark's machine played undisturbed. The only problem was that the tires going over various surfaces created frequencies of vibrations that would have to be filtered out in order for anyone to listen to the music. Other than that, the demonstration was a success. Within the week, Chrysler executive Lynn Townsend told Goldmark, "I must have it for the Chrysler."

In September 1955, Chrysler introduced the Highway Hi-Fi in its 1956 line of cars, including DeSotos, Plymouths, and Dodges. Located in a sponge-rubber-cushioned case (four inches high and less than a foot wide) mounted below the right center of the dashboard, it tapped into the radio's speaker and amplifier system with just the flip of a two-way switch. The 7-inch discs, despite their much slower speed and their small, 78-like hole in the center, could have been called 45s because each one was capable of holding up to 45 minutes of music, or an hour of speech, on each side. Six of them, included with the purchase of the Highway Hi-Fi, could fit into the unit's small storage area.

The original six records offered a full menu for the family, including several classical selections, the complete score of Broadway's *Pajama Game*, Walt Disney's *Davy Crockett* with Fess Parker, singing cowboy Gene Autry and his faithful horse Champion, orchestral pop, and dramatic readings from Bernard Shaw's *Don Juan in Hell* by a cast of Hollywood and Broadway stars. Over the next couple of years Columbia added roughly thirty-six more records, ranging in price from $2.95 to $4.95, heavy on the light classics, operas, show tunes, and popular melodies performed by the orchestras of Michel Legrand, Morton Gould, Sammy Kaye, Percy Faith, Paul Weston, and André Kostelanetz. Although young adults would have been ideal customers for the Highway Hi-Fi, there were no rock 'n' roll, rhythm & blues, hip modern jazz, or country & western records to attract them.

Using the basic principle of the modern jukebox playing mechanism, the pickup and record were firmly held in place together. "Using a new principle of design worked out by CBS Laboratories, the player and position of the stylus on a record are not affected by the angle of a car, its highway speed, or even severe cornering," said the Chrysler brochure.

According to an October 1955 Chrysler press release: "The pickup arm, though conventional in appearance, moves only in a horizontal plane. Hence, there is no problem of the arm itself bouncing when the car travels a rough road. Only the stylus can move vertically, and this is spring-loaded to hold the point against the record with a pressure of two grams. The pickup arm is also counterweighted, so that its center-of-mass is at the pivot point. This offsets the tendency of the arm to swing in response to fast acceleration, heavy braking and hard turning . . . . [I]t has proved extremely difficult to jar the arm off the record or even make the stylus jump a groove."

A 1956 Plymouth sales brochure assured buyers, "While you're driving, you can operate the Highway Hi-Fi with complete safety . . . no need to take your eyes from the road. Just pull out the drawer that's within easy reach of your right hand. Press the tab and swing the stylus arm and it automatically positions itself on the record. When [the] record has finished, press the tab when you wish and swing the arm to 'off' position."

According to Goldmark, there remained a problem of getting the Highway Hi-Fi fully up and running. "Columbia Records was interested in supplying records, but only if Chrysler placed an order for 20,000 machines, so they could sell that many records to start with. Chrysler seemed to be willing to oblige. So CBS Electronics went ahead." But it limited its preliminary production to only 18,000 units.

"Somehow this nice cultural addition to American autointoxication didn't take off with the kind of sales we had expected," said Goldmark. "There were complaints from both sides about the way the record players worked. But the chief underlying reason for the middling response, I think, lay in the fact that Chrysler and Columbia Records failed to do proper marketing by not advising potential customers how to obtain additional records. Dealers failed to stock them, and little or no attempt was made to see that they did."

Clearly both companies had to commit to the future to make the system work. But neither did. "Seeing the slow sales," said Goldmark, "the auto company relaxed its promotion." Columbia responded by limiting production of new music on super-slow records. By 1958 the Highway Hi-Fi was dead. It had been too much of a limited system, available only from authorized car dealers, confined to Chrysler products and not transferable to other models—a serious design flaw that, strangely, nobody at Chrysler or CBS, not even Goldmark, seems to have considered. If you traded in your Dodge for a Ford, you lost your record player *and* your record collection, because they couldn't be played on any other system. It also didn't help that the repertoire of recordings, available only from Columbia Records, ignored the most adventurous music on the 1956–57 pop charts.

In 1959 RCA stepped in with a cheaper, more customer-friendly, automatic-changing 45-rpm car system for Chrysler's 1960 Plymouths and DeSotos that otherwise used many of Goldmark's features. It not only played the ordinary 45s from your record collection, but it could stack and play fourteen of them at a time, and if you wanted to replay one of them, all you had to do was hit a switch on the front panel. According to a contemporary automotive writer named Jack Greenfield, "The device is actually an upside-down version of a conventional 45-rpm changer. It is similar in operation to many commercial 45-rpm jukeboxes in that the pickup is held by spring tension against the underside of the record being played. Tracking pressure is high compared to conventional 45-rpm units."

Along with the player came a unique spoken 45 by Steve Allen, who hosted a weekly, Plymouth-sponsored NBC variety show from late 1959 to mid-1960. Entitled "Come Along For a Ride in the Solid New Plymouth" (Solid Plymouth PLY 101), the disc featured Allen, who fancied himself a hipster, giving a sales pitch above his own soft piano backing: "Howdy, this is Steve Allen. No—wait a minute, don't go looking in the glove compartment. I'm not there. I'm really not in the car at all. Not personally, that is. But you've got to admit, that RCA auto Victrola's a fooler. You know, I enjoy sitting at my piano. I guess any, uh, musician does. But you! Man, you're really in solid—sitting behind the wheel of a new solid '60 Plymouth. That's really a thrilling spot. Yeah, I know I'll never forget my first ride. Solid, man. Really solid! There are some things you just don't expect from a low-priced car. And that's why the first ride in a solid '60 Plymouth is such a surprise . . ."

Unfortunately, even with Steverino at the wheel, RCA's 45 automobile player lasted only a year. Apparently the stacking-and-playing system was so complicated that it tended to break down in many different ways. Playing a full range of personal music in cars wouldn't be practical until the development of Bill Lear's eight-track tape format five years later.

During its short run, though, the RCA player, and other models produced by ARC and Norelco, were very popular with cruisers who could create their own rock 'n' roll and R&B shows on the road. It also provided an important impetus for collecting 45s, especially in the car-obsessed Los Angeles area, as cruisers heard and tracked down songs, and even paid more than retail for some songs they heard from other cruisers. Some record stores, like the legendary Wenzel's Music Town in Downey, also dubbed certain non-45s from LPs to metal acetates to be enjoyed as one-of-a-kind cruiser discs, thus accounting for certain weird combinations of songs credited to Dick Dale or the Rolling Stones on handwritten labels pasted onto 45-rpm metallic discs. Other stores in and around East L.A. handled "low rider" 45s, like "Angel Baby" by Rosie & the Originals or "Sad Girl" by Thee Midniters on the Good Old Gold, Blackjack, and many other "mystery" labels. These bootleg singles, pressed for the in-dash record player trade, still show up at swap meets throughout Southern California.

Despite the short active life of his slow-speed record player, Peter Goldmark had the last laugh. "As a spin-off from the new record technology, I developed for the Library of Congress a seven-inch record that plays four hours of spoken word and rotates at 8.31 rpm. This came into being because of my association with Recording for the Blind, an organization that has brought the beauties of the spoken word into the homes of thousands of blind students. We used the identical tone arm as we did in the automobile, so that it could be pummeled around a bit without distorting the sound."

There was another type of record called the flexi-disc, or flexi, found mostly in magazines and cereal boxes, that went back at least before World War II. In the late fifties, *Mad* magazine probably came up with the most popular flexi ever, called "It's a Gas," featuring a cheesy instrumental combo whose musical pauses were filled by loud, obnoxious belches. A children's publisher, John C. Winston Company, produced a couple dozen *Magic Talking Books* in the late fifties. And several music magazines came with Evatone soundsheets containing multi-disc sets from the Longines Symphonette Society. In the 1960s there were even "talking" baseball cards, as well as Motown cards featuring the label's many recording stars. All of these flexis were cheap, soft plastic good for a dozen or so plays before the stylus began eating out the grooves.

The most famous flexi series was a line of Top 40 hits from Philco called Hip Pocket Records. The plastic 45-rpm records were four inches in diameter, had two songs on one side only, came inside colorful sleeves, and were available for 69 cents at local Ford dealers (Philco was a division of Ford Motors) and Woolworth's department stores. Over fifty different titles were issued between 1967 and '69. Philco began with songs leased from the Atlantic, Mercury, and Roulette labels, but in 1968 several smaller companies, including Scepter and Wand, signed on. Philco even produced a stylishly designed, rectangular Miniature Radio Phonograph, model S-1378WH, that could play Hip Pockets or regular 45s.

They were sold in record envelopes, roughly six by five inches, which touted the discs' portability ("25 to 50 Hip Pocket records can be carried in pocket or purse"), their value as greeting cards suitable for mailing, and their durability ("Drop them or sit on them . . . they are almost indestructible"). Most important, they didn't sound like what you'd expect from cheap, almost paper-thin plastic. "Don't let the small size fool you . . . the sound is amazingly big." These sleeves were generally simple in design, with a listing of the two tracks and a photo of the artist or band.

All flexi-discs were issued in mono, which in some cases meant they were the only available alternate mixes of the stereo originals, most notably Neil Diamond's "Solitary Man" (HP-17), which Bang Records, a Mercury subsidiary, had released only in stereo in 1966. (Philco/Ford also released Diamond's "Girl, You'll Be a Woman Soon" and "Cherry Cherry" on HP-5.)

Among other Hip Pocket releases were Tommy James & the Shondells' "I Think We're Alone Now" (HP-1), the Doors' "Light My Fire"/"Break on Through" (HP-9), the Five Americans' "Western Union" (HP-10), John Fred & the Playboys' "Judy in Disguise" (HP-25), the Seeds' "Pushin' Too Hard" (HP-26), and Chuck Berry's "Maybellene"/"Roll Over Beethoven" (HP-34), taken from Mercury Records' mid-1960s remakes rather than the Chess Records originals from 1955 and '56. Even folk acts like Joan Baez and the Rooftop Singers were included. In all, Philco/Ford released forty-one pop Hip Pockets (the final one being the Isley Brothers' "Twist and Shout") and twelve children's singles.

Banking on Hip Pocket records being the next big thing, the Americom company came out with a competing series called Pocket Disc records, sold in vending machines for fifty cents, whose roster was the Beatles (four releases in all) and other artists from the group's Apple label, including Billy Preston and Mary Hopkins. Most of the 4-inch records, contained in generic red or blue covers, had a simple white Apple logo on a black background.

By 1969 the flexi-plastic, 4-inch 45 was a bust, and even though it was sometimes later used as a promotion, as when the Eva-Tone company pressed up a dozen or so Beatles flexi-45s as give-aways at Musicland record stores in the early eighties, the industry's abandonment of vinyl pretty much dumped the flexi down the black hole of history. Today, Hip Pocket singles are worth about $15 in mint shape, whereas the less-successful Americom discs can run from $200 to more than $1,000 if they're in pristine condition. The Musicland Beatles discs run from $10 to $30.

CHAPTER 14

The 12-Inch Single

T hough he's not a household name, Tom J. Moulton owns a significant piece of real estate in musical history. He was the first guy to dislodge the 7-inch 45 from its preeminence in the music marketplace.

Born in the early 1940s and raised in Schenectady, New York, Moulton fell so deeply in love with R&B music that he quit high school to work in a record store. "I wanted to become a disc jockey, and then my idol was caught in a pay-off scandal in the late fifties," he told Discoguy, an online disco historian, "and that absolutely destroyed me. I mean, how anybody could take money to play a record was beyond me. I thought they were playing it because they loved this new song, and that's what I thought I wanted to do—I wanted to turn people on to music."

Near the end of the sixties, Moulton was still carrying a torch for black music, only now it was called *soul* and moving toward *funk*. He was spending a weekend at Fire Island, a trendy gay enclave on Long Island known for its colorful nightclub culture, when he watched mostly white people like himself dancing with abandon as a club deejay played hard-driving black music. The only thing that bothered him was that the songs were just three minutes long. "It's a shame," he said later, "because the minute the song is over [the deejays] start mixing in this other song and [people] don't know whether they should dance to the new song or keep dancing to the old one." It broke the magic mood and sent many of the dancers off the floor. "I said, 'There's got to be a way to make it longer where you don't lose that feeling. Where you can take them to another level.' And that's when I came up with this idea to make a tape.

Moulton spent several days mixing and weaving his favorite dance songs together in such a way that he could keep a steady groove going for forty-five minutes. By luck he met and gave his tape to the owner of Fire Island's popular Sandpiper club, who in turn handed it to his floor deejay. A couple of weeks later the deejay called Moulton in the middle of the night and asked, "Can you make another tape—the people are getting wild for this tape."

By the early seventies Moulton had carved out a record promotion niche for himself. Most promoters visited radio stations to convince disc jockeys and program directors to play their companies' records. But Moulton was going to trend-setting dance club deejays around the New York City area, because dance singles were getting their reputations, their buzz, via the nightclub grapevine, not through radio play. Instead of flogging factory singles, Moulton dispensed special promo discs of company recordings he had remixed from the original tapes, emphasizing the beats for the dance floor. Working with an engineer named José Rodriquez at Media Sound Studio, he cut 7-inch test pressings that became so much livelier than the regular released music that eventually he could demand—and receive—mixing credit on the label.

One day when Rodriquez ran out of 7-inch blanks, they pressed up Moulton's club discs on a few 10-inch records. "I said, 'It looks so ridiculous, this little tiny band [of grooves] on this huge thing. What happens if we just, you know, make [the recording area] bigger?' [José] goes. 'You mean, like spread the grooves? Then I've got to raise the [sound] level.' I said, 'Go ahead, raise the level.' And so he cut it at +6. When I heard it I almost died. I said. 'Oh my God, it's so much louder and—listen to it! Why don't we cut a few more?'"

This time Moulton decided to try a 12-inch blank for a 45-rpm remix of "So Much for Love" by a Salsoul Records funk group called Moment of Truth. "That was the birth of the 12-inch single," Moulton later declared. (If "So Much for Love" was ever issued on 45, the press run was very limited.)

Talking with writer Brian Chin, Moulton said he liked cutting dance songs on 12-inch singles "because 45s were geared for radio, they were all 'middle' [range], and you couldn't cut a lot of [bass] onto the record. A lot of [45s] didn't have the fidelity and sounded terrible. But you were playing them for the songs, not the fidelity." On the dance floor, however, nobody was listening to the songs per se; they were dancing to the beat, the groove, the energy, the sheer excitement of sound pulsing out of huge speakers. Club deejays wanted lots of bottom end—bass lines and resonant beats—that made the room throb and the dancers ecstatic. But all that aural information required wider grooves, and if Moulton tried to put that kind of wide-groove mix on a 45, the song would last only a minute or two before the needle ran into the dead wax. He needed the larger palette.

By 1974, as disco music gained wider popularity, top record labels were hiring Moulton to re-configure their dance records because he had enough cachet among club deejays that his name on the label guaranteed exposure. One of his first disco hits was Gloria Gaynor's "Never Can Say Goodbye" (MGM 14748). Moulton, however, claims he never abandoned the 7-inch record. "I would do a 12-inch version of [a song], but then I always did a single version," he told Discoguy. "There was always a short version and a long version. You're going into the store to buy that [7-inch] record because you heard it on the radio. Why not have the option of being able to buy a longer version of the same song?" But the 45 was still the more important record for him, sales-wise. "I would do the 12-inch first. Then I would take all the great elements of the things that made it spectacular and put them in the single [7-inch] version. That's why the single versions were always so good."

Unfortunately for the 45, many of the record companies that specialized in dance records during the disco craze didn't agree. At first, they released special-mix 12-inch discs to the most influential deejays only for promotion, while the 7-inch versions carried on as the commercially available format. (Among the earliest promo 12-inch singles were Calhoon's "Dance, Dance, Dance" (Warner/Spector 0405) and Frankie Valli's "Swearin' to God" (Private Stock 45021), both in 1975. A year later, Rolling Stones Records released a 12-inch promo of the Rolling Stones single "Fool to Cry," with a B-side ["Crazy Mama"] different from the one on the 45 version ["Hot Stuff"]— even though both records had the same 19304 release number.) Companies pressed only a handful of 12-inch singles to create artificial demand and enhance their snob appeal. But in 1976, when Salsoul Records released the first commercial 12-inch 45-rpm record—Double Exposure's "Ten Percent"—to the public for $2.98, it was obvious that the disco scene was setting its own record medium.

Even so, companies continued to depend on the donut disc if they wanted radio play and sales beyond the hardcore cognoscenti. They'd put an instrumental set-up of the song on the A-side and the vocal performance on the B-side. Some deejays would mix two 45s of the same song back and forth on their turntables to get an uninterrupted dance track. But clearly the 7-inch single was not up to the demands of disco. People wanted to get out there and boogie-oogie-oogie till they just couldn't boogie no more, 'cause that's the way, uh-huh, uh-huh, they liked it, and the 12-incher, also called a "maxi-single," was the record for the job. (Though the 12-inch single played at 45 rpm, it was never designated as a "45," not even after it usurped the 7-inch disc's position in the industry.)

Disco music thrived for about six years. There were 15,000 disco clubs around the United States at its peak and about four hundred hit records, including several No. 1 singles by the Hues Corporation, the Bee Gees, Johnny Taylor, and KC and the Sunshine Band, among others. Not even Rick Dees's No. 1 1976 single—a 45—called "Disco Duck" (Fretone 040; reissued on RSO 857) could hobble it. But by decade's end the party was wearing down and wearing thin. The disco scene had devolved into flamboyant excess, and the major record companies had flooded the market with mostly lame stuff. In 1979 the disco film *Sgt. Pepper's Lonely Hearts Club Band* flopped so badly, it actually killed the recording career of the Bee Gees. By 1980 a "Disco Sucks" campaign was in full riot and radio stations were holding public burnings of disco records. Most of the melting vinyl was 12-inch.

But that only drove disco back into the clubs, where it was transformed into disco with different names, such as *garage* (from the legendary New York club Paradise Garage), *house* (from Chicago's

Warehouse), *hi energy* (Hi-NRG), *Euro*, and just plain *dance*. And almost none of this music was on 7-inch 45s.

By 1982, record stores were routinely setting aside 12-inch single sections. One of the first major recordings to establish the 12-inch single with general consumers was Michael Jackson's 1983 No. 1 song, "Billie Jean," from his multiplatinum *Thriller* album. The version issued on 45 (Epic 03509 and 03575—the second release being a one-sided disc) was about five minutes long—nearly the same length as the slightly different mix on the album. But the 12-inch "Billie Jean" was an "extended" dance mix, six and a half minutes long, with a lot more volume in the grooves. That

Who said disco was tacky? Drummer Norman Connors concocted this studio abomination for Buddah Records (560) in 1977.

same year, the Clash's 12-inch version of "Rock the Casbah," with a colorful sleeve and a dub (instrumental) mix of the song on the flipside, sold 100,000 copies—half a million units less than the 45 (Epic 03245) version, but significant enough to point to a new retailing trend in mainstream rock. More importantly, on the "urban music" scene that year, the 12-inch Tommy Boy Records single of "Planet Rock" by New York hip-hoppers Afrika Bambaataa & the Soul-Sonic Force went gold.

Nothing heralded the end of the 45's dominance more than hip-hop, the most important musical innovation in the last quarter of the twentieth century. Originally recorded on top of disco rhythms and funk beats, hip-hop needed plenty of boom room in the wax, plus enough length to keep people dancing. Bambaataa (nee Lance Aasim), who was rapping over pre-recorded electro-funk beats at New York City clubs as early as 1970, is considered to be the one who started hip-hop as a cultural and musical phenomenon, though he himself didn't record until 1980. Never interested in a pop career, he restricted himself to 12-inch singles, which by then was the format of choice (along with tape cassettes) among urban black youth.

It was still early enough, however, that in order for hip-hop to cross over to the white, suburban market, companies had to press 45s. Thus, the first commercial rap single, Fatback's "King Tim III (Personality Jock)" (Spring Records 199), was released on both 7- and 12-inch records. The song entered the R&B charts in early October of 1979.

Then a record company owner named Sylvia Robinson, who had sung on several fifties hits as half of Mickey & Sylvia, took rap into the mainstream. She said later that when she first saw several kids at a party rapping into a microphone over instrumental tracks, she had no idea what was going on. All she knew was that the people on the dance floor loved it. Attuned to the commercial realities of the late seventies disco world, she eschewed the militant street rappers and instead assembled a faceless studio trio called the Sugarhill Gang to record a slick, well-crafted song called "Rapper's Delight," based on the rhythm track, especially the bass line, of Chic's recent No. 1 disco 45, "Good Times" (Atlantic 3584).

Aiming at both the urban and crossover markets, Robinson's company, Sugar Hill Records, released "Rapper's Delight" on both 12-inch and 7-inch singles, with different mixes and catalog numbers: Sugar Hill 542 for the 12-inch single, 755 for the regular 45. Though *Billboard* and *Cashbox* tabulated both sizes together (sales reached two million copies), it was the traditional 45 single that turned "Rapper's Delight" into the first Top 40 rap song in early 1980, setting the musical direction for the next two decades and beyond. But from then on, Sugar Hill generally released 45s only after a 12-inch single showed crossover potential, so that by 1982, even an R&B hit like "The Message" by Grandmaster Flash and the Furious Five was released almost exclusively on 12-inch. Only when Sugar Hill was going straight for the white market, as with Grandmaster Flash's "The Nasty" (775) or Spoonie G's "Monster Jam" (765), would it release a heavy run of 45s. By 1985, when Grandmaster Flash sued the company into bankruptcy over unpaid royalties, Sugar Hill Records had already phased out the smaller single.

Likewise, when Mercury Records became the first major label to exploit the growing hip-hop movement by scooping up ex–Furious Five member Kurtis Blow (*née* Curtis Walker), it tailored its pressing patterns to whether the singles had across-the-board hit potential. Since Blow rapped over a disco track on his first single, "Christmas Rappin'," in late 1979, it was promoted as a dance single—on 12-inch only; but his next release, "The Breaks," showed enough wider appeal that Mercury put it out on both 45 (76075) and 12-inch. Though it reached only No. 87 on the pop charts, "The Breaks" gradually sold more than a million copies, becoming the first gold rap single.

As hip-hop continued going mainstream and successful labels like Tommy Boy and Def Jam were swallowed up by conglomerates, the 45 remained the vehicle for reaching pop audiences across the country with groups like the Force M.D.s, the Beastie Boys, Run-D.M.C., N.W.A. and LL Cool J until about 1988, when Public Enemy's "Don't Believe the Hype" (Def Jam 07934) and the Fat Boys' "The Twist (Yo, Twist)" (Tin Pan Apple 887 571-7) were the last big hits on 7-inch.

That year a short-lived trade publication called *Black Radio Exclusive* put out a special rap issue with a chart devoted to record speeds and formats, showing that of twenty-five new singles, only six were on 45, while fourteen were on 12-inch vinyl. The remaining five singles were on cassette, which by then was increasingly taking over the 45's job in hip-hop. For example, a year later 2 Live Crew's scandalous "Me So Horny" on the indie Luke Skyywalker label reached No. 26 on the charts without being pressed on 45. (The label name was shortened to "Luke" in mid-release when George Lucas threatened a lawsuit.)

Interviewed in 1991 (the year that Interscope Records and Death Row Records dominated the rap scene without issuing any singles on 45), a Los Angeles club deejay, Nu-Mark of Jurassic 5, discussed rap records with one of the authors. "I have about 200 45s. Deejays see

Many early Los Angeles rap artists and others recorded for a local vanity label, Malaco, a Hollywood pressing plant. Artists like the young Ice-T paid for their own 45s.

them, grab them for the fun of it. Capitol keeps 45s in mind because they have old-school tradition in mind. They do it for every release, I would say tops they probably press about 2,000 [45s]. Generally for hip-hop stuff, [45s] sound worse [than 12-inch] . . . . Once 12-inch came along, why are we doing 45s? Sound is way wider, that's for sure [on 12-inch]."

By the early nineties the most popular hip-hop music was *gangsta rap*, which avoided the 45. Songs like Dr. Dre's "Nuthin' But a G Thang," Cypress Hill's "Insane in the Brain," 2Pac's "I Get Around," and Ice Cube's "It Was a Good Day" became hits on cassette singles and 12-inchers only, though occasionally a miniscule number of 45s might be pressed up if the song were popular enough. It was a replay of the era between 1958 and 1960, when the last of a handful of record labels pressed tiny runs of 78s of their major hits to service what was left of the few jukeboxes still playing the 10-inchers, right up until Barrett Strong's early 1960 hit, "Money (That's What I Want)" (Anna Records 1111)—probably the last Top 20 record on 78 in the United States. And like those late rock 'n' roll 78s, hip-hop 45s are likely to be collectibles in the near future, much more valuable than their 12-inch counterparts.

CHAPTER 15

The End of the Single

T he single is dead. Long live the single," wrote Chris Willman in a 1987 *Los Angeles Times* article. The truth is that the Music Monopoly (*i.e.*, the five major record conglomerates), Big Radio, and even the chart makers have tried to kill off the single altogether. And yet, no matter how many times they drive a stake through its heart, the single manages to struggle upright from its coffin in new configurations.

The single got its first look at the future in the late 1960s when the emerging free-form FM radio format, aimed more at young adults than teenagers, showed that it could popularize cuts from "progressive rock" LPs without the need for corresponding 45s, or at least get a hit-worthy song moving to the point where the record company decided it warranted a single to cross it over to a more general audience.

Then the 12-inch vinyl single began supplanting the 45 in the seventies. In 1975 came the pre-recorded audiocassette tape—which within eight years would be outselling vinyl LPs—followed by its mid-eighties offshoot, the cassette single, or *cassingle*. In 1987, when A&M Records released the first major cassingle, Bryan Adams's "In the Heat of the Night" and "Another Day," at the same $1.98 price as the picture-sleeved 45 (2921), A&M's marketing general manager Bob Reitman explained, "This is the first generation that doesn't have a turntable. And singles are a teen and preteen item. Very seldom are singles an adult item, except in the country market." Sales of 45s had dropped so precipitously since 1977—the last great year for vinyl—that the idea of a 45 selling a million copies by itself, according to one Arista Records executive in 1987, was "almost unheard of."

MCA pushed cassingles to the mainstream teen market by adding bonus tracks. For example, pop star Tiffany's "I Saw Him Standing There" on 45 (MCA 53285) had the standard B-side, "Mister Mambo," but the cassingle (issued one number higher on 53286) contained a third track, or "C-side," called "Gotta Be Love." MCA similarly added a bonus song to the Jets' "Make It Real" cassingle (53317) that wasn't included on the 45 (53311).

By this time the Record Industry Association of America (RIAA) was reporting that the tape cassette had become the most popular configuration, comprising nearly sixty-two percent of all units shipped nationwide. In 1989 Tommy Boy Records had the first Top 40 hit issued exclusively on cassingle, De La Soul's "Me Myself & I." Tommy Boy's sales director, Steve Knutson, told *Rolling Stone* that bypassing a vinyl release may have angered some fans, but it avoided the high returns of 45s. "I really believe we would have shipped 50,000 [45s] and gotten back 45,000," he said.

(In 1988 George Harrison reportedly recorded "Handle With Care" as a throwaway to fulfill the requirement for a C-side on his upcoming cassingle. But executives at his record company, Dark Horse, were so impressed with the track that they convinced Harrison to hold it back and cut an entire album with the famous musicians who had, as a favor, collaborated with him on the song. Had the single been a 45, Harrison might never have recorded "Handle With Care" with his friends, and the Traveling Wilburys—with Harrison, Roy Orbison, Tom Petty, Bob Dylan, and Jeff Lynne—might not have formed as a recording and touring group.)

Insiders were telling the *Los Angeles Times* that the 45 was over. "Vinyl will be history . . . . Most chain record stores will not be carrying vinyl. I think it has one more Christmas after this, perhaps," said Mitch Perliss of Music Plus, a retailer with fifty-six record shops. Russ Solomon, president of the Tower Records store chain, foresaw "vinyl remaining viable only until about 1992." Skid Weiss, national director of communications for WEA (Warner-Elektra-Atlantic), told Cox News, "The demise of the 45 is a certainty. It's a dinosaur, an extinct configuration. It's going to be an extinct species."

By now the CD—the wafer-thin, aluminum-coated polycarbonate disc developed jointly by Sony in Japan and Philips/PolyGram in Holland—had become the industry's main format all across the board. Capable of holding nearly eighty minutes of music, the CD first arrived in America in 1983 with, ironically, a GRP Records album called *In the Digital Mood*, by the 1940s Glenn Miller Orchestra. During that first year, 800,000 CDs were sold in this country; three years later, sales topped fifty million. Fifteen years later, in 2001, annual domestic sales reached $12.2 billion.

For a time in the early nineties, A&M Records tried to push the CD-3 single (a mini-compact disc, three inches in diameter), but it proved to be too expensive (five dollars) and incompatible with most regular CD players without a special adapter. When the industry eventually got around to burning singles into the same five-inch CD that carried albums, the CD-3 was doomed. So was the cassingle. An RIAA report revealed: "More musicassette singles were actually returned as un-salable than were shipped in 2001." Half a million of them, in fact. The cassingle disappeared almost overnight, never to be seen again.

"Indeed, the cassette is close to being fast-forwarded into the technological graveyard," Anthony DeBarros wrote in *USA Today* in November 2001. "It may have helped nearly kill vinyl in the eighties and made eight-tracks little more than an unpleasant memory, but now its own vital signs are desperate: Last year, albums on tape made up just 5% of music sales, according to the Recording Industry Association of America, down from 63% in 1987."

Though the record industry touted the CD as a natural technological progression from analog to digital recording, vinyl fans and cynics claimed that it was merely a ploy to make people buy their record collections all over again. In 1993 Sony president Norio Ohga confirmed their suspicions when he told reporters that he had guided the CD onto the market to reinvigorate sales, not to deliver more convenience or better sound quality. "At the time we developed the compact disc, the LP market was saturated and the cassette market was beginning to slow down," he said. "We knew we needed a new carrier." And a more profitable one. According to Stan Cornyn, a marketing executive at Warner-Elektra-Atlantic who was instrumental in converting the conglomerate's various record companies to compact discs, "The profit this new configuration could bring to [our] business was too good to believe; it was like this week your paycheck got doubled; it was like *whee!* Everything about CDs cost like LPs: the same cost to record, the same cost to market, soon even the same cost to make." Yet record companies doubled the price of albums when they converted them from vinyl to CD. Comedian Paul Reiser, hosting the 1995 Grammy Awards, summed it all up nicely when he quipped, "A little message to the industry. I bought tapes to replace my records, then I bought CDs to replace my tapes. If you change one more time, I swear, we're all gonna buy sheet music and hum!"

With the success of the CD album, companies released fewer singles—on any format. If you rushed into a record shop to get that one great song you'd heard ten minutes ago on the radio, there was a good chance you wouldn't find it unless you wanted to buy an entire CD with a lot of filler on it. The *Los Angeles Times* announced that singles sales totaled only $31 million in 2001, "down a whopping 41% from 2000, according to SoundScan." In fact, SoundScan—the industry's computerized system that precisely maps record sales at retailers' cash registers—has been a determining factor in the decline of the single since being introduced nationally in early 1992, because it proved in black and white that singles were sometimes cutting into the sales of the industry's more profitable albums and denying them the more efficient way of gouging their customers.

During the week of February 23, 2002, only twenty-three recordings in the Top 40 had been released as singles—five on CD and eighteen on vinyl. The remaining seventeen hits, including Alanis Morissette's "Hands Clean" and No Doubt's "Hey, Baby," were available only on albums, which of course were overpriced at roughly $18. In some cases companies initially released a single to stimulate radio play and buyer interest, then pulled it from stores when the song started climbing the charts, so that it wouldn't interfere with album sales. Many insiders became upset with this new imbalance between singles and albums. One prominent record distributor, Carl Rosenburg, head of Top Hits in Buffalo, New York, noted, "I think they're losing a whole generation of record buyers."

It was no coincidence that younger music fans were abandoning traditional record stores by retrieving their favorite music directly from Internet file-sharing programs like Napster and burning their own private singles and albums into blank CDs, which, by the way, outsold pre-recorded commercial CDs for the first time in 2002. "You either have to steal it off the Internet or you just don't buy it at all," Rosenburg said. Pam Horowitz, president of the National Association of Record Merchants, agreed. "We have been in a song-driven marketplace for a number of years," she

In case you can't tell from the label, this is Jennifer Lopez's "I'm Real" (Epic 79662), a limited 45 release from 2001 and a clear illustration of how modern pop artists, with their various publishing and recording deals, coproducers, cowriters, comixers, multicity studios, lifestyle counselors, and hangers-on, have become too big, too glitzy, too important for the 7-inch single.

told a conference of record shop owners in the autumn of 2002, "and yet the availability of singles continues to decline. When there is no way for the consumer to purchase just the one song they want, why are we all surprised that they take advantage of the widely available alternative?"

Los Angeles Times pop music critic Robert Hilburn observed in early 2002 that the declining availability of singles has completely changed the definition of a hit. As an example, he noted that Mariah Carey had more No. 1 singles (fifteen) than anyone else since the Beatles (twenty). "On the list of meaningless pop statistics, that's No. 1 with a bullet," Hilburn wrote. And not just because her label, Columbia, had been selling her singles as loss leaders—generally at 49 cents—in the first weeks of release in order to create the impression that Carey was flashy hot. The larger problem was a lack of consensus of what a No. 1 single really was, because radio had broken down into such restrictive niches that any one single rarely got wide exposure. A few decades earlier, when Top 40 radio stations offered more diverse playlists, whatever happened to be at the top of the heap that week was heard by a large segment of the American population. Anyone not familiar with "Rock Around the Clock" (1955), "I Want to Hold Your Hand" (1964), "Love Can Keep Us

Supposedly the acetate for Afroman's "Because I Got High" (Universal 440015282) was found in a trash can. Released in 2002, the 45 label strains to contain the Parental Advisory, the bar code, and the Social Security–length release number.

Together" (1975) or "What's Love Got to Do With It" (1984) during those singles' time at No. 1 was hiding under a rock. But nowadays, as Hilburn pointed out, "There are many No. 1 records each week, one in each format . . . . The result: Singles can become No. 1 some weeks by selling as few as 15,000 copies." According to *Billboard*'s chart director, Geoff Mayfield, in 2002 and early 2003 the average weekly sum for the nation's top-selling single was only 22,000 units.

Moreover, since *Billboard* had reduced the importance of single sales and increased the weight of airplay when compiling its weekly Hot 100 chart, 1,000 radio listeners (as tabulated by Arbitron and other major survey groups) now had as much impact as the sale of one single. This methodology removed one of the last incentives for record companies to issue singles, which in turn made the number of radio "listener impressions" an even more significant factor in ranking songs. All a record company had to do was buy its way into heavy rotation at key radio stations—not a hard thing to do in today's Big Radio monopoly in which one conglomerate alone, Clear Channel Communications, owns a staggering 1,200 stations and can blanket the country with any song, regardless of whether a single is available or not. That may explain why there has been such a streak of anonymous No. 1 recordings since the early nineties.

For now, the 45—indeed, all vinyl—is dead as far as the record conglomerates are concerned. According to the RIAA, only 4.4 million vinyl singles, mostly 12-inch, were shipped to distributors in 2002, down from 5.5 million the year before. But the CD single isn't faring much better. Only 4.5 million were sold during the same period. If there's a future for the single, it will likely be in the form of a record company-sanctioned digital download from online record stores or a DVD, complete with an electronic press kit and music videos. But Glen Ward, president of Virgin Records' U.S. operations, isn't optimistic. "My nervousness is if we don't [revive the single] now," he told *Billboard* in March 2003, "the industry could lose the market forever."

CHAPTER 16

The 45 Will Rise Again!

Former Motown recording engineer John Matousek tells a story he heard from a Capitol executive a dozen years ago about how the company officers were approached by a major jukebox operator wanting to know, "What will it take for you guys to keep making 45s, because I've got all these jukeboxes I have to keep servicing." They told him, "It'll cost you $1.32 per record and we'll ship only to eight distributors." "Make it ten," the jukebox man said, and they had a deal. It was a losing financial arrangement that merely kept the operator's last remaining 45-rpm jukeboxes on life support, but he was determined to service a few die-hard customers. Just as a few roadhouses and cafes had hung on to their cranky old 78 jukeboxes until the bitter end in 1960, so too were a few enclaves now clinging to their 45-rpm Seeburgs and Wurlitzers. As late as 1993 there was still a 45 jukebox market out there, because Virgin Records released Janet Jackson's No. 1 hit, "If" (SK-17446), on 45 exclusively for the trade—with the words "For Jukeboxes Only" printed on the label in clear type.

Still, over the past several years the major labels have issued a limited number of 45s with mixes or versions not available elsewhere. In 1999, Atlantic Records released a Tori Amos single (7-84412) with alternate mixes of two songs from her *From the Choirgirl Hotel* CD that year. In 2001, Epic issued a "Clean Version" of the "Murder Remix" of Jennifer Lopez's "I'm Real" (Epic 79662), featuring Ja Rule. At the end of 2002, Mercury Records released a single of Shania Twain's "I'm Gonna Getcha Good" (088 172 272-7) with a country version on one side and a pop version on the other—both with the same vocals but different instrumental backing.

But the labels on these new 45s look almost nothing like the simple presentations found on vintage singles. Take the Jennifer Lopez 45. The label is a clutter of tiny, illegible print. All that's recognizable from more than several inches away is the title "I'm Real" and the bar code, certainly a modern intrusion not found on any old 45s. The casual shopper would have no idea who the artist was unless he recognized the crimped J-Lo logo at the top, nor which company had put it out unless he held a magnifying glass up to the label and found its name buried in the blur of print. The rest of the Lilliputian typeface details all the minutiae that goes into modern record production, such as the half-dozen songwriters and publishers, the various musicians and the record companies whose courtesy allowed them to participate, the producers and executive producers and sub-producers and tertiary producers, the various management companies, the recording studios, the engineers, the mixers—all for just one song. And all this information is crammed onto a 45 label. Nothing else reveals so clearly how today's corporate pop music has outgrown the modest 45.

Finding the few remaining 45s of 2003 recordings can be a problem. Most national chains such as Wherehouse don't stock them. Others, like Tower Records, maintain only a tiny singles section, generally far back in a corner containing a mere handful. Generally one has to go to smaller, specialty stores to find new and old 45s.

One of the few remaining distributors for major label 45s is Norwalk Records in Norwalk, California, southeast of Los Angeles. According to the company's singles buyer, Ron Vermette, there were only four 45s available in the "adult Top 40" and eight in the "adult contemporary" Top 20 in early 2003. "It's unusually weak, because there's nothing for the past two months," Vermette said in late January.

"Our 45 customers have jukeboxes in their home or are collectors or disc jockeys. About seventy percent of our 45 sales are for jukeboxes." Adult hits are still being pressed on 45, he said, because "people who get jukes in their home are middle-aged, they remember 45s and they have the money to spend on records. Kids don't know anything about 45s."

Vermette, who started collecting records in 1950, got into the business at a one-stop distributor in 1975. He stayed there until it closed in 1987, then moved to Norwalk Records, currently the only store in Southern California that makes an effort to stock all the hits currently available on 45.

"All the big labels were still putting out 45s until the end of [2002]," he said. "Generally, a big label does 2,000 units on a pressing. We'd only start with an order from fifty to one hundred. If it wasn't a big hit, I'd start with twenty-five. We would get two or three currents a week. It was sporadic with adult-oriented top hits on 45. With R&B and hip-hop, Dru Hill is the only hip-hop 45 right now."

As far as hip-hop is concerned, Vermette said, the 45 is dead. "Most of rap and hip-hop were commercially available until three years ago. We had N.W.A. and some of the others that are no longer commercially available, but one hip-hop store came in and bought all of them."

His main 45 trade is oldies. "[Collectables] has kept the oldie alive, that's still going pretty good. But I'm getting worried about the new releases. It's been two months since any 45s have come out."

Collectables Records in Narberth, Pennsylvania, is probably the world's biggest 45 manufacturer these days, though its primary product is CDs. In fact, Collectables has the 45 field pretty well sewed up. A company spokesman declined to talk with the authors about the company's present line of 45s, but Vice President Melissa Greene-Anderson told writer Oliver Wang in 1999 that Collectables controlled almost ninety percent of the 45 market: "Until five to seven years ago, we were selling six million units a year" from more than 10,000 outlets. But she admitted that by 1999 the market had dropped precipitously and that only 500 stores still carried 45s, most of them small, specialty outlets rather than national or regional chains.

Today, Collectables depends mainly on its mail-order arm, Nina's Discount Oldies, to sell its line of several thousand "factory fresh" 45 reissues of everything from the Andrews Sisters' "Beer Barrel Polka" (Collectables 90189) to Bachman-Turner Overdrive's "Takin' Care of Business" (04245), plus Michael Jackson, Elton John, and even New Kids on the Block.

Although Collectables sometimes reissues the original A and B sides together, such as Buddy Holly's "Peggy Sue" and "Everyday" (90043), mostly it combines two of an artist's best known hits—such as the Bobby Fuller Four's "I Fought the Law" and "Love's Made a Fool of You" (03199)—or brings together two separate one-hit wonders, such as Cannibal & the Headhunters' "Land of 1000 Dances" on one side, with Larry Verne's "Please, Mr. Custer" on the other (03124). For the 1980s pop group the Knack, Collectables put the original 45 version of "My Sharona" on one side and the longer LP version on the other (06296). Collectables reissue 45s retail at $2.50, but offers them to "serious collectors" who buy 500 or more at $1.50, even though Collectables singles have no value to real collectors, unless they're looking for something expendable to play on their 45 jukeboxes. On the other hand, some of the company's expensive specialty items—for example, a 2001 BMG/Collectables box set of Elvis Presley's No. 1 RCA hits on 45 reproductions of the originals, with bonus copies of his first five singles with the original Sun Records labels—are of interest to nobody *but* collectors.

According to Vermette at Norwalk Records, Collectables presses 200 singles at a time, just enough to keep the hits available. "On some they haven't gotten rights [renewed] to press new ones. It's hit and miss. I have sheets of hundreds of records that I fax to them that I'd like twenty-five to fifty copies of that they haven't been able to repress."

Those requests that haven't been filled include fifty copies of Bill Doggett's "Honky Tonk" and thirty-five copies of Donnie Elbert's "Have I Sinned"—which have fallen out of Collectables' catalog because of expired leasing rights. "The list of what's not available gets longer and longer," says Vermette. "There were 250 records on this request list that were on the label in the last few years and have since become unavailable, and this is just the Collectables list. The last time I talked to them, they said that to get rights for some records they had to press 500 of them and it wasn't worth their while."

It all looks pretty bleak, and yet history may give the 45 and its "groove technology" the last laugh. Whatever else you might think of vinyl, it has a permanence lacking in tape and CDs, whose surfaces (magnetic oxides on tape, plastic coating on CDs) are bound to them by glue, and even the best binders begin breaking down within twenty-five or thirty years. It remains to be seen how the CD will hold up at age thirty or forty. But whatever its longevity, some record producers are already reacting against the sterile, crystalline quiet of digital audio by adding the ambient sound of vinyl—hiss, pops, ticks, scratches—to modern recordings by rapper Eminem, country singer Toby Keith, alt.rock band Wilco, R&B singer Lamya, and other artists, in hopes of adding some "character." Spectrasonics, a Burbank, California, company, has even developed a software called Stylus for turning back the clock in the recording studio.

"There's almost too much clarity [with digital recordings], so you hear everything separately . . . and sometimes that's a little distracting to the music," Stylus inventor Eric Persing told the *Los Angeles Times*. "Some aspects of older recordings make them a more pleasant way to listen to the music . . . . It's not considered just a sound effect any more. The sounds that a record player makes have really become part of the lexicon of musical sound."

Most music originally released on 45, particularly the hits and the catalogs of hit-making artists, has been reissued on CD over the past twenty years, prompting many people to sell off their vinyl collections. The liner notes on early CD reissues generally made a point of extolling the ultra-modern fidelity that had been unavailable when the recordings were first released on wax, and there's no doubt that many of the familiar old tunes did sound like new. Engineers running original studio tapes through modern digital systems revealed nuances that had been entirely lost the first time around.

However, much of the vintage music you hear on CD today is not what folks were once listening to on their hi-fis and stereos. For example, the Zombies' 1964 hit, "She's Not There" (Parrot 9695 in the U.S., Decca in the U.K.), was a monaural mix-down from a four-track studio tape. Included in the original mono version was a drum rhythm that had been added after the group recorded live in the studio. But when "She's Not There" was revived for a stereo Zombies album five years later (after the group had broken up), the engineers went back to the live tracks and remixed them into stereo, but omitted the overdubbed drums. When CDs arrived in the early 1980s, it was this stereo mix that became the standard version. Modern listeners may hear this newer, totally live remix and declare it superior to the original—and indeed it could be. But it is essentially a different recording, not the 45-rpm "She's Not There" that reached high into the charts forty years ago.

These stereo remixes for CD became more problematic when engineers went back to the two- and three-track studio tapes used before stereo became the norm for commercial records. Since mono was still the 45 sound as late as the mid 1960s, producers used multitracking as a way to better control the recording process, not as a means to capture stereo. When singers and musicians recorded live together in the studio, there was a greater chance of mistakes requiring numerous retakes, so it became common to record the musicians first on one track, then add the lead vocal, the background vocals, and any extra instruments, such as strings, and finally mix everything down into mono. On at least two 1961 hits—Kathy Young with the Innocents' "A Thousand Stars" (Indigo 108) and Cathy Jean & the Roomates' "Please Love Me Forever" (Valmor 007), the lead singers never met their backup groups until the sales of their singles sent them on tour together. So the studio tapes, though multitrack, were not stereo. When compilers later went

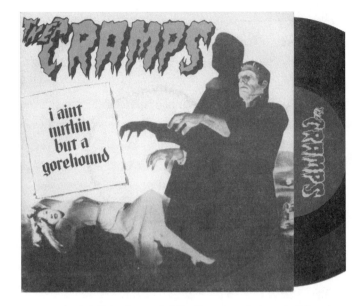

Late '70s psychobilly has kept rockabilly alive; even today's psychobilly artists want to be on 45s.

back to these tapes and tried to update them for the CD age, they put one or two tracks on one channel and the remaining track(s) on the other, because there was no way to credibly blend them into stereo. The result was a two-track mono, with (for example) the rhythm section in one ear and the vocals in another—altogether an unpleasant listening experience. Rhino Records, the Los Angeles oldies reissue label now owned by Warner Bros., was sometimes guilty of creating these abominations, but it was not alone.

Even when the tracks are amenable to being mixed into stereo, they still result in a product different from the original because the voices and instruments no longer have the same relationship to each other. Also, flubs and clams that were hidden in the original mixes suddenly jump out at the listener, a problem expressed in Keith A. Singer's lament to *Discoveries* magazine in February 2003: "The song 'You Baby' by the Turtles appears to have some distortion in the rhythm guitar, audible from one channel and not present on my original mono 45 [White Whale 227] and original mono album. All CDs (including Rhino's) seem to have the distortion. It appears that the distortion is on the stereo but not the mono take of the song."

Another problem with going back even to a mono studio tape (the one that actually captured the performance directly) and creating a new master tape (from which records and CDs are made) is that it's nearly impossible for a new engineer to match the equalization, compression, reverb, and ambience of the original recording, whether in mono or stereo. For example, MCA's current CD version of Bill Haley and His Comets' "Rock Around the Clock" is not as tight or as bright as the single that changed the musical landscape back in '55. When both Rhino Records in the U.S. and Bear Family Records in Germany separately reissued the recordings of Frankie Lymon & the Teenagers in the 1990s, they failed to add the heavy echo and reverb to "Teenage Love" that had so characterized the 45 original (Gee 1032) and had a great effect on producer Phil Spector developing his later, echo-laden Wall of Sound. Granted, something is always lost in the translation from one "language" to another, but essentially this amounted to a rewrite of rock 'n' roll history. Likewise, many of Fats Domino's 1950s singles had been slightly speeded up and echo-enhanced to compensate for the "dead sound" of the ill-designed New Orleans studio where he recorded, yet whoever mastered the 1990s reissues of this material took it straight off the studio spools, much to its detriment. The new recordings lacked much of the excitement of the original cuts.

Worse, many young engineers feel obliged to update old recordings for new listeners. Don Bolles, former drummer of the punk rock group the Germs and now a record collector, told *Los Angeles Times* writer Jim Washburn, "A lot of the engineers remastering stuff for CD seem only to be trying to impress people, pumping the bass and the highs, and they lose the warmth and what the artist intended it to sound like. It's like putting Toyota tail lights on the back of a '57 Chevy."

The good news is that any medium-sized city has at least one or two stores that still sell vinyl, and they're usually the hippest record stores in town. Billions of 45s of every possible musical genre, from 1949 to the present, exist in the world, and more continue to be pressed up every day by indie operations, because many young artists outside the pop mainstream demand it. "Any cool band on an indie label wants to have a 45 out," says Andy Framzle, who owns two Vinyl Fetish retail stores in Hollywood. "It's a badge of honor with garage and punk bands especially, because the major labels have killed the 45 and these [artists] look at the 45 as a symbol of independence and rebellion against corporate music. The rockabilly and surf bands want to have a 45 out because those are traditionally 45 genres, so it's cool to be on 45. They still want a CD, but the 45 is the thing they'll brag about."

Framzle admits that despite the name of his stores, he sells more CDs than vinyl, but there are still plenty of buyers who come in for records. "People looking for new wave and dance and hip-hop want 12-inch," he says, "but for punk, soul, and funk they want 45s. I sell more 12-inch records than 45s, but they don't hold their value as well. My guess is that 45s are your best value if you're collecting. Especially punk 45s, they were pressed in small batches and they're highly desirable now, so they're only gonna go up and up." Overall, the main source of new 45s is import singles, he says, nearly all of which come with artistic picture sleeves. "45s reign supreme," says Framzle.

In February 2003 *USA Today* reported that retro turntables and record players were selling better than ever. Crosley Radio, which makes reproductions of forties and fifties record players, claimed it sold 400,000 the previous year and expected to sell even more in 2003. One of Crosley's hot items is the 4-in-1 Entertainment Center, which, at $299, contains a CD player, cassette deck, AM/FM radio, and a turntable that plays at all three speeds, including 78. Geoff Mayfield, director of charts at *Billboard*, said that Crosley's turntable sales reflected increased sales of vinyl records, which rose 6.4 percent from 2001 to 2002.

The 45 is very much alive!

CHAPTER 17

The 50 Most Expensive 45s

T hough a few companies continue to press 45s, mostly in small numbers, and countless thousands of people all over the world still play them, 45s have become collectibles—cultural artifacts from an earlier time. And the folks who own and lovingly tend their old 45s and search endlessly for more are collectors.

In the summer of 2002, a record collector paid $30,000 for the only known surviving copy of King Oliver's 1923 jazz recording of "Zulu's Ball" on Gennett Records. One can only imagine how gingerly that frail, nearly 80-year-old 78 was handed from the seller to the buyer. What's harder to imagine is why anyone would pay that much money for a slab of brittle shellac recorded in the pre-microphone period when 78s sounded tinny and scratchy. But once a dedicated record collector decides he must have something, hardly anything can stop him. So far, no 45 has sold for that much, but the numbers are climbing, and over the last few years several buyers have approached the $20,000 ceiling and cracked it at least once.

To the hardcore collector-gatherer, prized records are like bottles of fine wine: They're admired, bragged about, and stashed away in a controlled environment, but never used for their intended purpose. No collector would ever put a spotless, shiny-as-new, vintage 45 on a record player and lower the needle. The most he'll do is don a white glove on rare occasions and slide his darling little baby from its sleeve to gaze upon the flawless sheen of the plastic and the brightness of the label, which will likely bring back a memory or two of his idyllic teen years. He'll be careful not to exhale near the precious surface. If he's got the consummate collectible, enclosed in its original shrinkwrap, he'll merely admire the label peeping through the round hole in the sleeve, for opening it up and looking at the virgin vinyl is the last thing he would do. Notice, by the way, that we use the masculine pronoun. There may be a few *she* 45 collectors, but they're so rare as to be collectibles themselves.

Among collectors there is a standard grading system that runs from *mint* to *poor*, with *near mint*, *very good plus*, *very good*, *good*, and *fair* in between. By mint they mean unplayed and unblemished in every way—a perfect 10, something spirited from the pressing plant or the record store and put away for posterity. Generally when collectors speak of mint they really mean near mint records, because mint is an ideal, extremely difficult to find with records made forty and fifty years ago. Even the tiniest flaw in the wax or on the label detracts from a 45's mint possibilities, regardless of whether or not it affects the sound of the recording—because a mint 45 isn't supposed to be played anyway. The other various gradings are subjective, and they often lead to problems when, say, a collector buys a 45 from an eBay seller who claims it's VG+, when in fact it's more like a fair.

More important than grading, of course, is the combination of rarity and desirability. There may be a mint, hard-to-find copy of Tina Robin's 45 of "Everyday" on Coral 9-61935 out there, but nobody's looking for it. On the other hand, even a battered copy of the Hornets' "I Can't Believe" on States 127 is worth over $1,000 to a handful of doo-wop aficionados.

Value is based on one standard: How much is a collector willing to pay for a given single? The prices below are for near-mint copies unless stated otherwise, and they can change at any time. If there are only three buyers willing to pay $5,000 for a specific record, its price will likely go down after all three buyers have obtained their copies. Then again, once those three copies have sold for $5,000 apiece and the word gets around, other collectors may start to feel there's something missing in their lives if they don't get one for themselves. Then yet again, if a collector happens to track down the owner of the obscure record company and comes up with ten more mint copies, suddenly the value plummets. (Wise collectors who discover such caches of previously ultra-rare 45s will silently hoard them and sell the singles one by one, a year or two apart.) Overall, however, 45s seem destined to increase in value because new 45 collectors are coming into the hobby everyday, while the supply of old singles remains roughly the same. Prospective 45 collectors should also know that most valuable 45s have been bootlegged (obviously not originals) and counterfeited (hard to discern from the originals).

One major collector and high-end seller we contacted was John Tefteller, whose periodic record auctions can be found at www.Tefteller.com and in *Discoveries* magazine. Offering his opinion on what the ten most valuable 45s might be if they can be found in mint condition, Tefteller told us, "I think these are not only the most significant but also the most recognizable and the most likely to hold these values or more in the coming years. In short, these are not fad records that sell for a lot and then drop in price as the years go on. I am probably the first and only dealer you would ask that would include blues in my top ten, but it deserves to be there and those prices are real. I would buy any or all of these at the prices listed, if I needed them for my collection."

Though 1960s and '70s soul and funk 45s have shown the hottest growth in record collecting in recent years, Tefteller thinks their high prices are an aberration. "These records do not have the long term stable price structure that the classic fifties stuff has and may or may not wind up being fad records," he said. Whether that's true or not remains to be seen, but they have not yet reached the stratosphere of early doo-wop singles.

Tim Neely, author of the *Goldmine Price Guide to 45 rpm Records*, says that where eBay and other online auctions have depressed the value of LPs, "the market for 45s remains strong." And thanks to a feeding frenzy for rare 45s in the 1990s, "the market has stabilized" and "many of those choice items are now in possession of people who want to keep them for awhile. Thus, their availability on the open market is drying up." That in turn may move tomorrow's collectors to concentrate on late 1970s and 1980s singles, which also happen to be closer to the years they grew up in.

Here are fifty of what are probably the most expensive 45s.

1. "Do I Love You (Indeed I Do)"/"Sweeter as the Days Go By" by Frank Wilson (Soul 35019), 1965

Less than four copies of this 45, released on a Motown subsidiary, are known. Wilson, a producer-songwriter at Motown, was given an ultimatum by company president Berry Gordy Jr. to choose between being a vocalist and a staff producer. Wilson chose the latter, prompting Gordy to kill the 45's nascent release. Gordy then recorded the voice of his white female protégé, Chris Clark, over Wilson's track, wiping away his voice in the process. Eventually a copy of Wilson's original found its way into the hands of a British club deejay who turned the record into a local dance hit. Another copy in mint condition, apparently lifted from the Motown files in a completely illicit transaction, sold at auction in England for roughly $23,000. A lesser-condition 45 sold not long ago for $12,000.

2. "Anna"/"Ask Me Why" by the Beatles (Vee-Jay 8), 1963

Released only as a special promotional record for disc jockeys, less than ten copies are known to exist because Vee-Jay changed its mind and decided to go with the Beatles' own "Please Please Me" instead of their remake of R&B singer Arthur Alexander's "Anna." Owners of this 45 have been known to turn down offers of $12,000 to $15,000, which makes it possibly a $20,000 item. *Goldmine*, the international collectors magazine, puts the value closer to $10,000. Copies are generally in near-mint condition since this 45 never hit the multiplay commercial market. Vee-Jay's first official Beatles release, "Please Please Me"/"Ask Me Why" (498), in May 1963—ten full months before Beatlemania arrived in the States—goes for between $1,600 and $12,000, whether the label spells the group's name as Beatles or Beattles. A white-label promo copy of "Please Please Me" with a slight pressing flaw in the wax recently sold for $12,000. Incidentally, their producer George Martin's ultra-rare 1964 instrumental soundtrack 45 of "A Hard Day's Night"/"I Should Have Known Better" (United Artists 750), complete with picture sleeve, sells for around $1,000.

3. "That's All Right"/"Blue Moon of Kentucky" by Elvis Presley (Sun 205), 1954

Elvis's 1954–55 Sun recordings are cultural touchstones, and the five singles from his year and a half at the company are now holy relics—especially the 45s, which had smaller press runs than the 78s. Many collectors claim the rarest and most valuable is the third release, "Milkcow Blues"/"You're a Heartbreaker" (211), but *Goldmine* claims it's worth only $5,000, whereas Presley's very first single, "That's All Right," is $6,000—maybe more. (A mint 45 of "That's All Right" did sell to an overseas collector a few years ago for $17,000, but *Goldmine* calls that "an aberration." Whatever.) "Good Rockin' Tonight"/"I Don't Care If the Sun Don't Shine" (210) goes for $3,000, "Baby Let's Play House"/"I'm Left, You're Right, She's Gone" (217) for $3,000, and "I Forgot to Remember to Forget"/"Mystery Train" (223) for a mere $2,500, because it sold more than the others and spent five weeks at No. 1 on the country charts in early 1956, sharing sales with RCA Victor's late 1955 reissue (47-6357) in the first months after Presley left Sun Records.

4. "I Can't Believe"/"Lonesome Baby" by the Hornets (States 127), 1953

Early doo-wop 45s have been valuable since the 1960s. They were almost always released on independent R&B labels, which generally pressed tiny runs of 45s in the early 1950s. These companies sometimes used the slightly more expensive red vinyl, which had a quieter sound because there were fewer impurities than in black vinyl—hence its greater value beyond visual aesthetics. In the late 1990s a red vinyl copy sold at auction for $15,000. A black vinyl copy is worth only $8,000. The value of this record derives not only from its rarity, but also because States was an important R&B, blues, and doo-wop label, and this is the rarest of all its titles. "I Can't Believe" was the only single by this obscure Chicago group before its lead vocalist, Johnny Moore, moved on and later joined the Drifters, where he sang "Under the Boardwalk" (Atlantic 2237) and several other hits.

5. "Rocket 88"/"Come Back Where You Belong" by Jackie Brenston (Chess 1458), 1956

This was a signpost release indicating (at least in hindsight) that rock 'n' roll was dead ahead. Brenston was merely the singer in pianist Ike Turner's band, but his name was put on the label and Turner's was omitted completely. Still, it's considered Ike Turner's first single. Recorded at Sun Studio in Memphis and leased to Chess Records in Chicago, it was a major 1951 R&B hit on 78 but not released on 45 at that early date. Not until five years later did Chess press it up on a few 45s with the original silver-top Chess label graphics, making it a weird sort of original. Collector fever for this donut disc began in Pittsburgh, a hotbed of R&B even today. A 45 recently sold for close to $10,000. John Tefteller thinks a mint copy could go for over $20,000.

6. "There Is Love in You"/"What'll You Do Next" by the Prisonaires (Sun 207), 1954

Led by tenor Johnny Bragg, this Ink Spots–inspired vocal group came by its name honestly: The five members were prisoners at Tennessee State Penitentiary near Nashville, and when Sun Records producer Sam Phillips wasn't recording them with a tape recorder at the prison, they were put in chains and driven under guard to the studio in Memphis at the other end of the state. This tender, soaring ballad—their last of four singles for Sun—is worth over $15,000 in mint shape, according to Tefteller. *Goldmine* more conservatively puts the figure at $12,000. A red vinyl 45 of their first Sun single and only R&B hit, "Just Walking in the Rain"/"Baby Please" (Sun 186), goes for around $5,000. Upon Bragg's release from prison in 1955, he formed the Marigolds, whose Excello Records 45s are also fairly valuable.

7. "Rockin' Chair Daddy"/"The Great Musical Menagerist" by Harmonica Frank (Sun 205), 1954

Hillbilly singer Frank Floyd's claim to fame was that he could play a small harmonica in one side of his mouth while he sang out of the other. These were probably the most bizarre recordings ever to come out of Sun Studio. According to Tefteller, a mint 45 could sell for over $15,000, but any copy you're most likely to find will be more in the ballpark of $2,000.

8. "My Bonnie"/"The Saints" by Tony Sheridan & the Beat Brothers (Decca 31382), 1962

This is by far the rarest of the Beatles' first American singles, mostly because it's not a very good record, but also because even if the Beatles had been popular at this early date, their name wasn't on the label. Besides, they were only providing instrumental accompaniment and background vocals for Sheridan, an ordinary vocalist. A deejay copy is rare, a commercial copy is close to impossible to find. Even copies with handwriting on the label can fetch over $10,000. Decca reluctantly agreed to release this 45 for its British parent company in 1962, but when the single got a bad reception from distributors, most copies were destroyed, which is why most known 45s are promos. When Beatlemania struck the U.S. in 1964, both sides were reissued on MGM 13213, worth only $50 or so unless you've got a $300 deejay copy.

9. "Wipe Out"/"Surfer Joe" by the Surfaris (DFS 11/12), 1963

The A-side is surf-rock's national anthem. Combined with an equally popular B-side, this is about the only surf record still being played on oldies radio. The record company's name was simply the initials of the Southern California group's manager, Dale F. Smolin, who personally pressed up 45s for them to sell at concerts. The versions here are both longer than the hit versions. The local Princess label leased the tapes, edited them down to a shorter, radio-friendly length, and issued two different

45s—long versions and short versions—under the same release number, Princess 50. (The shorter versions are marked by "RE-1" in the run-off grooves of both sides.) Then Dot Records picked up the shorter versions of the two songs and turned them into a two-sided national hit (Dot 16479). On the original DFS single, "Surfer Joe" has an extra verse about Joe being put on KP duty at Camp Pendleton, and "Wipe Out" is just longer. *Goldmine* says it's worth $3,000, but Steve Propes thinks a mint copy could go as high as $12,000. The Princess uncut 45 is worth $400, while its edited sister might go for half that.

The Princess single of "Wipe Out" was the second release of this surf classic, but not until Dot Records picked it up did the single become a surf anthem and Top 5 hit.

10. "For Your Precious Love"/"Sweet Was the Wine" by Jerry Butler & the Impressions
(Vee-Jay 280), 1958

This was an early major hit by a recording quartet that went on to become an important 1960s and '70s soul-funk group led by Curtis Mayfield. Jerry Butler would also have his own string of hits and later become a successful Chicago politician. What makes this 45 so rare is that the million-seller was released on Vee-Jay's subsidiary label, Abner Records (1013), which is worth only $40 today in mint shape, after being released on another subsidiary label (Falcon 1013), now worth only $60 near mint. Until recently, nobody outside the company knew that Vee-Jay had briefly, perhaps mistakenly, released a small run of "For Your Precious Love" under the main imprimatur, which is why even a marked-up copy sold not long ago for over $3,000. A near-mint would bring $8,000, says *Goldmine*. A mint copy is worth $10,000, says Tefteller.

11. "Blue, Can't Get No Place With You"/"Cheatin' Baby" by the Coins (Gee 10), 1954.

This single by an obscure doo-wop group is worth about $2,000 near mint, but Tefteller thinks a mint copy, if found, would fetch over $10,000. The Coins' follow-up, "Look at Me Girl" (Gee 11), is worth over $2,000 if its B-side is "S.R. Blues." If not, the 45 is worth only $600.

12. "I Wanna Be Your Man"/"Stoned" by the Rolling Stones (London 9641), 1964

This 45, slated to be the Stones' American debut, wasn't officially put out because the B-side's title was thought to be drug related, even though it was little more than a cop on Booker T. & the MG's' "Green Onions"—and an instrumental at that. Yet ultra-rare commercial copies do exist, worth $9,000 in the right condition. Promo copies are also rare and can bring $1,000 or $1,500, depending on the label color. The A-side, a Beatles song written by John Lennon and Paul McCartney, was reissued on London 9657 as the B-side of the group's first official U.S. single, a remake of Buddy Holly's "Not Fade Away."

13. "Annie Kicked the Bucket" by the Nu-Tones (Hollywood Star 798), 1954

One of many answers to the Midnighters' milestone recording of "Work With Me Annie," this 45 from a Los Angeles one-shot label was pressed and released in very small quantity, mostly 78s, and almost no 45s are known to exist. A copy found at Jane's Records in Santa Monica sold not long ago for $9,000, but a near-mint could probably go a grand higher.

14. "Country Boy"/"All Night Long" by Muddy Waters (Chess 1509), 1952

McKinley Morganfield, a.k.a. Muddy Waters, was the first major Mississippi-born singer-guitarist to electrify the Delta blues, and his recordings remain popular beyond record collectors and blues aficionados. *Goldmine* says "Country Boy," Muddy's first confirmed 45 on Chess Records, should go for $2,500; a mint, red vinyl copy, says Tefteller, is worth at least $8,000.

15. "I Really Don't Want to Know"/"Get With It" by the Flamingos (Parrot 811), 1955

This is the rarest of the super-rare 1954–55 singles by this enormously important R&B vocal group from Chicago, long before their time on the pop charts. Red vinyl is worth $8,000, black vinyl $5,000 to $7,000, depending on how near mint it is. The group's other red vinyl 45s on Parrot Records go for around $1,600. Red vinyl copies of their earlier Chance Records 45s, in 1953, are also in the $1,500 to $3,000 range.

16. "The Stars Will Remember"/"Come Back My Love" by the Buccaneers (Rama 21), 1954

Tefteller claims that a mint copy of this 45 will go for $8,000. *Goldmine* puts a near-mint copy at $2,000, along with the Buccaneers' next single, "In the Mission of St. Augustine" (Gee 24). Their first single, "Dear Ruth"/"Fine Brown Frame," is worth $4,000 on Southern Records 101, but only about $600 on its Rainbow Records 211 reissue—both from 1953.

17. "Why Must I Wonder"/"Sally Lou" by the Emeralds (Kicks 3), 1954

At an early 2003 auction sale, Tefteller was asking $7,500 for a mint copy of this rare Los Angeles vocal group 45 that *Goldmine* says is worth only $700. Out of the Emeralds came Billy Guy, who was later one of the lead vocalists for the Coasters.

18. "My Reverie"/"Let's Say a Prayer" by the Larks (Apollo 1184), 1951

The Larks was an important doo-wop group in the early days, when black records were still being released mostly on 78s. Overall, they may be the most collectible artists on 7-inch because all ten of their Apollo Records 45s are in the four-figure range. In early 2003 a mint copy of their most famous record, "My Reverie," a 1938 song based on Claude Debussy's *Reverie*, on a red vinyl 45 was selling for $7,500. Tefteller thinks it's worth $8,000 today. A near-mint red vinyl 45 of "Stolen Love"/"In My Lonely Room" (Apollo 1190) is tagged at $5,000, with the slightly more common black vinyl worth only half that much. "Little Side Car"/"Hey Little Girl" (Apollo 429) and "Ooh, It Feels So Good"/"Don't Believe in Tomorrow" (Apollo 430) were the Larks' first singles and first 45s, in 1951, and each is worth $4,000 today.

19. "Riding in the Moonlight"/"Morning at Midnight" by the Howlin' Wolf (RPM 333), 1952

Goldmine says this single by Mississippi blues growler Chester Burnett, a.k.a. Howlin' Wolf, doesn't exist on 45, but Tefteller claims it does—and costs $7,000 in mint shape. Two follow-up 45s, "Passing By Blues"/"Crying at Daybreak" (340) and "My Baby Stole Off"/"I Want Your Picture" (347), are worth $3,000 and $2,400, respectively. At the time, Howlin' Wolf was being recorded at Sun Studio in Memphis for Chess Records in Chicago, but RPM, a Los Angeles company, sneaked into town and recorded these tracks in a West Memphis garage. Another version of "Morning at Midnight" was released on Chess 1479 as "Moanin' at Midnight" in 1951.

20. "Wolf Call Boogie"/"Harmonica Jam" by Hot Shot Love (Sun 196), 1954

Before Sun Records turned to rockabilly, it was a Mississippi-to-Memphis blues label, but these raw hootin' and hollerin', rural-flavored sides by harmonica player Coy Love were already outside the blues mainstream. Elvis's first single changed everything at Sun just a few months later. *Goldmine* puts this 45 at $7,000.

21. "Can't Help Loving That Girl of Mine"/"I'm Coming Home" by the Hide-A-Ways (Ronni 1000), 1954

This Philadelphia release never got beyond the city limits. It was considered the rarest group 45 of them all until a couple of copies were uncovered, with some collectors suspecting that other copies are awaiting being found, but a 45 is worth $6,000 nonetheless.

22. "219 Train"/"My Gal" by the Moonglows (Chance 1161), 1954

This is the rarest 45 by this definitive vocal group on the Chance label, which itself is super-rare among 45 collectors. That accounts for its $6,000 price tag even though it was only released on black vinyl. The Moonglows' other 1953–54 Chance 45s, and an earlier 1952 single on the Champagne label, are also valuable, especially on red vinyl ($3,000). "219 Train" caught the group at their best during their formative years.

23. "(Let's Dance) The Screw," Parts 1 & 2 by the Crystals (Philles 111), 1964

The story of this 45 is strange but true. The Crystals, a female vocal group best known for their 1962 No. 1 record, "He's a Rebel" (Philles 106), enjoyed several hits in the early sixties, so when producer Phil Spector (the Phil in Philles Records) wanted to dissolve his acrimonious partnership with Lester Sill (the Les in Philles), he agreed as consideration to give Sill the ownership of the Crystals' next 45, sure to be a big hit. The result was a record with no commercial potential: To make sure that the single would garner no royalties for Sill, Spector merely chanted the title over and over above an instrumental track for nearly six minutes, while a vocal group (probably the Crystals, but with Spector you never knew) sang in the background. The B-side was more of the same. No more than six deejay copies escaped, and Sill refused to release the single commercially. Spector still ended the partnership, however. According to Tim Neely, a light blue label will fetch $6,000, a white label only $4,000. If Lester Sill had kept a few copies, he could have enriched himself (and thumbed his nose at Spector) by selling them later to collectors.

24. "God Save the Queen"/"No Feelings" by the Sex Pistols (A&M 7284), 1977

Though we've confined our list to American 45s, this U.K. release has a significance for U.S. punk rock collectors, so we're making it the exception. American A&M Records' British division seemed anxious to release this single by the London punk rock group on the heels of their first single, "Anarchy in the U.K." (EMI 2566). But after the Sex Pistols went on a BBC TV show and shouted expletives at the host and everyone else, the national press expressed outrage, calling them "foul-mouthed yobs." A&M executives immediately cancelled the group's contract, which meant they had to scrap the new 45s they'd pressed up. Funny, with lyrics like "God save the queen, she ain't no human being," one has to wonder why A&M was surprised. Virgin Records wisely stepped in, signed the group, and reissued the single with a new B-side (Virgin 181). It went almost to the top of the U.K. charts despite the song being banned from the BBC. The A&M single is worth $6,000 in primo shape today. According to Andy Framzle, owner of the Vinyl Fetish retail stores in Hollywood, the value of "God Save the Queen" is only the beginning for punk rock 45s from the late seventies and early eighties, which are shaping up to be the major collectibles of the future.

25. "Golden Girl"/"Big Wig Walk" by the Marbles (Lucky 002), 1954
Issued by a small Los Angeles black label operating out of a record store, this group, led by Johnny Torrance, soon became the Jewels whose "Hearts of Stone" (R&B 1301) was one of the earliest doo-wop hit songs. A mint copy of "Golden Girl" recently sold for $5,000.

26. "Tell the World"/"Blues at Three" by the Dells (Vee-Jay 134), 1955
Hardly any copies of the first 45 by this important Chicago R&B/soul vocal group are known to exist, but a red vinyl copy will go for $5,000, black vinyl for $2,000. None of their other singles even come close, except for "Darling, I Know" (Checker Records 794), an earlier 45 they recorded under the name the El Reys, which is worth $1,200.

27. "Ooby Dooby"/"Tryin' to Get to You" by the Teen Kings (Je-Wel 101), 1956
This was the earliest single by Roy Orbison, cut at Norman Petty Studios in Clovis, New Mexico, for a small Texas label before he re-recorded it at Sun Records in Memphis. Both versions sound much the same, but his Sun remake of "Ooby Dooby" became Roy's first hit and is now considered a rockabilly classic. The B-side was a song originally recorded by a black vocal group called the Eagles (Mercury 70391) and first redone in 1954 by Elvis Presley at Sun Records but not released until 1956 (RCA 47-6639). The Teen Kings' 45 has two different Je-Wel labels: one is sub-credited as "Vocal Roy Oribson," the other correctly as "Vocal Roy Orbison." But both are worth the same $4,000, the highest price of any non-Elvis rockabilly 45.

28. "Count Every Star"/"I'm Gonna Paper All My Walls With Your Love" by the Ravens (National 9111), 1950

This was the first 45 release by this landmark group that, along with the Orioles, practically invented the 1950s black harmony style. It's also their only 45 on National Records (out of their twenty-one singles for the label). Doo-wop collectors value this song because it was remade as a hit by the Rivieras (Coed 503) in 1958. Worth $3,000 in near-mint condition, it's so sought after that collectors will pay half that for a VG+.

29. "Every Beat of My Heart"/"All Night Long" by the Royals (Federal 12064), 1952

The Royals are best remembered as the vocal group that evolved into Hank Ballard & the Midnighters. Every Royals 45 on Federal Records is valuable, but their first five singles in 1952 are all in the four-figure range, especially this one on blue vinyl ($3,000), as well as their blue vinyl 45 of "Moonrise"/"Fifth Street Blues" on Federal 12088 (also $3,000). Other early 45s, including the black vinyl copies of the above two singles, are in the $1,500–$2,500 range. "Every Beat of My Heart" is the first rendition of a song that would later be important in the early career of Gladys Knight & the Pips. The flip side, "All Night Long," features forties blues-shouting legend Wynonie Harris on a vocal bridge.

30. "Red Sails in the Sunset"/"Be Anything, But Be Mine" by the Five Keys (Aladdin 3127), 1952

This 45 by another important early doo-wop group is considered the best of their very rare sides, which accounts for its $6,000 price tag ($3,000 in merely VG shape). Another single, "These Foolish Things"/"Lonesome Old Story" (Aladdin 3190) from 1953, is worth $4,000. The Five Keys' other 1951–53 Aladdin 45s all go from $800 to $1,000.

31. "Bye Bye"/"Someone's in Love" by the Cosmic Rays, with Le Sun Ra & Arkestra (Saturn 222), 1960

This 1960 doo-wop recording by eccentric jazz legend Sun Ra goes for $3,000. A follow-up single, "Daddy's Gonna Tell You No Lies"/"Dreaming" (401), is worth $2,000.

32. "Stealin'"/"Don't Ease Me In" by the Grateful Dead (Scorpio 003-201), 1966

This very first 45 by San Francisco's favorite acid jammers is very sought after by Deadheads-in-the-know, normally not a population known to seek out 45s by anyone. *Goldmine* estimates its worth at $1,000, but it may go as high as $3,000. The Grateful Dead's only other valuable 45 is "Dark Star"/"Born Cross-Eyed" (Warner Bros. 7186), worth $500 if it's in a picture sleeve.

33. "Walk–Don't Run"/"Home" by the Ventures (Blue Horizon 101), 1960

Issued on a Tacoma, Washington, vanity label by members of the guitar-driven instrumental group itself, "Walk-Don't Run" (note the hyphen) became not just a smash after being reissued as "Walk—Don't Run" (with a dash replacing the hyphen) on Dolton Records 25, but a phenomenon that sent a generation of boys scurrying into music shops to buy guitars. The price of this original 45 is about $2,500.

34. "Optical Sound"/"Calm Me Down" by the Human Expression (Accent 1226), 1967

The Human Expression was a Sunset Strip band that has been compared to the Doors, but it recorded only three singles. This was the second. Regular-issue 45s of "Optical Sound" are actually worth less than the group's first single, "Love at Psychedelic Velocity" (both are valued only in the $100 to $200 range), but promotional 45s of "Optical Sound" are sought after because they don't have the psychedelic effects that were later added to the commercial copies. When collector Don Haley found a mint promo copy in an Elko, Nevada, thrift shop for 50 cents and put it on eBay in early 2003, it sold for over $2,300.

35. "Cool Off Baby"/"Almost" by Billy Barrix (Shreveport, Chess 1662), 1957

This is hands down the rarest rockabilly release of all, on Shreveport Records or Chess Records (normally a blues and R&B label), but especially on Shreveport, which rockabilly collector Dick Blackburn says he's never seen or knows anything about. We don't even know the release number. The song is unremarkable—it's simply a reworking of Elvis's "I Wanna Play House With You"—but it has a great studio sound with the slap bass mixed up front and two amazing guitar solos. The Chess Records reissue is as valuable as the Shreveport original—$2,000 or more. Barrix, a Tennessee native, apparently made only two other 45s, billed as Curley Barrix, for Dunwich Records in 1966.

36. "Box Top"/"Calypso Love Cry" by Ike Turner with Little Ann/Ike Turner with Fred Sample (Tune Town 501), 1959

This was the first time on record for Anna Mae Bullock, soon to become Anna Mae Turner when she married guitarist-bandleader Ike, who in turn renamed her Tina. Almost no originals are known to exist of this homemade single on a one-off St. Louis label. It's not even listed in the Tina Turner discographies. But if you find a copy, it's worth $2,500. Tina appears only on one side of the record.

37. "Doll Face"/"I Feel So Good" by the Vibranaires (Chariot 103, After Hours 103), 1954

After this primitive-sounding doo-wop 45 was released, almost the entire stock was lost when the Harlem location where they were being stored suspiciously went up in flames. The Chariot 45 is worth $2,000, the After Hours single around $2,500 (because it's on red vinyl). This same group's second single, "Stop Torturing Me"/"Stop Jibing, Baby" (Chariot 105, After Hours 105), credited to the Vibes, is worth about $2,000.

38. "The Fat Man"/"Detroit City Blues" by Fats Domino (Imperial 5058), 1952

Domino's very first record, an R&B hit in 1950 despite its murky recording, was released on 78 only, but Imperial Records issued it on 45 two years later when the company made the transition to the smaller format. A pristine copy is worth $2,000, but be careful because "The Fat Man" has been counterfeited. Domino's next most valuable 45 is his second single, "Korea Blues"/"Every Night About This Time" (5099), also released exclusively on 78 before being reissued on 45 two years later in 1952. A near-mint copy fetches $800.

39. "Looking For Love"/"I'll Be Yours" by Karen Carpenter (Magic Lamp 704), 1966

This is an early Carpenters release, featuring both Karen and Richard Carpenter though it's credited only to Karen, several years before the world heard of this soft-rock brother and sister duo. Only a few copies exist, and collectors will pay $2,000 for it in any reasonable condition. One 45 rests in the lobby of the Carpenter Center Theater at Long Beach State where they both went to school.

40. "In the Still of the Nite"/"The Jones Girl" by the Five Satins (Standord 200), 1956

This all-time favorite doo-wop recording, taped in a Hartford, Connecticut, church basement, is most familiar on Ember Records (1005) out of New York City, but it was originally released on Hartford's local Standord label, with "The Jones Girl" marked as the A-side. There were two pressings; one had the added label credit: "Produced by Martin Kuegell." If you've got that one, it's worth $2,000. The other is worth only $900. The group's first Standord single, "All Mine"/"Rose Mary" (100), is worth $700. The Ember hit single of "In the Still of the Nite" is worth $200 if the label is red and the number 6106A is etched in the dead wax. Otherwise it's a $30–$50 record.

41. "Nervous Wreck"/"No More Love" by Willie Nix & His Band (Chance 1163), 1954

"I've seen only two copies on 45, and even the 78 is super scarce," says John Tefteller, who tags Memphis blues singer/drummer Nix's Chance single at $1,500. *Goldmine* puts it at twice that much, $3,000, and says that an earlier 45, "All By Myself"/"Just Can't Stay" (Sabre 104), is worth $2,000.

Another of Nix's records, "Seems Like a Million Years"/"Baker Street Boogie," was reportedly released only as a 78 on Sun Records (179), yet it also goes for four figures, so one can only speculate what a 45 copy would be worth if it turned up.

42. "Oh Maria"/"I Hope These Words Will Find You Well" by Joe Alexander & the Cubans (Ballad 1008), 1955

Reputedly this was Chuck Berry's first recording—session files show that one of Alexander's sidemen was St. Louis guitarist Chuck Berryl, a pseudonym Berry used at that time. But even at $1,500, it's an uninteresting 45 that would be worth very little without its connection to rock 'n' roll's earliest poet.

43. "Tongue Tied Jill"/"Get With It" by Charlie Feathers (Meteor 5032), 1956

This is a definitive rockabilly performance by one of the genre's more desirable artists, recording for a company favored by rockabilly collectors because of its overall excellence. If the label is maroon, it's worth $1,500; if it's blue, divide by four. Feathers's 45s on the Flip, King, and Sun labels are all worth over $400.

44. "Boppin' High School Baby"/"Warrior Sam" by Don Willis (Satellite 101), 1959

This is the first single on the Memphis label that changed to Stax Records after another Satellite Records company sent them a cease & desist order. Stax became a fabled, world-class soul operation in the 1960s. This 45, one of the company's few non-R&B or soul releases, is rockabilly and nothing short of great, but when Stax established its black music direction, it dropped "Boppin' High School Baby" from its catalog like a brick, unwittingly bestowing a later value of $1,500 on the 45. Willis recorded only one other known single, for Style Records in 1964.

45. "Biscuit Bakin' Mama"/"Superstition" by Big Ed & His Combo (Checker 790), 1954

This one's an all-time great rocker by bluesman Eddie Burns, who recorded under various names. Being very tough to find on 45, it sells for $1,000 even in medium shape.

46. "Saddled the Cow & Milked the Mule"/"Ouch! Pretty Baby" by Roscoe Gordon (RPM 324), 1951

Rocking pianist and novelty blues singer Roscoe Gordon was known for playing in clubs with a succession of dancing chickens. (Actually, the trick was that he mildly electrified the top of his piano, forcing the chickens to lift their feet.) He also enjoyed a couple of hits. This single, one of his first recordings and almost certainly his first 45, is super rare. Tefteller claims only two exist, which makes it a $1,000 record.

47. "She's Gone"/"Strange Letter Blues" by Schoolboy Cleve (Feature 3013), 1954
Harmonica player Cleve White was accompanied on this country blues by the great Lightnin' Slim on guitar. Too bad Schoolboy Cleve rarely recorded. A mint copy is worth $1,000.

48. Any number of rockabilly records would fit here. Los Angeles rockabilly expert Dick Blackburn says that expensive rockabilly 45s tend to be much more obscure than high-priced doo-wop records. Also, rockabilly 45s don't hold their high values as consistently as blues records. "It doesn't have the cultural cachet, even though rockabilly collectors are just as fanatical as anyone else," says Blackburn. "For one thing, there are less of them, and until recently they were mostly Europeans. Maybe it has something to do with rockabilly's nonsense lyrics and its call to good times. It doesn't have the *gravitas* of R&B and blues. Plus, most rockabilly 45s came much later, starting around 1957 and going until '63. And there's no colored wax [vinyl] on early rockabilly records to make them more valuable. Another reason is that many of the best rockabilly records got spirited off to England before Americans got hip to their value." So how valuable are rare, sought-after rockabilly 45s? According to Blackburn, any of the singles below would fetch at least $1,500 in near-mint shape.

"I'm Doing All Right" by Jerry Hanson (Starday 560)

"Lobo Jones" by Jackie Gotroe (Vortex 102)

"Have Myself a Ball" by Bill Bowen (Meteor 5033)

"All Messed Up" by Jess Hooper (Meteor 5025)

"Knocked Out Joint on Mars" by Buck Trail (Trail 104)

"Gone Baby Gone" by David Ray Smith (Heart 250)

"Marlene" by the Sonics (Gaity 114)

"Goodbye Train" by Jim Foley (Lucky 1001)

"Bluest Boy in Town" by Phil Gray (Rhythm 101)

"Big Sandy" by Bobby Roberts (Sky 101)

"I'll Be Leaving You" by Turner Moore (Mellotone 1500)

"Eager Boy" by the Lonesome Drifter (K 5812)

"Bad Bad Boy" by Bobby Lollar (Benton 101)

"She's My Baby" by Leon Holmes (Peach 597)

"Rockin' on the Moon" by Deacon & the Rock N' Rollers (Nau-Voo 804)

"Rock-Ola Ruby" by Sonee West (Nor-Va-Jak 1956)

"Red Hot Mama" by Wayne Williams (Sure 1001)

"Gonna Have a Party" by Dickie Damron (Laurel 792)

"Dry Run" by Parker Cunningham (Rebel 700)

"Walkin' Talkin' Baby Doll" by the Three Ramblers (Ozark 716)

"Rock N' Roll Irene" by Buddy Miller (Security 108)

49. "At the Hop"/"Sometimes" by Danny & the Juniors (Singular 711), 1957

The A-side was going to be called "Do the Bop" until Dick Clark told them that the bop, a vigorous dance step, was over. When first released on Singular, "At the Hop" had a count-off at the beginning, but when ABC-Paramount Records picked up the record and reissued it nationally (9871), the engineers removed the first few seconds. The Singular 45, with the count-off intact, is obviously worth much more than ABC-Paramount's No. 1 version today, $1,000 in mint condition, whether the label credits band director Artie Singer or not.

Country singer Barbara Mandrell's homemade first 45, "Pan-Handle Rag," is so rare that it's not listed in discographies.

50. "Beggin' You" by the Royal Chessman (Custom Fidelity, no release #), 1969

An obscure Mexican-American vocal group recorded this 45 in a small El Monte, California, studio with the idea of selling or giving away copies at concerts around Los Angeles. The only known copy ended up with Steven Parent, the son of the people who owned the studio, who was carrying it with him in his car to play for a couple of labels around Hollywood. While visiting a friend who lived in the guest house at Roman Polanski's sprawling estate, Parent was murdered, along with Sharon Tate and others, by members of the Charles Manson family. According to the vocal group members, the LAPD impounded the car in which Parent was killed, and the original 45 might still be in an evidence locker, because they were never able to get it back. Meanwhile, an East Los Angeles bootlegger named Bootin' Bernie dubbed an acetate onto two of his labels, Riot and Angie, and sold the 45s on the street, making these the only copies that any living human being has heard. The group's leader, David Luna, now drives a bus and occasionally picks up Bootin' Bernie, who's no longer doing 45s, but Luna holds no grudges because he knows that without Bernie's bootleg there'd be no Royal Chessman on vinyl at all. No known original copies, no verified sales, great sound, and a direct connection to a notorious multiple murder—no other 45 can make that claim. A found copy's worth would be at least $2,000.

CHAPTER 18

Odd Lots, Odd Balls & Odds 'n' Ends

···

T hough 45s were generally mass-produced, even a major-label release could become a collectible item because of a mistake or a series of unexpected or strange events. Also, many 45s contained recordings, or specific versions of recordings, available nowhere else.

Today's record companies commonly release specialized versions of songs to fit into different radio niche markets. The most notable perhaps was a 2002 Shania Twain CD album that contained two different arrangements of each song behind the same vocal track—one country, the other pop. Both versions of the designated hit, "I'm Gonna Getcha Good," were also issued on a 45 (Mercury 088 172 272-7). During the 45 era, such promotional tactics were unheard of, mainly because an obvious remix pointed out the artificiality of the overall recorded performance. Also, radio formats were not so severely fragmented that companies felt compelled to appeal to more than one of them in order to have a hit record.

But differences did occur between the various formats, particularly after the LP—especially the "concept LP"—became the primary platform for rock artists in the late 1960s. Since the longer format encouraged these artists to jam endlessly, 45-rpm versions of LP tracks often had to be edited down to make them fit into tight Top 40 programming schedules, but they are too numerous and prosaic to mention here. More interesting are the mistakes and the censorial trimmings.

Up until multitrack recording became the standard in the late 1950s, artists usually recorded live in the studio, performing each song over and over—"Take 1, Take 2," *et al.*—until the producers felt they had a releasable take. Sometimes, to save money, they would record the musicians first, then have the singer or singers record numerous vocal takes over the same instrumental track, which allowed the producer the luxury of editing together the best vocal parts of each take without worrying about changes in the tempo or background. In more than a few cases, whether by accident or design, a different "take" of a particular song appeared on the 45 than on an LP.

This happened, for example, to both Buddy Holly and the Big Bopper, two of three early rock 'n' rollers (Ritchie Valens being the other) killed in a legendary 1959 plane crash. When Holly was under contract to Decca Records in 1956, he recorded three sessions in Nashville. At the second session in July, he cut two rockabilly songs, "That'll Be the Day" and "Rock Around With Ollie Vee," with his own Texas band. When Holly returned to Nashville in November, producer Owen Bradley wanted to record "Rock Around With Ollie Vee" again, only this time with Nashville session men, including alto saxophonist Ed "Dutch" McMillin. Both versions of the song remained unreleased until the following year, when Holly re-recorded a hit version of "That'll Be the Day" with the Crickets on Brunswick Records (55009), prompting Decca to cover it by releasing Holly's earlier version (30434). For the B-side, Decca picked "Rock Around With Ollie Vee," but instead of using the more exciting rockabilly cut from the "That'll Be the Day" session, it picked the slower, saxophone version, probably because it had a much more Nashville country sound. Eight months later, however, when Decca issued Holly's 1956 material on an album called *That'll Be the Day*, it included only the first "Rock Around With Ollie Vee," which eventually became a rockabilly anthem. The rare 45 version wasn't included on an album until the 1970s, long after Holly's death.

Meanwhile, Mercury Records, following the success of the Big Bopper's "Chantilly Lace" (71343) in 1958, released an album called *Chantilly Lace* that included two songs, "Walking Through My Dreams" and "It's the Truth Ruth," which Mercury released again the following year as posthumous singles. "Walking Through My Dreams," the B-side of the third Big Bopper single (Mercury 71416), was much different, looser and loopier, than the album version. For one, the Big Bopper (real name Jiles P. Richardson) on 45 humorously described his dream as being in cinemascope and in stereophonic sound, populated by movie stars Brigitte Bardot, Marilyn Monroe, and Zsa Zsa Gabor. "Now whatcha all doin' in my dream, you ain't s'pose to be on till tomorrow night!," he exclaimed. None of this was on the album version. For the follow-up single, Mercury used an obviously earlier take of "It's the Truth Ruth" (71415) that was not as tight as the album version. Subsequent Big Bopper albums, including a comprehensive 1989 CD package by Rhino Records, repeated Mercury's original album, but the alternate 45 versions of the two songs have never been reissued since 1959.

In a few cases different takes of a song appeared on the 45 and 78 releases. One unusual example was the song "Johnny Darling," by a Los Angeles doo-wop group called the Feathers. They recorded their first, rather crude version of the song in 1954 in a garage studio for the small black-owned Show Time label, but when the song started getting airplay in Los Angeles, a larger indie company, Aladdin Records, claimed rights to the quintet under a previous contract. Aladdin immediately sent the Feathers back into the studio with a professional band led by Johnny Otis and re-cut the song. As explained previously, when recording engineers made master tapes from raw studio tape, they treated 45s and 78s differently, because the larger 78 could handle more bass and greater highs in its wider grooves, whereas the 45 required more compression and equalization in order to accommodate the performance. Most likely, Aladdin originally mastered "Johnny Darling" only as a 78, to see how the record would fare, then decided to master a 45 version a couple of weeks later when its distributors reordered. But since the tape used to master the 78 was not immediately available, Aladdin used another take of the song altogether. Both singles had the same catalog number, Aladdin 3267. Meanwhile, Show Time Records still had its original performance of "Johnny Darling" on the market (with a different B-side than the Aladdin releases), which meant that there were three different versions of the same group singing the same song in the stores at the same time. (See more on the Feathers below.) Other examples of singles with different takes on 45 and 78 are "Money Honey" by Clyde McPhatter & the Drifters (Atlantic 1006), "A Beggar for Your Kisses" by the Diamonds (Atlantic 981), and "I Started Out" by the Chordells (Onyx 504).

A few 45s were mastered with a 78-rpm stylus that created a bigger groove. This happened at Sun Records on several releases, including "Just Walking in the Rain" (186) by the Prisonaires. The Fascinators' "The Bells of My Heart" (Your Copy 1135, 1954), the Five Emeralds' "I'll Beg" (S-R-C 106, 1953), and several singles by the Five Dollars and the Five Jets on Detroit's Fortune label were also recorded with 78 styluses.

Whirling Disc Records, a New York doo-wop label, in 1957 released the Channels' "I Really Love You" backed with "What Do You Do" (107). When the company went back to do a second pressing, it used a different take of both songs.

The deejay copies and some of the initial commercial pressings of Bob Dylan's 1965 hit, "Positively 4th Street" (Columbia 43389), had the wrong song on them. Though the label on the A-side said "Positively 4th Street," the recording was actually "Can You Please Crawl Out Your Window?" Columbia quickly fixed the problem, but when it followed up with "Can You Please Crawl Out Your Window" (backed with "Highway 61 Revisited") on the next single (43477), it used a different studio take.

In a few cases the beginning or ending of the song was excised from one pressing of a record to the next. That's what happened in 1958, when the word got back to ABC Paramount that radio stations were getting complaints about its latest hit record, "Stagger Lee" (9972), an updating of an old blues song by Lloyd Price. The objection was to the final verse in which "Stagger Lee shot Billy, oh he shot that poor boy so bad, till the bullet came through Billy and it broke the bartender's glass." Price went back into the studio and overdubbed a new verse over the original instrumental and choral tracks that completely eliminated the fight between Stagger Lee and Billy, along with earlier references to gambling. Fortunately, the unexpurgated version was already a hit and few copies of the remake were released.

In 1961 country singer Jimmy Dean had a No. 1 pop hit with "Big Bad John" (Columbia 42175), a reworking of the John Henry steel-drivin' legend. Near the end of this first release, Dean recited the line: "At the bottom of this mine lies one hell of a man," which stopped the single dead in its tracks at many radio stations. Dean was rushed back into the studio to recut that one line as "At the bottom of this mine lies a big *big* man" to make it acceptable. In 1959, Fabian's new 45, "Got the Feeling" (Chancellor 1041), was pulled from the market because the slurred opening sounded like a profanity. The opening was edited and that version charted.

Lou Christie's 1966 hit, "Rhapsody in the Rain" (MGM 13473), had to be changed when some radio stations objected to the lyric "We were makin' out in the rain/and in this car our love went much too far," Christie replaced it with "We fell in love in the rain/and in this car, love came like a falling star." You can tell the difference by looking at the numbers in the run-out grooves. Someone added the letters "DJ" to the pressing plant's original dead wax number 66-XY-308.

Singles taken from LPs and issued on 45 often had to be changed to accommodate the smaller format and different marketplace. The most famous example was Simon & Garfunkel's "The Sounds of Silence." Paul Simon and Art Garfunkel recorded the song accompanied only by Simon's acoustic guitar for their first album, *Wednesday Morning, 3 a.m.*, in 1965. When a Boston radio station began playing the cut and getting a good response, the duo's label, Columbia, decided to release it as a single. But producer Tom Wilson felt that since folk music, in particular Bob Dylan, had gone electric since Simon & Garfunkel were last in the studio, "The Sounds of Silence" would have to be electrified to survive in the marketplace. Wilson happened to be in the studio recording Bob Dylan's "Like a Rolling Stone" at the time, so when the session was over he asked the band to overdub an electric guitar, electric bass, and drums onto Simon & Garfunkel's LP track. The amped-up single (Columbia 43396) shot to No. 1 on January 1, 1966. (Incidentally, the B-side on the released single was "We've Got a Groovy Thing Going," but the flipside of the promo 45, pressed on red vinyl, had the original LP acoustic version of "The Sounds of Silence."

In 1979 the Knack had to make lyric changes to three different parts of "Good Girls Don't (But I Do)" (Capitol 4771) before the offending LP version could become a 45 follow-up to their No. 1 hit, "My Sharona."

"Tell the Truth"/"Roll It Over" by Derek and the Dominos was released as a single on Atco 45-6780 in 1970 in anticipation of Eric Clapton's upcoming *Layla and Other Assorted Love Songs* album, but when the producer, Phil Spector, left the project midway through to work with George Harrison, Clapton re-recorded "Tell the Truth" for the LP. The single's flipside, "Roll It Over," was scrapped altogether from the album and available only on 45. Spector then got Harrison to record a new version of "Roll It Over" for the ex-Beatle's *All Things Must Pass* triple LP.

Oftentimes 45s were mastered differently than their LP counterparts. Warner Bros. in 1963 released an album called *Live at Cisco's* by R&B tenor saxophonist Big Jay McNeely. The album, recorded at a club in a Southern California beach town, had the relaxed feel of a live show and the ambience of a place where people were dancing, smoking, drinking, and shouting. But when Warner Bros. released a 45, "You Don't Have to Go"/"Big Jay's Count" (WB 5401), from two of the live tracks, a little tinkering was needed to make them more immediate and radio-friendly. This included compressing the recording and adding echo to give it more presence.

Conversely, many labels that focused on making 45s issued LPs simply as ancillary items to cash in on hit singles. Detroit's Motown Records was famous for laboring over its 45s, experimentally mastering test pressings to achieve maximum impact coming out of small radio and phonograph speakers, but when it came time to master albums, the job was turned over to night engineers, who worked cheaply without tying up valuable studio time. As a consequence, Motown albums, whether by the Supremes or lesser artists, generally sound inferior to its 45s. The same could be said for another record factory, Cameo/Parkway, in Philadelphia, which carelessly cranked out numerous Chubby Checker dance albums whose songs, particularly on stereo LPs, were taken directly off the raw, unbalanced two-track studio tapes instead of the more carefully crafted 45-single master tapes.

Occasionally, the producer or artist made a last-minute change in the song for the final release, or halted the release altogether, yet copies of the original version got through, resulting in two different 45s of the same recording. "Shop Around" by the Miracles (Tamla 54034) was originally recorded with a prominent guitar part, but a week or so after its release, Motown president Berry Gordy had a change of heart. After selling a token number of the earlier take, he remixed the song. This new version replaced the earlier single and went on to become the group's first major hit, in 1960. The first version can be identified on sight by H55518A etched in the dead wax. The second version is marked simply as L-1 instead. Both versions have been found on the horizontal lines and the "globes" label. (For their album version of "Shop Around," the group's alto, Claudette Rogers, sang lead instead of Smokey Robinson. She later became his wife.)

Also at Motown, producer Frank Wilson recorded his own voice on "Do I Love You (Indeed I Do)." But after several promo 45s were pressed, Berry Gordy convinced Wilson his future lay in producing, not singing, and instead recorded the voice of white vocalist Chris Clark over Wilson's track for a 1966 single, shortened to "I Love You" (V.I.P. 25041). (See more on this record in Chapter 17.)

In 1962 the Beatles appeared on their first single, "My Bonnie"/"The Saints" (Decca 31382), as a backup group, billed as the Beat Brothers, for singer Tony Sheridan. Taken from a live show, the recording originally featured a spoken German introduction for its German release and an English introduction for British buyers. Decca then released an edited version (with the English intro) thirteen seconds shorter for the American market, and yet another version without the introduction. Each was released in both mono and stereo—all under the same Decca serial number. (There was also a deejay issue with a pink Decca label.) Two years later, the single was reissued on MGM 13213, as the Beatles with Tony Sheridan. The titles were lengthened to "My Bonnie (My Bonnie Lies Over the Ocean)" and "The Saints (When the Saints Go Marching In)." Another song from the Sheridan-Beatles session was "Sweet Georgia Brown" (Atco 6302), released in 1964, which was different from the original British Polydor NH 52-906 single. For the American updated version, Tony Sheridan overdubbed new lyrics that referred to the Beatles. Incidentally, when Sheridan's "Sweet Georgia Brown" was originally released in 1962 on a German EP called *Ya Ya* (Polydor 21485), it was an entirely different version without the Beatles singing background.

Speaking of the Beatles, their No. 1 British 45, "Love Me Do" (Parlophone 4983), and their No. 1 American 45, "Love Me Do" (Tollie 9008), were two separate recordings. The British version was recorded on September 4, 1963, with Ringo Starr on drums, but producer George Martin wasn't happy with his performance. When the group returned to the studio a week later, on September 11, a professional studio musician named Andy White sat in on drums while Ringo played tambourine. This second version was included on the Beatles' *Please Please Me* album, which was originally released in the U.S. by Vee-Jay Records, a black-owned Chicago company, in 1963. After the Beatles became a sensation in the United States a few months later, Vee-Jay pulled its own "Love Me Do" (*sans* Ringo) off the album and released it as a single on the subsidiary Tollie label.

John Lennon's 1969 single, "Cold Turkey" (Apple 1813), was originally pressed with a defective stamper with a skip in the song's third chorus, which abbreviated Lennon's pronunciation of "turkey" to "tea." When the problem was fixed, the pressings were resumed with a label whose lettering was printed in bolder type. Lennon, by the way, was a big fan of Rosie & the Originals' "Angel Baby" (Highland 1011), a Top 10 hit from 1961, which also had a skip from the defective acetate—but that skip stayed in the song and nobody seemed to notice.

Bill Buchanan and Dickie Goodman pioneered the so-called break-in record, featuring snippets of popular songs as gags within a story. Their first single, "Flying Saucer" (Luniverse 101), was a huge hit in 1956. On their follow-up 45, "Buchanan and Goodman on Trial" (102), the original release featured a brief sample of Fats Domino's "I'm in Love Again." When Domino's record company/publisher threatened a lawsuit, B&G replaced it with a bit from Jim Lowe's "The Green Door." The first 45 has signatures of Buchanan and Goodman in the dead wax; the second version does not.

When RCA Victor first released Elvis Presley's 1960 hit, "It's Now or Never" (47-7777), apparently an engineer used the wrong mix, because subsequent pressings contained an overdubbed piano not on the original. The rare original version can be identified by the numbers L2WW-0100-3S or L2WW-0100-4S in the trail-off wax. Likewise, on RCA's first pressing of Presley's gospel number, "He Touched Me" (74-0651), in 1972, the song was mistakenly mastered at 35 rpm. Subsequent pressings were at the correct speed. The slow version has AWKS-1277 stamped on the A-side's dead wax; the later one is marked APKS-1277. The first version is worth nearly twenty times more.

Finally, when Bruce Springsteen's "Cover Me" (Columbia 38-04561) went into its second pressing on 45, somebody at the company removed the Boss's spoken word introduction to the live B-side, "Jersey Girl." You can tell the two versions apart just by looking at the stamper number scratched into the run-out grooves on the "Jersey Girl" side; if the number ends in 2A, that's the trimmed version, which is far less valuable today.

In a few cases 45 releases were aborted, but only after a few copies or an early run escaped. For example, "He Hit Me (And It Felt Like a Kiss)," a Carole King song recorded by the Crystals (Philles 105) in 1962, was yanked from the company schedule as soon as producer/owner Phil Spector got the first backlash from radio programmers, who refused to play a record about domestic violence. Copies of the 45 are naturally hard to find. Two years later Spector also pulled back the release of Darlene Love's "Stumble and Fall" (Philles 123) at the last moment, and replaced it with the Ronettes' "Walkin' in the Rain," using the same Philles 123 catalog number. (Incidentally, the picture sleeve for this 45 changed "Walkin'" to "Walking"—and like many picture sleeves it's worth far more than the single itself.) In 1963 Spector also slipped out five or six promotional copies of the Crystals' "(Let's Dance) The Screw" (Philles 111), a totally noncommercial recording made to abide by the terms of a lawsuit. (See Chapter 17.)

In a similar vein, the Rolling Stones kissed off their label, London/Decca, in 1970 when they delivered a final recording to satisfy the terms of their expiring contract. The song, performed only by Mick Jagger and Keith Richards, was called "Cocksucker Blues," a.k.a. "Schoolboy Blues," the lament of a teenage male hustler hanging out on London's Leicester Square. London/Decca promptly stashed the tape away in its vault, but thirteen years later, when the company's German label was casting around for Rolling Stones rarities for its *Best of the Rest* box set, a one-sided 45 of "Cocksucker Blues" (no release number) was included as a "bonus single." A couple of weeks later, Decca recalled the box set, yanked "Cocksucker Blues," removed all references to it on the cover, and reissued a cleaner, R-rated *Best of the Rest*. The single is now one of the most prized Rolling Stones 45s.

Oftentimes subsequent pressings of a 45 (or simultaneous pressings done at another plant) had a different label, generally a change in typeface or placement of information. For example, Capitol used two pressing plants, one in Hollywood, the other in Scranton, Pennsylvania, to press Beatles singles in the mid-to-late 1960s, but the Hollywood plant used labels with more space between the lettering in "The Beatles," making it look much larger on the label—plus the catalog numbers were bigger and fatter. Neither variation is more valuable because so many 45s with each label were pressed up. But sometimes there were changes that fundamentally altered the rarity and value of the records. When Capitol's subsidiary label, Tower Records, released Ian Whitcomb's 1965

Phil Spector routinely put instrumental jams with obscure titles on the B-sides of singles, so disc jockeys would play only the intended hit sides.

hit, "You Turn Me On" (134), the Los Angeles pressing plant correctly printed its running time as 2:42 on the label, but the East Coast plant printed 2:15.

Roy Orbison's No. 1 smash, "Oh, Pretty Woman," was originally titled "Pretty Woman" when it was first released on Monument 851. But when Cole Porter's music publisher alerted Monument that the venerable Porter catalog already had a "Pretty Woman," Monument Records changed the title on subsequent pressings.

Peter, Paul & Mary's popular 1963 novelty, "Puff (The Magic Dragon)" (Warner Bros. 5348), was originally released simply as "Puff," which some wags took as a reference to marijuana. When kids started calling radio stations requesting "Puff the magic dragon," the company prudently lengthened the title on later pressings.

The Doors' 45 version of "Hello! I Love You, Won't You Tell Me Your Name" (Elektra 45635) was later shortened to "Hello! I Love You," which may have helped the song go to No. 1 in 1968. Motown Records did the same thing with the Supremes' 1963 single, "A Breath Taking, First Sight Soul Shaking, One Night Love Making, Next Day Heart Breaking Guy" (Motown 1044), reducing it to simply "A Breath Taking Guy" on subsequent singles, which are worth about one-fourth the money to collectors. Motown also first issued Junior Walker's 1965 hit as "Shot Gun" (Soul 35008), before quickly retitling it "Shotgun."

The B-side of Elvis Presley's 1963 hit, "Devil in Disguise" (RCA Victor 8188), was mistakenly titled on the label as "Please Don't Drag That String Along." Subsequent pressings got it right, as "Please Don't Drag That String Around," but of course the correctly worded single is worth a mere fraction of the original today.

The Penguins' "Earth Angel" (Dootone 348), one of the first major doo-wop hits in 1954–55, began selling so quickly that the tiny, black-owned record company could barely keep up with the demand. As Dootone's pressing plant ran out of the usual red label color, it used others, including blue, black, maroon, and finally yellow, assessed at varying values by collectors decades later.

This same problem came up when the Chicago black indie, Vee-Jay, got the American rights to the Beatles' first album and singles in 1963. When demand for the Beatles suddenly skyrocketed the following year, the small pressing plant that Vee-Jay used had to scramble to keep up with the release of "Please Please Me"/"From Me to You" (581). When it ran out of standard Vee-Jay labels, the plant made up makeshift labels with the words VEE JAY and VJ in block printing. According to *Goldmine*, there were at least fifteen different label variations of the single, including color changes. To confuse matters more, Vee-Jay's original 1963 release of "Please Please Me" had a different number (498), a different B-side ("Ask Me Why"), two different Vee-Jay logos, and two different spellings of the Beatles/the Beattles.

As for the misspelling, Vee-Jay had been practicing. Their first major hit, the Spaniels' "Goodnite Sweetheart, Goodnite" (107), in 1954 was one of the early doo-wop classics, but that didn't stop Vee-Jay from pressing up a batch of 45s with the group's name spelled Spanials on the label.

Ricky Nelson recorded his very first single, "I'm Walkin'" (Verve 10047), in 1957 just as the venerable jazz- and folk music–oriented record company was changing label designs. A few Nelson 45s were issued on Verve's old orange-yellow label, but most copies bore the updated black-and-white label. The same thing happened a couple of years earlier with Bill Haley and His Comets' "Rock Around the Clock" (Decca 29124), originally released in 1954. A year later, after the song was featured in the film *Blackboard Jungle*, Decca reissued the single with its newly designed, more modern looking label with block lettering instead of the early Victorian script, and "Rock Around the Clock" went to No. 1. The earlier label is obviously much rarer.

In several cases a group changed names in the midst of a release. For example, when Federal Records first issued its huge 1954 R&B hit, "Work With Me Annie" (12169), the vocal group was credited as the Royals. But since the company had recently acquired a more popular R&B group called the Five Royales, it changed the Royals to the Midnighters on later pressings. Thus, "Work With Me Annie" was issued first by the Royals, then, in an interim pressing, as "The Midnighters, formerly known as the Royals," and finally as the Midnighters.

Recordings were also reissued under different titles, such as Vince Castro's 1958 single, "Bong Bong (I Love You Madly)" (Apt 25007), a reissue of "Bong Bong" (Doe 102). Then, during the first Twist craze in 1960, Apt Records reissued its single under a new catalog number (25047) as "Bong Twist," even though there was no mention of twisting in the lyrics. The Twist craze got so hot in late 1961 and early '62 that many labels began reissuing material with that magic word appended to the title, including Billy Joe and the Checkmates' Top 10 hit, "Percolator (Twist)" (Dore 620).

In February 1966, Dore had success with another group called the Entertainers III, whose members were drawn from Billy Joe and the Checkmates. Their debut 45 was entitled "People Don't Look No More (Temptation Walk)" (Dore 749). Evidently, to cash in on the popularity of the Temptations vocal group on Motown, whose fancy footwork inspired the dance step, the title was rearranged to "Temptation Walk (People Don't Look No More)." The new title, and the decision to rename the group Entertainers IV, was enough to lift the song into the national soul Top 30.

In another instance, a vocal group called the Revels recorded a spooky song during the 1959 Stroll dance craze called "Dead Man's Stroll" (Norgolde 103), but when distributors and disc jockeys told the company that the title might be too macabre, Norgolde reissued the record—everything else being the same—as "Midnight Stroll," which went on to be a hit.

Record companies routinely used a different color label and sometimes a different design for the promotional 45s they sent to radio stations. In the case of Del Shannon's "Two Kinds of Teardrops" on Big Top Records (3143), the deejay label was not only yellow instead of the usual pink, but the title was slightly shortened to the ungrammatical "Two Kind of Teardrops." Likewise, the promo copy of Marvin Gaye's "How Can I Forget You" (Tamla 54190) shaved off the last word, "You." Could it be because Gaye had already used up his quota on another single called "You" (Tamla 54160)? No, Motown's promo label simply acknowledged that the song was a remake of Jimmy Holiday's "How Can I Forget" (Everett 2022), but someone decided the "you" made the song more personal.

When Atlantic Records first released Daryl Hall & John Oates' "She's Gone"/"I'm Just a Kid (Don't Make Me Feel Like a Man)" in 1973 with the catalog number 2983, the 45 went nowhere. But after the duo switched labels and became famous, Atlantic reissued the same record as 3332 three years later. The deejay copy, incidentally, had "She's Gone" on both sides, with a long and short version.

When the Rolling Stones' manager, Allen Klein, released their 1975 single, a remake of Stevie Wonder's "I Don't Know Why," on his own label (ABKCO 4701), he mistakenly credited the song to group members Mick Jagger, Keith Richards, and Mick Taylor. On subsequent pressings, the songwriters were correctly given as Wonder-[Paul] Riser-[Don] Hunter-[Lula Mae] Hardaway. The first pressing is worth twice as much (only about $10) as the second.

Then you've got those 45 releases that stand out because of something unique to them. One strange single was "Black Magic and Witchcraft" by a Midwestern group called the Comic Books on Citation Records (5001) in 1962. Because of a printing oversight, the labels arrived at the pressing plant without the group's name on them, so the producer made a rubber hand-stamp and individually added "The Comic Books" to each 45.

Apple Records, the Beatles' vanity label, had two label designs, one for each side of the record. The A-side logo was the outside of a shiny green apple and the B-side had a different logo showing the inside of an apple sliced in half on every Apple single—except one. When Apple released George Harrison's "My Sweet Lord" and "Isn't It a Pity" (2995) in 1970, both songs were considered so hit-worthy that the whole-apple logo was used on each side.

On quite a few releases there were different B-sides from one pressing to the next. (See Chapter 12 concerning the financial value of B-sides.) The reason was generally that the intended A-side was upstaged by the B-side, and if the B-side became the hit, record companies sometimes replaced the former A-side with a song they owned, in order to collect the royalties. The story of the Chords' "Sh-Boom" (Cat 104) is detailed in Chapter 12, but similarly Richard Berry's original 1956 version of "Louie Louie" (Flip 321) began as a flipside but moved to the top of the record when disc jockeys started playing it instead of the original A-side, his remake of the country song "You Are My Sunshine." Flip replaced the old A-side with another Richard Berry song called "Rock, Rock, Rock" that was company-owned. (Super-rare first versions of Berry's "Louie Louie" were mistakenly printed as "Louie Lovie.")

The B-side of Paul McCartney & Wings' 1974 hit, "Jet" (Apple 1871), was originally "Let Me Roll It," but because of John Lennon's involvement with the song, McCartney replaced it with "Mammunia" when the two were feuding. When Capitol Records reissued the single two years later (same serial number as Apple's), it restored "Let Me Roll It."

Donna Summers' 1975 smash, "Love to Love You Baby" (Oasis 401), was originally released with "Need a Man Blues" on the B-side, but when the single took off up the charts because of its popularity in disco clubs, Oasis reissued a new pressing with a dance remix of "Love to Love You Baby" on the flip.

Motown's Berry Gordy was notorious for making changes to singles that had already been released. The first single by the Miracles was Tamla 54028, but there were four different releases under that catalog number. The first one, released in March 1960, was "The Feeling Is So Fine," backed with "You Can Depend on Me." A month later the single was re-released with the same labels but with an alternate version of "You Can Depend on Me." That same month another single came out with an entirely different A-side, "Way Over There," and the B-side retitled "(You Can) Depend on Me."

And finally, two months later, Motown released the last version, with strings overdubbed onto the original mix of "Way Over There" and the B-side retitled yet again to a simple "Depend on Me." All are valuable, but they range from $60 (version #4) to $500 (version #2).

The biggest selling song of 1977 was "You Light Up My Life" (Warner/Curb 8455) by Debby Boone, which began in a film of the same name starring Didi Cohn, who lip-synched to commercial jingle singer Kacey Cisyk's recording of the song. After producer Mike Curb saw an advanced screening of the movie, he borrowed the song's instrumental tracks from songwriter Joe Brooks and over-dubbed Debby Boone's voice on top. At

Warner Bros. yanked this B-side from Debby Boone's "You Light Up My Life" (8455) and replaced it with a song it owned.

first the Debby Boone single was released on Warner Bros. 8455—with "He's a Rebel" on the B-side, credited to the Boones. Then, just a couple of weeks later, Warner Bros. pulled the B-side off, replaced it with Debby's previously issued "Hasta Manana" (formerly on 8355) and re-released "You Light Up My Life" with a new catalog number, 8446. The song topped the national charts for ten straight weeks, during which time Arista Records finally got around to issuing a 45 of Kacey Cisyk's original version (0287), crediting the performance to Original Cast of *You Light Up My Life* instead of Cisyk. Its sales were negligible.

Oftentimes a single on a small indie was picked up by a larger company and changed in one way or another. (See Chapter 17 for several examples.) "96 Tears" and its flipside, "Midnight Hour," were recorded in a Michigan living room by ? (Question Mark) and the Mysterians and released in 1965 on a Texas label (Pa-Go-Go 102). Before long, Cameo Records stepped in and bought the master, edited down the A-side to tighten it up, and reissued it on a single (428) that went to No. 1 in 1966. Seven years later, the company that bought the Cameo catalog reissued the unedited Pa-Go-Go version (ABKCO 4020) with a new B-side called "Can't Get Enough of You, Baby." A quarter of a century later, in 1997, members of the original group, including ? (Rudy Martinez), returned to the studio to record a note-for-note copy of "96 Tears" for a prominent oldies reissue company because ABKCO refused to lease the original hit, and that's the one (Collectables 4050) you're most likely to hear today. (ABKCO, owned by Allen Klein, almost warrants its own chapter, because it refuses to reissue most of the old hits in its catalog, prompting Collectables and others to hire the original artists and make note-for-note recreations, including the Animals' "We Gotta Get Out of This Place" and Chubby Checker's "The Twist.")

It was fairly common that an artist would record the same song for a couple of different labels, sometimes under different names. For example, Buddy Holly recorded "That'll Be the Day" (Decca 30434) without background vocals in 1956 before cutting the more famous 1957 version with the Crickets (Brunswick 55009). James Taylor recorded "Carolina on My Mind" in 1969 for Apple Records (1805), which released it twice with two different B-sides without much success. Meanwhile, Taylor recorded the song again for his 1970 Warner Bros. *Sweet Baby James* album, and that's the one that became the hit version despite not being released on 45 (probably because of Taylor's former Apple contract). Barry Manilow wanted so badly to make his song "Could It Be Magic" into a hit that he recorded it twice. The first time was when he was a member of the group Featherbed (Bell 45133, 1971). Only promo copies survive, with a mono version on one side and stereo version on the other. After getting signed to a major label in 1975, Manilow gave the song a second try (Arista 0126). As it was going to No. 1, Bell Records reissued the old Featherbed version under Manilow's name (45422) to cash in on Arista's success.

On one hit record, the A- and B-side labels were mistakenly reversed and nobody cared. When New Mexico producer Norman Petty recorded an instrumental group called the String-A-Longs, he sold the masters to Warwick Records. Since there were no vocals on either track to identify them, Warwick put the labels for the B-side, "Am I Asking Too Much" (Warwick 603), on the A-side of the 45, while the A-side label, "Wheels," was pressed onto the B-side. By the time Petty realized what had happened, the B-side tune masquerading as "Wheels" was getting good radio response, becoming a Top 5 hit in the first week of 1960. Petty quickly replaced "Am I Asking Too Much" with one of his own songs, "Tell the World," on the flipside of subsequent pressings. He issued "Tell the World" again with a new B-side, "For My Angel," first as by the String-A-Longs (Warwick 606) in 1960, and then as by Mickey Boyd & the Plain Viewers (7 Arts 700) in 1961. All these machinations allowed Petty to personally collect the extra publishing royalties.

The Capris' doo-wop classic, "There's a Moon Out Tonight," refused to die even though the group split and went their separate ways. The five Italian kids from Queens, New York, recorded the song and a B-side for the small Planet label (1010) in 1958, but nothing happened. Three years later a few collectors reissued the 45 as a limited pressing on Lost Nite 101. At that point a larger indie, Old Town Records, stepped in and reissued the single (1094) in late 1961. As it climbed the charts, the former members of the Capris put their lives on hold, got in touch with each other again and reformed the group to promote the single.

By 1960 some singles were being released in both mono and stereo versions, though mono was still more common. Sometimes the stereo was real, other times it was electronically "rechanneled" into fake stereo by splitting the signal according to frequencies. In many cases, especially at Liberty Records in Hollywood, there were two totally different recordings, one mono, one stereo. The most famous was the Fleetwoods' 1959 No. 1 hit, "Come Softly to Me," first released as a mono recording on Dolphin Records (1) in Seattle, Washington, then picked up by Liberty and released (55188) in its mono state. But Liberty also created a stereo version (77188) by recording the group's lead singer, Gary Troxel, shaking his car keys to create a "percussion" track for the original tape.

In the case of Del Shannon's "Little Town Flirt"/"The Wamboo" (Big Top 12-1308) in 1962, there were three different 45s: one with both sides in stereo, one with both sides in mono, and a deejay copy with "Little Town Flirt" on both sides—one mono, the other stereo. Shannon's stereo recordings later became valuable when Big Top lost the original stereo masters.

After mono went out of style in the late 1960s, companies nonetheless continued to supply disc jockeys with promotional 45s that contained a stereo mix of the plug song on one side for FM stations and a separate mono mix of the song on the other for AM. The mono mixes of many 1970s and eighties singles, such as Bruce Springsteen's "Born to Run" (Columbia 33323) and the Police's "Message in a Bottle" (A&M 2190), were exclusive to the promo 45s and remain available nowhere else.

Running times of songs were almost always listed on 45s so that disc jockeys could precisely slot a record into their tight schedules. Since long records cut in on revenues from commercials, Top 40 radio programmers avoided them, but Phil Spector, the mischievous Puck of pop music, got around this problem in 1964 when he released the Righteous Brothers' nearly four-minute-long "You've Lost That Lovin' Feelin'" (Philles 124) by printing a much shorter 3:05, instead of the real 3:50, on the label "by mistake." By the time radio program directors got wise, the song was already climbing the charts. Spector later sent out deejay copies of the Righteous Brothers' "Ebb Tide" (Philles 130—though the deejay copy was numberless) with nothing on the label except the Philles logo, a photo of Spector, and the title "Thanks For Giving Me the Right Time," a reference to the wrong timing of "You've Lost That Lovin' Feelin'."

One of the more unusual concept 45s was "High School, U.S.A." by singer Tommy Facenda, a veteran of Gene Vincent's Blue Caps. At various parts of the song, Facenda rattled off names of Virginia-area high schools like an auctioneer. Originally released by the Norfolk, Virginia-based Legrand label (1001), "High School U.S.A." was picked up by Atlantic Records, which immediately sent Facenda back into the studio to record twenty-seven more versions of the song over the same instrumental-choral track, only this time Facenda named high schools instead of cities. All twenty-eight versions were released under different numbers separate from Atlantic's regular numerical system. For example, the Virginia high schools version was 45-51, a New York City version was 45-52, and so on, up to Oklahoma (45-78). Among the other areas with their own "High School U.S.A." singles were Philadelphia (45-55), Detroit (45-56), Cleveland (45-62), New Orleans (45-68), Georgia/Alabama (45-70), Los Angeles (45-73), Texas (45-75), and Seattle (45-76). *Billboard* tabulated all the versions as one, and collectively they reached No. 28 on the charts in late 1959. All versions are worth roughly the same to collectors.

Also in 1959, Federal Records in Cincinnati released a 45 by Johnnie & Bill with two different takes of the same song, "On My Way to School" (12479). The faster B-side take was labeled "Teen Age Version." Among the truly rare though not generally sought-after 45s are special one-off promotional and advertising singles sent out to disc jockeys, distributors, or other special groups. For example, in the early 1950s Capitol sent all its retailers a 45 called "I Tawt I Taw a Record Dealer," by Mel Blanc, the voice of the popular cartoon character, Tweety Bird, whose catchphrase was "I tawt I taw a puddy tat."

Some early 45 bootlegs have become prized collectors items simply because they filled a void. A perfect example is the 45 single of the Five Sharps' "Stormy Weather" (Bim Bam Boom 103) whose history is described in Chapter 11. Even more valuable is Bill Haley and His Comets' "Rock Around the Clock"/"Crazy Man, Crazy" (Essex 103). Essex Records in Philadelphia was Haley's record label up until he signed with Decca in early 1954. The Comets' first hit, "Crazy Man, Crazy," had actually been issued on Essex 321 in 1953, but "Rock Around the Clock" was a Decca release that the owner of Essex had refused to record earlier because he hated the song's publisher. When somebody put out the bootleg in 1955 using an obviously phony catalog number, it conveniently combined two of Haley's most popular recordings onto a fantasy 45 that is worth more today than most of Haley's legitimate singles.

When artists suddenly broke through with a big hit, their earlier recordings often came back to haunt them. For example, when Johnny Ace became an R&B sensation for Duke Records in the early 1950s with a string of No. 1 hits, a record company in Los Angeles dug up an earlier Memphis session that Ace had played piano on and found that he'd sung one song, a rambling, pointless, and embarrassing thing called "Midnight Hour's Journey," that showed nothing of Ace's later charisma. The song duly came out on Flair 1015, blaring Johnny Ace's name on the label. Since there was no second Johnny Ace song on the tape, the company put another artist, Earl Forrest, on the flipside. Though the 1953 single didn't chart, it is by far Ace's most valuable 45 among collectors of his work.

Likewise, when the Platters signed with Mercury Records in 1955 and broke into the big time with "Only You (And You Alone)" (70633), their former label took the opportunity to unleash a clearly inferior version of the song (Federal 12244), complete with a whistling bridge, that it had previously deemed unworthy of release. Naturally, this is the version that's now a valuable collector's item.

One of the most seasoned rock 'n' roll artists of the 1950s was Big Joe Turner, a black blues shouter who had first recorded in 1939, so when he was suddenly enjoying a 1956 hit with "Corrina Corrina" (Atlantic 1088), Decca Records went back into its vaults and released a definitely non–rock 'n' roll version (29924) of Turner singing the song with jazz pianist Art Tatum's group in 1941. And Danny Flores, who recorded as a vocalist under his own name before he became better known as Chuck Rio, the saxophonist of the Champs and composer of the group's 1958 hit, "Tequila" (Challenge 1016), was surprised to find his old Danny Flores single, "No Matter What You Do" (RPM 491), had come back onto the market under the name Chuck "Tequila" Rio (Kent 303). The same thing happened to Dion & the Belmonts after their first hit, "I Wonder Why" (Laurie 3013), in May 1958; another label dug up Dion's earlier, much inferior single, "The Chosen Few" (Mohawk 105), recorded with the Timberlanes, then reissued it as by Dion & the Timberlanes (Jubilee 5294). And finally, when Brenda Holloway had her first hit record, "Every Little Bit Hurts" (Tamla 54094), in early 1964, her previous label resurrected a song she'd done two years earlier on an excellent doo-wop 45 called "Echo," backed with "Hey Fool" (Donna 1358). Since her old label had recorded four songs with her, it duly reissued the remaining two but, instead of wasting them on just one Brenda Holloway 45, it spread them out over two singles and put "Echo" on the B-side of both of them, feebly disguising it as "Echo-Echo-Echo" (Donna 1366) and "More Echo" (Donna 1370).

In 1959, "Midnight Express" by Willie Tremaine was issued on the new Swastika (1001) label, until a pressing plant employee suggested a name change. "Midnight Express" was thus reissued on Cuca (1001), a more acceptable label name.

Perhaps the weirdest 45 reissue was Joe Jones's "You Talk Too Much"/"I Love You Still," a 1960 hit first released on the tiny New Orleans Ric label (972). When Jones was touring to promote the single, he met Morris Levy of Roulette Records, who prevailed upon Jones to re-record an almost identical version of both songs. Roulette's 45 (4304) combined with the original Ric single to score an impressive No. 3 on the charts, but Roulette increasingly dominated sales. How Levy got Jones to sign with him without a whimper from Ric Records remains a mystery, unless one is aware that Levy was a front man for New York's Genovese crime family.

If nothing else, these oddball singles show how volatile and spontaneous the music industry used to be during the 45 era. With today's corporate control, however, those days are probably gone forever.

Sources

BOOKS

Bronson, Fred, *The Billboard Book of Number One Hits*. New York: Billboard Publications, 1985

Canby, Edward Tatnall, *Saturday Review Home Book of Recorded Music and Sound Reproduction*. New York: Prentice Hall, 1952

Cornyn, Stan with Paul Scanlon, *Exploding: The Highs, Hits, Hype, Heroes, and Hustlers of the Warner Music Group*. New York: HarperCollins, 2002

Dawson, Jim & Steve Propes, *What Was the First Rock 'N' Roll Record?* Boston, MA: Faber & Faber, 1992

——, *Nervous Man Nervous*. Milford, NH: Big Nickel Publications, 1994

——, *The Twist*, Boston, MA: Faber & Faber, 1995

Drake, Spencer, editor, *45 RPM: A Visual History of the Seven-Inch Record*. New York: Princeton Architectural Press, 2002

Fisher, Eddie, with David Fisher, *Been There, Done That*. New York: St. Martin's Press, 1999

Gart, Galen, *The History of Rhythm & Blues, Vol. 1—1948–1950*. Milford, NH: Big Nickel Publications, 1986

——, *The History of Rhythm & Blues, Vol. 1—1951*. Milford, NH: Big Nickel Publications, 1991

——, *The History of Rhythm & Blues, Vol. 2—1952*. Milford, NH: Big Nickel Publications, 1992

——, *The History of Rhythm & Blues, Vol. 3—1953*. Milford, NH: Big Nickel Publications, 1989

——, *The History of Rhythm & Blues, Vol. 4—1954*. Milford, NH: Big Nickel Publications, 1990

——, *The History of Rhythm & Blues, Vol. 5—1955*. Milford, NH: Big Nickel Publications, 1990

Gart, Galen & Roy C. Ames, *Duke/Peacock Records*. Milford, NH: Big Nickel Publications, 1990

Goldmark, Peter C., *Maverick Inventor: My Turbulent Years at CBS*. New York: Saturday Review Press, 1973

Lyons, Eugene, *David Sarnoff*. New York: Harper & Row, 1966

McCoy, William & Mitchell McGeary, *Every Little Thing—The Definitive Guide to Beatles Recording Variations, Rare Mixes & Other Musical Oddities, 1958–1986*. Ann Arbor, MI: Popular Culture, Ink., 1990

Neely, Tim, Goldmine Price Guide to 45 rpm Records (3rd edition). Iola, WI: Krause Publications, 2001

Osborne, Jerry, *Popular & Rock Records, 1948–1978*. Phoenix, AZ: O'Sullivan, Woodside & Co., 1978

——, *Elvis Word For Word*. New York: Harmony Books, 2000

Paley, William S., *As It Happened: A Memoir*. Garden City, NY: Doubleday, 1979

Sarnoff, David, *Looking Ahead: The Papers of David Sarnoff*. New York: McGraw-Hill Book Co., 1968

Schicke, C.A., *Revolution in Sound*. Boston: Little, Brown & Co., 1974

Shaw, Arnold, *Honkers and Shouters*. New York: Macmillan Publishing Co., 1978

Sherman, Michael W., *The Collector's Guide to Victor Records*. Dallas, TX: Monarch Record Enterprises, 1992

Vourtsis, Phil, *The Fabulous Victrola 45*. New York: Schiffer Books, 2002

Wile, F.W., *Emile Berliner: Maker of the Microphone*. New York: Bobbs Merrill Co., 1926

World's Greatest Artists Are on RCA Victor 45 rpm Records (record catalog, form 2K 2385). Camden, NJ: Radio Corp. of America, RCA Victor Division, 1949

MAGAZINE ARTICLES

Bauder, David, "Are Pop Singles on the Way Out?" *Los Angeles Times*, March 1, 2002, p.F29

Caida, Joe, "On and Off the Soapbox; or, Some Random Thoughts Re the Record Evolution," *The Billboard*, December 4, 1948, p.3

——, "Lowdown on New RCA Disk," *The Billboard*, January 8, 1949, p.3

——, "Let's Not Get Dizzy on New Record Speeds; They're Here," *The Billboard*, January 15, 1949, p.3

——, "Some Support From Buffalo & Memphis and Rock From L.A.," *The Billboard*, February 5, 1949, p.3

Christman, Ed, "Labels Give Singles Another Try," *Billboard*, March 15, 2003, p.1

——, "RIAA Says 2002 Shipments Off 11.2%," *Billboard*, March 15, 2003, p.4

Cummins, Gordon, "Best Selling EPs of the Big Beat Era," *Now Dig This*, March 2002, p.20

Dawson, Jim, "Return of the 45," *L.A. Weekly*, December 21–27, 1979, p.61

———, "Valens: The Forgotten Story," *Los Angeles Times*, February 3, 1980, p.100

DeBarros, Anthony, "Digital Music: Fast Forwarding Tapes to Oblivion," *USA Today*, November 28, 2001, p.E1

Edwards, Louis, "David Sarnoff," *Practical Knowledge*, February 1949, p.14

Hilburn, Robert, "The 12-Inch Record Is on a Hot Roll," *Los Angeles Times*, February 13, 1983, Calendar p.66

———, "The Not-So-Big Hit Single," *Los Angeles Times*, February 17, 2002, Calendar, p.7

Horowitz, Is, "45 Disks Gain Edge Over 78 Pop Singles," *The Billboard*, February 26, 1955, p.27

Isom, Warren Rex, "Before the Fie Groove and Stereo Record and Other Innovations," *Journal of the Audio Engineering Society*, Oct./Nov. 1977, V.25, p.10/11

Knoedelseder, William K., "Compact Discs Are Music to the Ears of the Record Industry," *Los Angeles Times*, January 11, 1987, p. IV–1

Kubernik, Harvey, "Phil Spector," *Goldmine*, February 22, 2002, p.14

Kuipers, Dean, "Where Do You Buy?" *Los Angeles Times*, December 19, 2002, p.E36

Leigh, Spencer, "Shakers, Fakers and Takers," *Now Dig This*, March 2002, p.8

Lewis, Randy, "Pop Gets Crackle, Snap Back," *Los Angeles Times*, December 18, 2002, p.A1

Miller, Chuck, "Victory Music: The Story of the V-Disc Record Label (1943–49)," *Goldmine*, February 1999

Moonoogian, George A., "The Giant That Started It All," *Record Exchanger*, Vol. 4, No. 3, 1975

Neely, Tim, "25 of the Most Collectible Phil Spector Records," *Goldmine*, February 22, 2002, p.19

Newman, Ralph M., "The 5 Sharps: Even More to the Story." *Discoveries*, June 2001, p.35

Rosen, Craig, "Flipping Over Flip Sides," *Los Angeles Times*, December 1, 1984, p.V–1

Simon, Bill, "Low-Priced Kidisks Boom Biz," *The Billboard*, May 28, 1949, p.18

Tefteller, John, "Poor Economy: Red Hot Record Sales," *Discoveries*, March 2003, p.40

Timburg, Scott, "A Toast to a Man Who Left His Imprint on L.A.," *Los Angeles Times*, August 10, 2002, p.F2

Wallerstein, Edward, "The Development of the LP," *High Fidelity*, April 1976, p.26

Wang, Oliver, "Life at 45 rpm," *San Francisco Bay Guardian*, July 7, 1999, p.56

Washburn, Jim, "Vinyl Lovers Still Seek Out Stacks o' Wax," *Los Angeles Times*, December 1, 1993, p.F1

Webman, Hal & Alan Fischler, "The Record Year," *The Billboard NAMM Trade Show and Convention Section*, June 19, 1948, p.14

Weiser, Norman, "New Disks Not to Affect Jukes," *The Billboard*, April 2, 1949, p.133

———, "15,000,000 45 RPM's Set For Juke Use in 1952; Hiked Production, Distribution to Shoot Figure Higher in 1953," *The Billboard*, April 19, 1952, p.16

Willman, Chris, "Record Firms Try Again With Cassette Singles," *Los Angeles Times*, March 19, 1987, p.VI–1

Wilson, Tony, "Tot Tallow's Take Terrific: Kidisk Sales 20% of Total," *The Billboard*, May 1, 1949, p.16

Wilson, Tony & Jerry Wexler, "Specialized Disk Sales Advance," *The Billboard NAMM Trade Show and Convention Section*, June 19, 1948, p.20

Advertisement: "After 10 Million Phonographs—After 1 Billion Records...," *The Billboard*, April 2, 1949, p.35–38

Advertisement: "What's All This About a Record War?" *The Billboard*, March 12, 1949, p.27

"Artists Mitt RCA's 45 R.P.M," *The Billboard*, December 18, 1948, p.22

"Battle of Webs Boils On; NBC Holds Harris; CBS Adds," *The Billboard*, January 29, 1949, p.5

"Bogus Platters on Market," *The Billboard*, April 10, 1948, p.17

"Cap, Mercury, Decca, Coral Still in Debate," *The Billboard*, January 8, 1955, p.11

"Cap Springs With 45 in April," *The Billboard*, February 12, 1949, p.36

"CBS's Battle for Survival," *The Billboard*, December 18, 1948, p.3

"Chain Store Execs Approve Disk Cuts, Dislike Confusions," *The Billboard*, January 22, 1955, p.13

"Col.'s New LP Player to Bow," *The Billboard*, May 14, 1949, p.20

"Col.'s 7-In. LP Prices & Catalog: Waxery Issues Rates for New Microgrooves," *The Billboard*, January 15, 1949, p.20

"Columbia's Diskery, CBS Show Mircogroove Platters to Press; Tell How It Began," *The Billboard*, June 26, 1948, p.3

"Columbia's First LP Disks Ready, Pop to Longhair," *The Billboard*, September 11, 1948, p.17

"Columbia's New 7-Incher, To Expand Its 33-1/3 Line Across Board, Is Due Soon," *The Billboard*, January 8, 1949, p.13

"Dealers Slashing Prices on Victor, Columbia Labels," *The Billboard*, March 12, 1949, p.23

"Distribs Sold on LPs, But Big Sales Bally Lies Ahead," *The Billboard*, July 3, 1948, p.19

"'53 Disk Sales Hit All-Time Peak of $205,000,000," *The Billboard*, May 8, 1954, p.13

"45 R.P.M. Hues Add Sales Hypo," *The Billboard*, February 19, 1949, p.18

"45 R.P.M. Prices Are Announced By RCA Victor," *The Billboard*, March 13, 1949, p.28

"45's and LP's Check Slump in Wax Sales," *The Billboard*, May 21, 1949, p.3

"General, The," *Time*, July 23, 1951, p.74

"Hypoing LP Acceptance, Says Columbia," *The Billboard*, February 19, 1949, p.17

"Kidisk Boom Still Soaring; New Pressers," *The Billboard*, May 8, 1949, p.3

"Kidisks Draw Play in Cap's First 45 Issue," *The Billboard*, March 19, 1949, p.18

"Majors Sell 7 Tot Wax at 25c Level," *The Billboard*, August 31, 1949, p.15

"Micro-Groove Disk Rush Is On," *The Billboard*, June 5, 1948, p.3

Options and Accessories catalog for 1957 Dodge, Highway Hi-Fi booklet #DMA 3296

"Philly to Plug 78-R.P.M.; Player to Sell at Cost," *The Billboard*, January 8, 1949, p.17

"Phono Makers Rush to Cash In on 33-1/3 Idea," *The Billboard*, June 5, 1948, p.17

"Phono Men See RCA Cut Cueing Demse of 78s," *The Billboard*, January 8, 1955, p.11

"Player in Every Home; Bldg. Project Installs RCA Sets as Regular Equipment," *The Billboard*, June 25, 1949, p.3

"Pubs, Artists, MPTF Views Vary on Prices," *The Billboard*, January 8, 1955, p.11

"RCA Pitches to Juke Ops," *The Billboard*, June 25, 1949, p.15

"RCA Plans Super-Speed Delivery on 45 R.P.M. Hits," *The Billboard*, June 6, 1949, p.3

"RCA Revamps Staff to Set Big 45 Push," *The Billboard*, July 2, 1949, p.3

"RCA Winning LP Fight With Col For Cap's Hand," *The Billboard*, February 5, 1949, p.20

"Revolutionary Disk Marvel by Columbia," *The Billboard*, May 29, 1948, p.3

"Shellac Housecleaning Paving Way for New Type Disks; Col Reported Readying 25% Slash," *The Billboard*, March 26, 1949, p.23

"Survey Indicates LP Sales Okay; Only a Minority Feel 45 R.P.M. Will Hurt Business," *The Billboard*, March 5, 1949, p.37

"Tempo Records Are First Out on 78, 33-1/3 and 45," *The Billboard*, March 5, 1949, p.18

"3-Speed Phono Mad Whirl," *The Billboard*, February 26, 1949, p.3

"Victor Distribs Tee Off Drive on 45 Disks," *The Billboard*, March 12, 1949, p.21

"Victor Skeds Key Sessions Promoting 45," *The Billboard*, February 19, 1949, p.17

INTERNET ARTICLES

Amato, Ivan, "Leo Baekeland," www.time.com/time100/scientist/profile/baekeland.html

Brock-Nannestad, George, "Why 78, 45 and 33⅓ Record Formats?" www.history-of-rock.com/record_formats.htm

Copeland, Peter, "Why 78, 45 and 33⅓ Record Formats?" www.history-of-rock.com/record_formats.htm

Diehl, David, "Royale 45 RPM EPs," http://www.hensteeth.com/royale45.html

Discoguy, "This Is Tom Moulton," http://www.disco-disco.com/tributes/tom.html

Flexi Disk Museum, http://www.wfmu.org/MACrec/

Katuna, Norm, "Birth of the 45 R.P.M. Record," www.history-of-rock.com/fortyfive_birth.htm

Kelsey, Steve, "Downstairs Records—Your Steps to Music: The RCA Victor 45 RPM Phonograph,"
    www.downstairsrecords.com/about/rpm.html

Neely, Tim, "The 45—In the Beginning," www.geocities.com/vinylagogo/45history.html

Worsley, Roger, "Why 78, 45 and 33-1/3 Record Formats?" www.history-of-rock.com/record_formats.htm

Acknowledgments

··

Jim Dawson thanks Mary Katherine Aldin, Mark Atnip, Dick Blackburn, Edgar Bullington, Ray Campi, Peter Copeland of the British Library National Sound Archive, Doctor Demento (Barry Hansen), eye in the sky Bob Doerschuk, Todd Everett, Art Fein, Jean-Claude Ferland, Doug Fieger, Andy Framzle, Marv Goldberg, Libbie Goold, Peter Guralnik, Hunter Hancock, Fred "Skip" Heller, Dick "Huggy Boy" Hugg, our editor Richard Johnston, Kate Karp, Steve Kelsay, Richard Knoppow, Harvey Kubernik, Allen Larman, Golden Bill Leibowitz, Greg Loescher, Greil Marcus, Rip Masters, our production editor Amy Miller, Chuck Miller, Harry Narunsky, Tim Neely, Michael Ochs, Ray Regalado, Earl Reinhalter, Jeff Riley, Gene Sculatti, Brian A. Singer, Phil Spector, Gloria Stanford, John Tefteller, Billy Vera, Frank Weimann of the Literary Group, Ian Whitcomb, Jonny Whiteside, Bill Windsor (www.45s.com), and Alexander Zah.

Steve Propes thanks these helpful collectors, researchers, and fellow fans of the 45: Don Barrett, Tom Bennett, Steve Brigati, John Broven, Jim Cooprider, Tony D'Amico, Gerry Diez, DJ Nu-Mark of Jurassic 5, Richard Gibson, Pete Grendysa, Don Haley, Danny Holloway, Louis Iacueo, Rollye James, Ruben Molina, Peter Muldavin, Gary Myers, Larry Orr, Jim Philbrook, Paul Politi, Phil Powell, Eric Predoehl, Lane Quigley, John Raino, Mike Saito, David Somerville, Bill Soon, Mike Vague, Ron Vermette, Tom & Maxine Wenzel, and Barry Wickham. Thanks as well to these 45 enthusiasts who helped out: Bob Beban, Al Blaazer, Bill Bugge, Maggie Cattwo, Chester Coleman, Dik de Heer, Mark Dintenfass, Dean Farrell, Roger Ford, Jim Hauser, Greg Ioannou, Harry Krentz, Todd Lucas, Don McLaughlin, Phil Millstein, Bob Moke, Gary Nichols, Scott Parker, Joe Pecoraro, Roy Phillips, Michel Proost, Steve Rood, Clay Stabler, Peter Staehli, Tapio Vaisanen, and Gary West.

Both authors also thank Galen Gart, Bruce Grossberg, Norm Katuna, Dave Marsh, Opal Louis Nations, Bob "the Bopper" O'Brien, Sylvia Propes, and George Townsend.

About the Authors

JIM DAWSON, a native of Parkersburg, West Virginia, has written extensively on early rock 'n' roll and rhythm & blues for magazines and newspapers, and contributed liner notes for over 150 albums and CDs. He also wrote the internationally infamous *Who Cut the Cheese? A Cultural History of the Fart*. Dawson currently lives in Hollywood.

STEVE PROPES, born in Berkeley, California, is a writer and record collector with a large library of vinyl and the host of an Internet radio program, *The Steve Propes 45 Show* (www.cerritos.edu/wpmd), on which he plays nothing but 45s. He lives in Long Beach, California, with his wife Sylvia, and they have two grown daughters.

Dawson and Propes are the authors of Faber & Faber's now legendary *What Was the First Rock 'n' Roll Record?* that *Mojo* dubbed "one the most impressive musical reads of [1993]."

Index

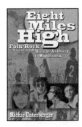